# Teach Yourself
# Office Microsoft® 2000

VISUALLY™

Visual™

*From*
**maranGraphics™**

&

Hungry Minds™ HUNGRY MINDS, INC.
New York, NY ♦ Cleveland, OH ♦ Indianapolis, IN

# Teach Yourself Microsoft® Office 2000 VISUALLY™

Published by
**Hungry Minds, Inc.**
909 Third Avenue
New York, NY 10022

Copyright© 1999 by maranGraphics Inc.
5755 Coopers Avenue
Mississauga, Ontario, Canada
L4Z 1R9

Library of Congress Catalog Card No.: 98-75595

ISBN: 0-7645-6051-4

Printed in the United States of America

11

Distributed in the United States by Hungry Minds, Inc.

Distributed by CDG Books Canada Inc. for Canada; by Transworld Publishers Limited in the United Kingdom; by IDG Norge Books for Norway; by IDG Sweden Books for Sweden; by IDG Books Australia Publishing Corporation Pty. Ltd. for Australia and New Zealand; by TransQuest Publishers Pte Ltd. for Singapore, Malaysia, Thailand, Indonesia, and Hong Kong; by Gotop Information Inc. for Taiwan; by ICG Muse, Inc. for Japan; by Intersoft for South Africa; by Eyrolles for France; by International Thomson Publishing for Germany, Austria and Switzerland; by Distribuidora Cuspide for Argentina; by LR International for Brazil; by Galileo Libros for Chile; by Ediciones ZETA S.C.R. Ltda. for Peru; by WS Computer Publishing Corporation, Inc., for the Philippines; by Contemporanea de Ediciones for Venezuela; by Express Computer Distributors for the Caribbean and West Indies; by Micronesia Media Distributor, Inc. for Micronesia; by Chips Computadoras S.A. de C.V. for Mexico; by Editorial Norma de Panama S.A. for Panama; by American Bookshops for Finland.

For general information on Hungry Minds' products and services please contact our Customer Care Department within the U.S. at 800-762-2974, outside the U.S. at 317-572-3993 or fax 317-572-4002.

For sales inquiries and reseller information, including discounts, premium and bulk quantity sales, and foreign-language translations, please contact our Customer Care Department at 800-434-3422, fax 317-572-4002, or write to Hungry Minds, Inc., Attn: Customer Care Department, 10475 Crosspoint Boulevard, Indianapolis, IN 46256.

For information on licensing foreign or domestic rights, please contact our Sub-Rights Customer Care Department at 650-653-7098.

For authorization to photocopy items for corporate, personal, or educational use, please contact Copyright Clearance Center, 222 Rosewood Drive, Danvers, MA 01923, or fax 978-750-4470.

For information on using Hungry Minds' products and services in the classroom or for ordering examination copies, please contact our Educational Sales Department at 800-434-2086 or fax 317-572-4005.

Please contact our Public Relations Department at 212-884-5163 for press review copies or 212-884-5000 for author interviews and other publicity information or fax 212-884-5400.

For authorization to photocopy items for corporate, personal, or educational use, please contact maranGraphics at 800-469-6616. Screen shots displayed in this book are based on pre-release software and are subject to change.

## Trademark Acknowledgments

## Permissions

The 3-D illustrations are the copyright of maranGraphics, Inc.

| U.S. Corporate Sales | U.S. Trade Sales |
| --- | --- |
| Contact maranGraphics at (800) 469-6616 or Fax (905) 890-9434. | Contact Hungry Minds at (800) 434-3422 or (650) 655-3000. |

# Some comments from our readers...

"I have to praise you and your company on the fine products you turn out. I have twelve of the *Teach Yourself VISUALLY* and *Simplified* books in my house. They were instrumental in helping me pass a difficult computer course. Thank you for creating books that are easy to follow."

  —*Gordon Justin (Brielle, NJ)*

"I commend your efforts and your success. I teach in an outreach program for the Dr. Eugene Clark Library in Lockhart, TX. Your *Teach Yourself VISUALLY* books are incredible and I use them in my computer classes. All my students love them!"

  —*Michele Schalin (Lockhart, TX)*

"Thank you for all the hard work it took to put *Teach Yourself Microsoft Office 2000 VISUALLY* together. I love this book! The colors are beautiful and the text is simple to understand. Thank you so much for helping people like me learn about computers. The Maran family is just what the doctor ordered. Thank you, thank you, thank you."

  —*Carol Moten (New Kensington, PA)*

"I would like to take this time to compliment maranGraphics on creating such great books. Thank you for making it clear. Keep up the good work."

  —*Kirk Santoro (Burbank, CA)*

"Thank you, thank you, thank you....for making it so easy for me to break into this high-tech world. I now own four of your books. I recommend them to anyone who is a beginner like myself. Now....if you could just do one for programming VCR's, it would make my day!"

  —*Gay O'Donnell (Calgary, Alberta, Canada)*

"I write to extend my thanks and appreciation for your books. They are clear, easy to follow, and straight to the point. Keep up the good work!"

  —*Seward Kollie (Dakar, Senegal)*

"What fantastic teaching books you have produced! Congratulations to you and your staff. You deserve the Nobel prize in Education in the Software category. Thanks for helping me to understand computers."

  —*Bruno Tonon (Melbourne, Australia)*

"Over time, I have bought a number of your 'Read Less, Learn More' books. For me, they are THE way to learn anything easily.

  —*José A. Mazón (Cuba, NY)*

"I was introduced to maranGraphics about four years ago and YOU ARE THE GREATEST THING THAT EVER HAPPENED TO INTRODUCTORY COMPUTER BOOKS!"

  —*Glenn Nettleton (Huntsville, AL)*

"Compliments To The Chef!! Your books are extraordinary! Or, simply put, Extra-Ordinary, meaning way above the rest! THANK YOU THANK YOU THANK YOU! for creating these.

  —*Christine J. Manfrin (Castle Rock, CO)*

"I'm a grandma who was pushed by an 11-year-old grandson to join the computer age. I found myself hopelessly confused and frustrated until I discovered the Visual series. I'm no expert by any means now, but I'm a lot further along than I would have been otherwise. Thank you!"

  —*Carol Louthain (Logansport, IN)*

maranGraphics is a family-run business
located near Toronto, Canada.

**At maranGraphics**, we believe in producing great computer books—one book at a time.

Each maranGraphics book uses the award-winning communication process that we have been developing over the last 25 years. Using this process, we organize screen shots, text and illustrations in a way that makes it easy for you to learn new concepts and tasks.

We spend hours deciding the best way to perform each task, so you don't have to! Our clear, easy-to-follow screen shots and instructions walk you through each task from beginning to end.

Our detailed illustrations go hand-in-hand with the text to help reinforce the information. Each illustration is a labor of love—some take up to a week to draw!

We want to thank you for purchasing what we feel are the best computer books money can buy. We hope you enjoy using this book as much as we enjoyed creating it!

Sincerely,

*The Maran Family*

Please visit us on the web at:
# www.maran.com

# CREDITS

**Author & Architect:**
Ruth Maran

**Copy Development:**
Kelleigh Wing
Wanda Lawrie

**Project Manager:**
Judy Maran

**Editing &
Screen Captures:**
Roxanne Van Damme
Cathy Benn
Raquel Scott
Janice Boyer
Michelle Kirchner
James Menzies
Frances Lea
Emmet Mellow

**Layout Designer:**
Treena Lees

**Illustrators:**
Russ Marini
Jamie Bell
Peter Grecco
Sean Johannesen
Steven Schaerer

**Screen Artist:**
Jimmy Tam

**Indexer:**
Kelleigh Wing

**Post Production:**
Robert Maran

**Editorial Support:**
Michael Roney

# ACKNOWLEDGMENTS

maranGraphics™

Thanks to the dedicated staff of maranGraphics, including
Jamie Bell, Cathy Benn, Janice Boyer, Francisco Ferreira,
Peter Grecco, Jenn Hillman, Sean Johannesen, Michelle Kirchner,
Wanda Lawrie, Frances Lea, Treena Lees, Jill Maran, Judy Maran,
Maxine Maran, Robert Maran, Sherry Maran, Russ Marini,
Emmet Mellow, James Menzies, Steven Schaerer, Raquel Scott,
Jimmy Tam, Roxanne Van Damme, Paul Whitehead
and Kelleigh Wing.

Finally, to Richard Maran who originated the easy-to-use
graphic format of this guide. Thank you for your
inspiration and guidance.

# TABLE OF CONTENTS

## *3* EDIT A DOCUMENT

## *4* FORMAT TEXT

## *5* FORMAT PAGES

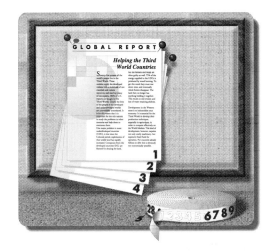

## *6* WORKING WITH TABLES

# TABLE OF CONTENTS

## USING EXCEL

## 6 PRINT A WORKSHEET

## 7 WORKING WITH CHARTS

## USING POWERPOINT

## 1 GETTING STARTED

## 2 EDIT SLIDES

# TABLE OF CONTENTS

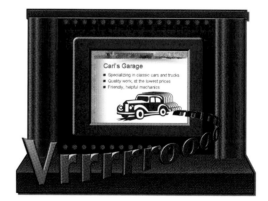

# USING ACCESS

# TABLE OF CONTENTS

# USING PUBLISHER

## USING OUTLOOK

### 1 EXCHANGE E-MAIL

### 2 MANAGE INFORMATION

## MICROSOFT OFFICE AND THE INTERNET

### 1 MICROSOFT OFFICE AND THE INTERNET

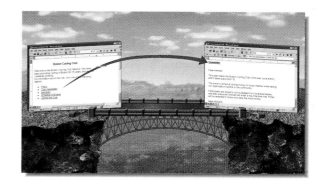

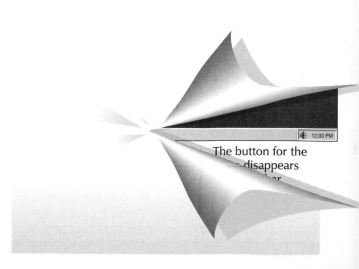

The button for the
...disappears

# INTRODUCTION TO MICROSOFT OFFICE 2000

**Microsoft® Office 2000 is a collection of programs that can help you accomplish various tasks.**

All Microsoft Office 2000 programs share a common design and work in a similar way. Once you learn one program, you can easily learn the others.

## Word

Word is a word processing program that helps you quickly and efficiently create documents such as letters, memos and reports.

## Excel

Excel is a spreadsheet program you can use to organize, analyze and attractively present data, such as a budget or sales report.

## PowerPoint

PowerPoint is a program that helps you plan, organize and design professional presentations. You can use your computer screen, 35mm slides or overhead transparencies to deliver a presentation you create.

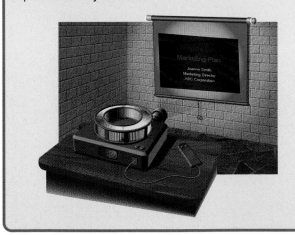

## Access

Access is a database program that allows you to store and manage large collections of information. Databases can contain business or personal information, such as client orders, expenses, addresses or music collections.

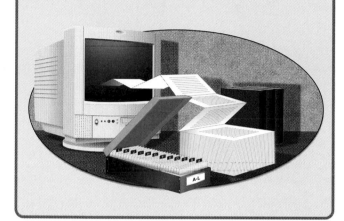

## Publisher

Publisher is a desktop publishing program that helps you design professional publications, such as banners, brochures, catalogs, flyers, invitations and newsletters.

## Outlook

Outlook is an information management program that helps you manage your e-mail messages, appointments, contacts, tasks and notes.

## Microsoft Office and the Internet

Each Microsoft Office program provides features that allow you to take advantage of the Internet. You can save Microsoft Office documents as Web pages, which allows you to place your documents on the Internet.

# MICROSOFT OFFICE 2000 EDITIONS

**There are several editions of Microsoft Office 2000 available.** | The available Microsoft Office 2000 editions include Standard, Small Business, Professional and Premium.

Standard          Small Business          Professional          Premium

**Each edition contains a different combination of programs.**

| Programs | MICROSOFT OFFICE 2000 EDITIONS | | | |
|---|---|---|---|---|
| | Standard | Small Business | Professional | Premium |
| Word | ✔ | ✔ | ✔ | ✔ |
| Excel | ✔ | ✔ | ✔ | ✔ |
| PowerPoint | ✔ | | ✔ | ✔ |
| Access | | | ✔ | ✔ |
| Publisher | | ✔ | ✔ | ✔ |
| Outlook | ✔ | ✔ | ✔ | ✔ |
| FrontPage | | | | ✔ |
| PhotoDraw | | | | ✔ |
| Internet Explorer 5.0 | | | | ✔ |
| Small Business Tools | | ✔ | ✔ | ✔ |

# USING THE MOUSE

**A mouse is a handheld device that lets you select and move items on your screen.**

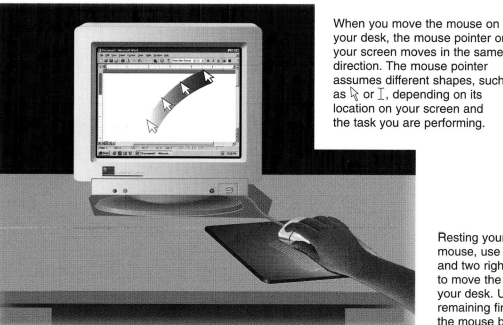

When you move the mouse on your desk, the mouse pointer on your screen moves in the same direction. The mouse pointer assumes different shapes, such as $\c$ or $\mathrm{I}$, depending on its location on your screen and the task you are performing.

Resting your hand on the mouse, use your thumb and two rightmost fingers to move the mouse on your desk. Use your two remaining fingers to press the mouse buttons.

## MOUSE ACTIONS

**Click**

Press and release the left mouse button.

**Double-click**

Quickly press and release the left mouse button twice.

**Right-click**

Press and release the right mouse button.

**Drag**

Position the mouse pointer ($\c$) over an object on your screen and then press and hold down the left mouse button. Still holding down the button, move the mouse to where you want to place the object and then release the button.

# START A PROGRAM

You can start an
Office program to
perform a task such
as creating a letter,
analyzing financial
data or designing
a presentation.

## START A PROGRAM

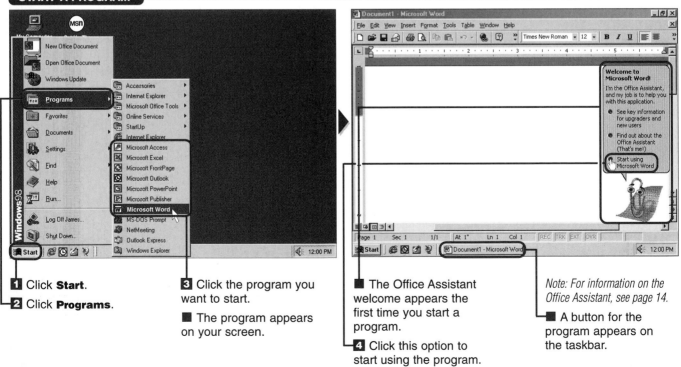

**1** Click **Start**.

**2** Click **Programs**.

**3** Click the program you
want to start.

■ The program appears
on your screen.

■ The Office Assistant
welcome appears the
first time you start a
program.

**4** Click this option to
start using the program.

*Note: For information on the
Office Assistant, see page 14.*

■ A button for the
program appears on
the taskbar.

6

# EXIT A PROGRAM

When you finish using a program, you can exit the program.

You should always exit all programs before turning off your computer.

## EXIT A PROGRAM

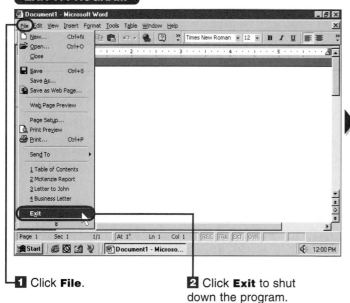

**1** Click **File**.

**2** Click **Exit** to shut down the program.

■ The program disappears from your screen.

■ The button for the program disappears from the taskbar.

7

# SELECT COMMANDS USING MENUS

You can select a command from a menu to perform a task in an Office program. Each command performs a different task.

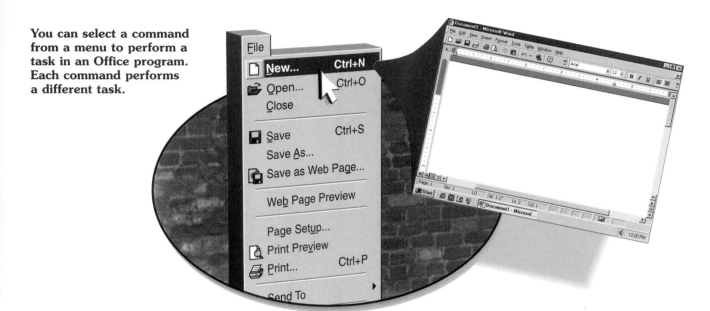

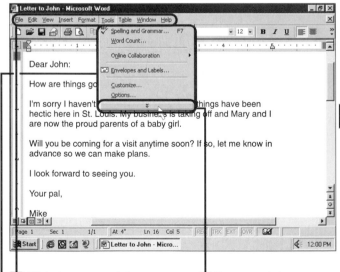

**1** Click the name of the menu you want to display.

■ A short version of the menu appears, displaying the most commonly used commands.

**2** To expand the menu and display all the commands, position the mouse ⏸ over ⯆.

*Note: If you do not perform step 2, the expanded menu will automatically appear after a few seconds.*

■ The expanded menu appears, displaying all the commands.

**3** Click the command you want to use.

*Note: A dimmed command is currently not available.*

■ To close a menu without selecting a command, click outside the menu.

**?**

**How can I make a command appear on the short version of a menu?**

When you select a command from an expanded menu, the command is automatically added to the short version of the menu. The next time you display the short version of the menu, the command you selected will appear.

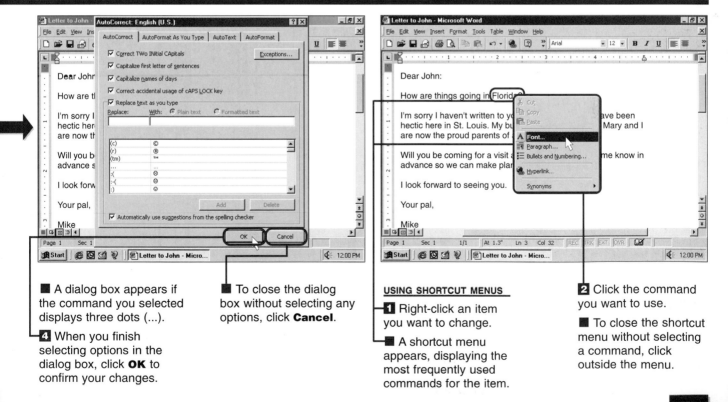

**Expanded menu**

**Short menu**

■ A dialog box appears if the command you selected displays three dots (...).

**4** When you finish selecting options in the dialog box, click **OK** to confirm your changes.

■ To close the dialog box without selecting any options, click **Cancel**.

**USING SHORTCUT MENUS**

**1** Right-click an item you want to change.

■ A shortcut menu appears, displaying the most frequently used commands for the item.

**2** Click the command you want to use.

■ To close the shortcut menu without selecting a command, click outside the menu.

# SELECT COMMANDS USING TOOLBARS

**A toolbar contains buttons that you can use to select commands and access commonly used features.**

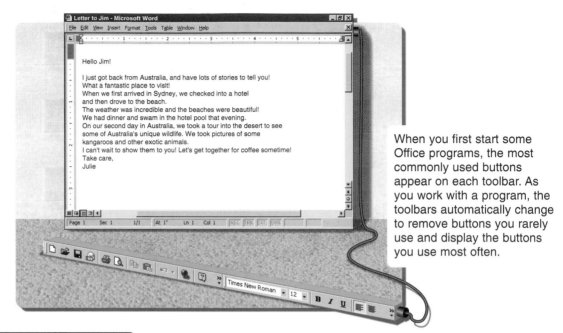

When you first start some Office programs, the most commonly used buttons appear on each toolbar. As you work with a program, the toolbars automatically change to remove buttons you rarely use and display the buttons you use most often.

## SELECT COMMANDS USING TOOLBARS

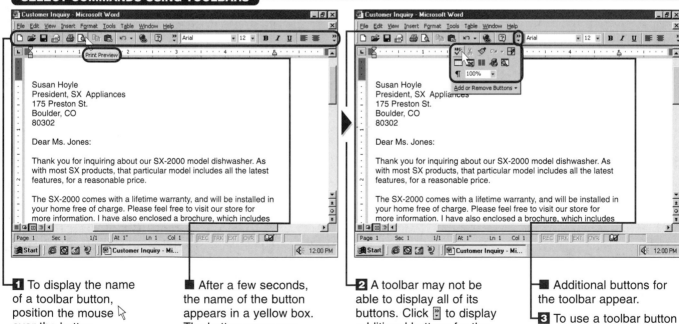

**1** To display the name of a toolbar button, position the mouse ⌖ over the button.

■ After a few seconds, the name of the button appears in a yellow box. The button name can help you determine the task the button performs.

**2** A toolbar may not be able to display all of its buttons. Click ▓ to display additional buttons for the toolbar.

■ Additional buttons for the toolbar appear.

**3** To use a toolbar button to select a command, click the button.

# DISPLAY OR HIDE A TOOLBAR

Each Microsoft Office program offers several toolbars that you can display or hide at any time. Each toolbar contains buttons that help you quickly perform common tasks.

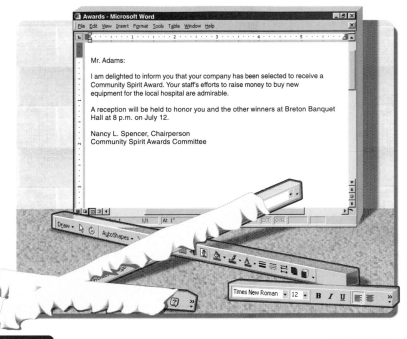

When you first start an Office program, one or more toolbars automatically appear on your screen. You can choose which toolbars to display based on the tasks you perform most often.

## DISPLAY OR HIDE A TOOLBAR

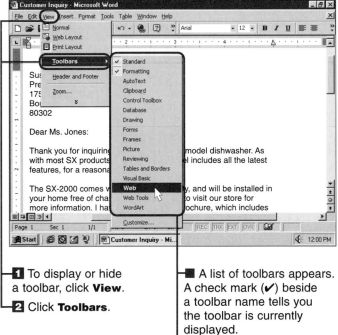

■1 To display or hide a toolbar, click **View**.

■2 Click **Toolbars**.

■ A list of toolbars appears. A check mark (✔) beside a toolbar name tells you the toolbar is currently displayed.

■3 Click the name of the toolbar you want to display or hide.

■ The program displays or hides the toolbar you selected.

# SIZE A TOOLBAR

You can increase the size
of a toolbar to display
more buttons on the
toolbar. This is useful
when a toolbar appears
on the same row as
another toolbar and
cannot display all
of its buttons.

If several toolbars are displayed on
the same row, you cannot size the
leftmost toolbar. You also cannot size
a toolbar that appears on its own row.

## SIZE A TOOLBAR

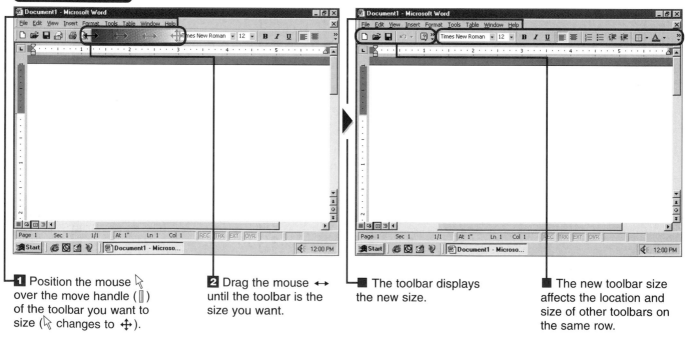

**1** Position the mouse ▷
over the move handle ( ▐ )
of the toolbar you want to
size ( ▷ changes to ✛ ).

**2** Drag the mouse ↔
until the toolbar is the
size you want.

■ The toolbar displays
the new size.

■ The new toolbar size
affects the location and
size of other toolbars on
the same row.

# MOVE A TOOLBAR

You can move a
toolbar to the top,
bottom, right or left
edge of your screen.

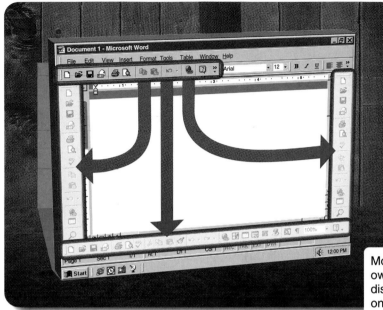

Moving a toolbar to its
own row allows you to
display more buttons
on the toolbar.

## MOVE A TOOLBAR

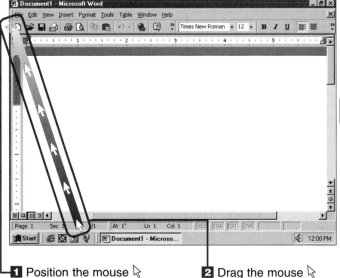

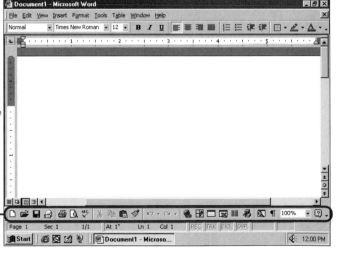

**1** Position the mouse ⇖
over the move handle (▯)
of the toolbar you want to
move (⇖ changes to ✛).

**2** Drag the mouse ⇖
to where you want the
toolbar to appear.

■ The toolbar appears
in the new location.

13

# GETTING HELP

If you do not know how to perform a task, you can ask the Office Assistant for help.

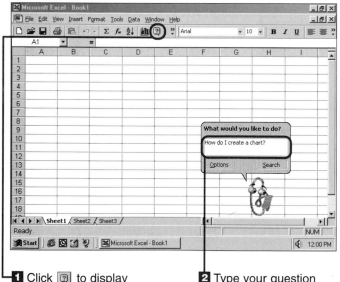

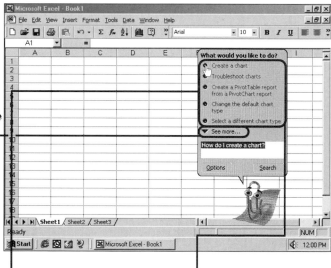

**1** Click  to display the Office Assistant.

*Note: If ▩ is not displayed, click ▩ on the Standard toolbar to display all the buttons.*

**2** Type your question and then press the **Enter** key.

*Note: If the question area does not appear, click the Office Assistant.*

■ A list of help topics related to your question appears.

■ If more help topics exist, you can click **See more** to view the additional topics.

*Note: If you do not see a help topic of interest, try rephrasing your question.*

**3** Click a help topic of interest.

**?**

**Why do some words in the Help window appear in blue?**

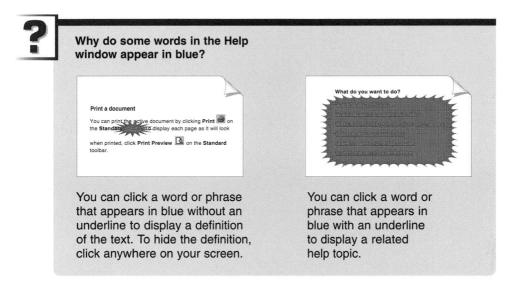

You can click a word or phrase that appears in blue without an underline to display a definition of the text. To hide the definition, click anywhere on your screen.

You can click a word or phrase that appears in blue with an underline to display a related help topic.

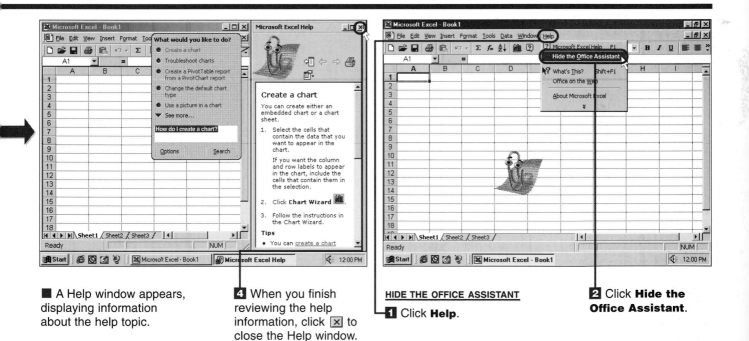

■ A Help window appears, displaying information about the help topic.

**4** When you finish reviewing the help information, click ⊠ to close the Help window.

**HIDE THE OFFICE ASSISTANT**

**1** Click **Help**.

**2** Click **Hide the Office Assistant**.

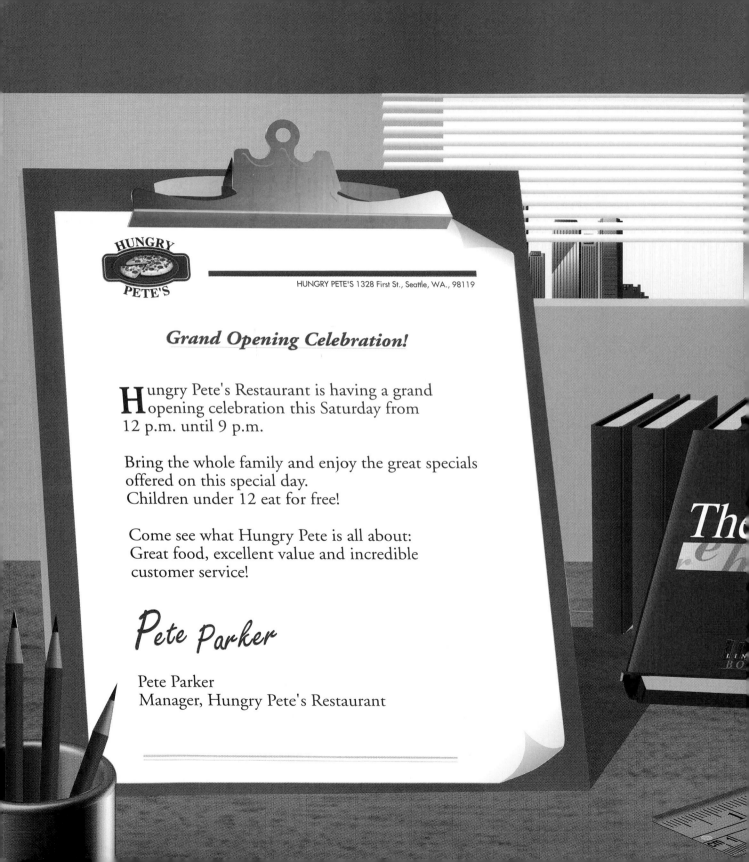

HUNGRY PETE'S 1328 First St., Seattle, WA., 98119

## *Grand Opening Celebration!*

**H**ungry Pete's Restaurant is having a grand opening celebration this Saturday from 12 p.m. until 9 p.m.

Bring the whole family and enjoy the great specials offered on this special day.
Children under 12 eat for free!

Come see what Hungry Pete is all about:
Great food, excellent value and incredible customer service!

*Pete Parker*

Pete Parker
Manager, Hungry Pete's Restaurant

# Using Word

# INTRODUCTION TO WORD

Word is a word processing program you can use to efficiently produce professional-looking documents, such as letters, reports and essays.

## Editing

Word offers many time-saving features to help you edit text in a document. You can add or delete text, rearrange paragraphs and check for spelling and grammar errors. Word remembers the last changes you made to a document, so you can undo changes you regret.

## Formatting

You can format a document to enhance the appearance of the document. You can use various font sizes, styles and colors to make important text stand out. You can also use bullets to separate items in a list, add page numbers or center text.

## Creating Tables

You can create tables to neatly display information in a document. You can use one of Word's ready-to-use designs to enhance the appearance of a table.

# START WORD

When you start
Word, a blank
document appears
on your screen.
You can type text
into this document.

## START WORD

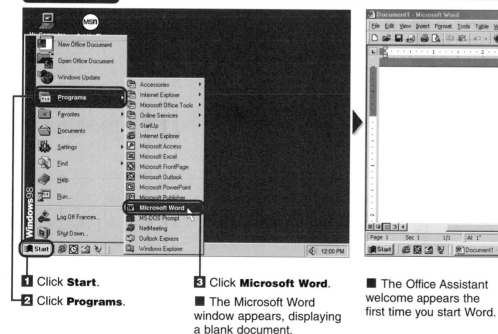

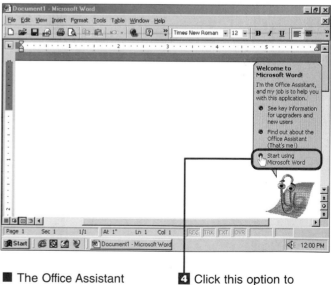

**1** Click **Start**.

**2** Click **Programs**.

**3** Click **Microsoft Word**.

■ The Microsoft Word
window appears, displaying
a blank document.

■ The Office Assistant
welcome appears the
first time you start Word.

**4** Click this option to
start using Word.

*Note: For information on the
Office Assistant, see page 14.*

# THE WORD SCREEN

The Word screen displays several items to help you perform tasks efficiently.

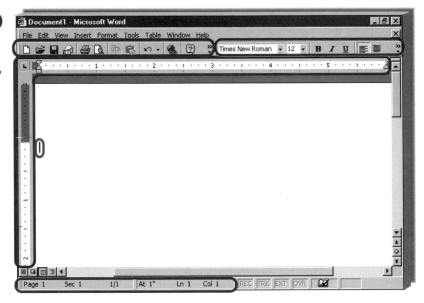

**Standard Toolbar**

Contains buttons to help you select common commands, such as Save and Print.

**Insertion Point**

The flashing line on the screen that indicates where the text you type will appear.

**Formatting Toolbar**

Contains buttons to help you select common formatting commands, such as Bold and Underline.

**Ruler**

Allows you to change margin and tab settings for the document.

**Status Bar**

Provides information about the area of the document displayed on the screen and the position of the insertion point.

**Page 1**

The page displayed on the screen.

**Sec 1**

The section of the document displayed on the screen.

**1/1**

The page displayed on the screen and the total number of pages in the document.

**At 1"**

The distance from the top of the page to the insertion point.

**Ln 1**

The number of lines from the top margin to the insertion point.

**Col 1**

The number of characters from the left margin to the insertion point, including spaces.

# ENTER TEXT

**Word allows you to type text into your document quickly and easily.**

Word automatically underlines misspelled words in red and grammar errors in green. The underlines will not appear when you print your document. To correct misspelled words and grammar errors, see page 48.

## ENTER TEXT

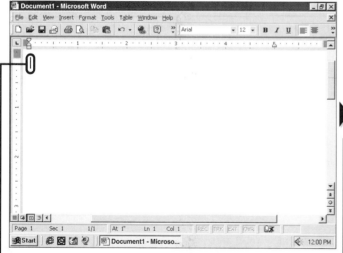

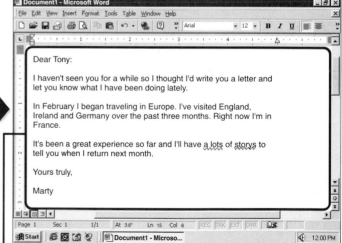

■ The text you type will appear where the insertion point flashes on your screen.

**1** Type the text for your document.

■ When you reach the end of a line, Word automatically wraps the text to the next line. You only need to press the **Enter** key when you want to start a new paragraph.

*Note: In this example, the font of text was changed to Arial to make the document easier to read. To change the font of text, see page 52.*

# SELECT TEXT

Before performing many tasks in Word, you must select the text you want to work with. Selected text appears highlighted on your screen.

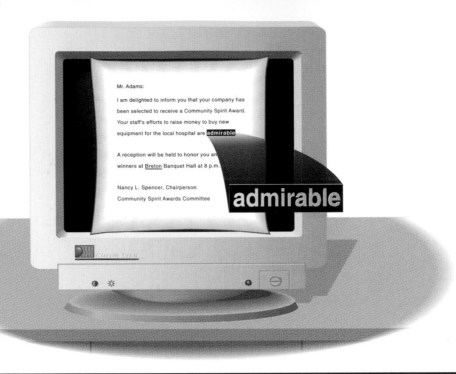

admirable

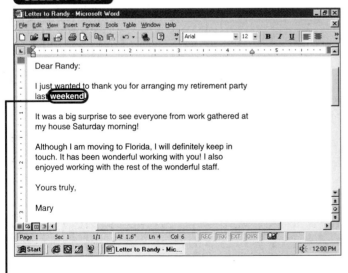

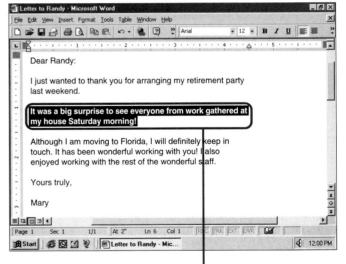

**SELECT A WORD**

**1** Double-click the word you want to select.

■ To deselect text, click outside the selected area.

**SELECT A SENTENCE**

**1** Press and hold down the Ctrl key.

**2** Still holding down the Ctrl key, click the sentence you want to select.

**?**

**How do I select all the text in my document?**

To quickly select all the text in your document, press and hold down the `Ctrl` key as you press the `A` key.

Mr. Adams:

I am delighted to inform you that your company has been selected to receive a Community Spirit Award. Your staff's efforts to raise money to buy new equipment for the local hospital are admirable.

A reception will be held to honor you and the other winners at Dreton Danquet Hall at 0 p.m. on July 12th.

Nancy L. Spencer, Chairperson
Community Spirit Awards Committee

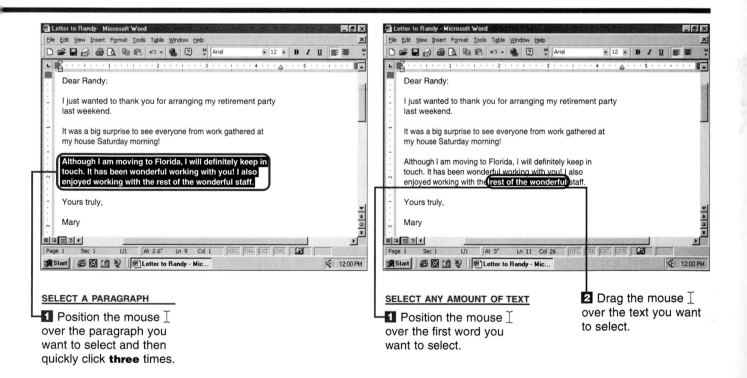

**SELECT A PARAGRAPH**

**1** Position the mouse I over the paragraph you want to select and then quickly click **three** times.

**SELECT ANY AMOUNT OF TEXT**

**1** Position the mouse I over the first word you want to select.

**2** Drag the mouse I over the text you want to select.

# MOVE THROUGH A DOCUMENT

You can easily move to another location in your document.

If you create a long document, your computer screen may not be able to display all the text at once. You must scroll through your document to view other parts of the document.

## MOVE THROUGH A DOCUMENT

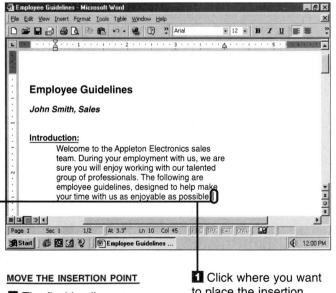

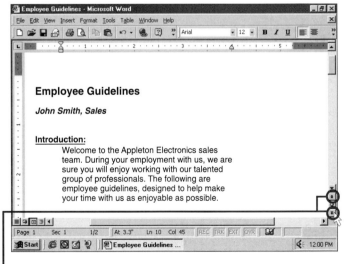

### MOVE THE INSERTION POINT

■ The flashing line on your screen, called the insertion point, indicates where the text you type will appear.

**1** Click where you want to place the insertion point.

*Note: You can also press the*
←, →, ↑ *or* ↓ *key*
*to move the insertion point one character or line in any direction.*

### DISPLAY PREVIOUS OR NEXT PAGE

**1** Click one of the following buttons.

⬆ Display previous page

⬇ Display next page

**How do I use a wheeled mouse to scroll through my document?**

A wheeled mouse has a wheel between the left and right mouse buttons. Moving this wheel lets you quickly scroll through your document. The Microsoft IntelliMouse is a popular example of a wheeled mouse.

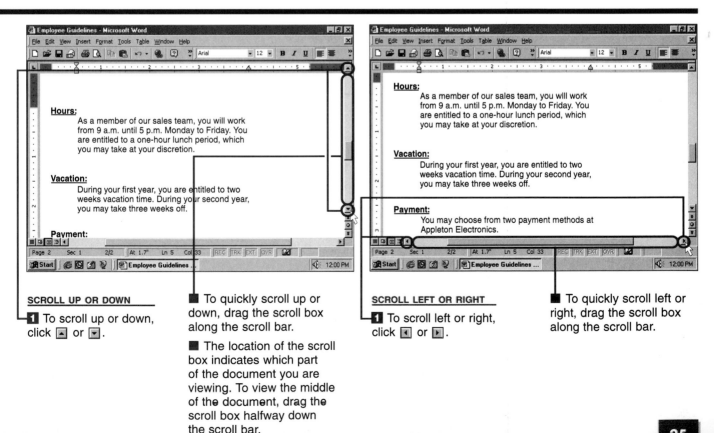

**SCROLL UP OR DOWN**

**1** To scroll up or down, click ▲ or ▼.

■ To quickly scroll up or down, drag the scroll box along the scroll bar.

■ The location of the scroll box indicates which part of the document you are viewing. To view the middle of the document, drag the scroll box halfway down the scroll bar.

**SCROLL LEFT OR RIGHT**

**1** To scroll left or right, click ◄ or ►.

■ To quickly scroll left or right, drag the scroll box along the scroll bar.

# CHANGE THE VIEW

Word offers four ways to display your document. You can choose the view that best suits your needs.

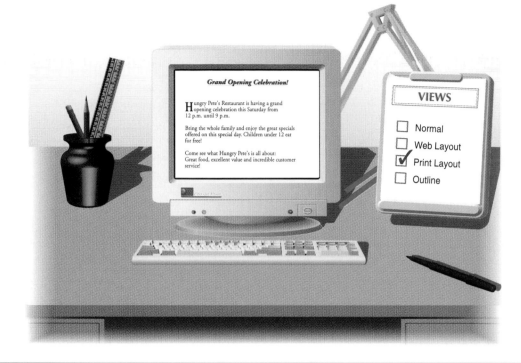

VIEWS

- ☐ Normal
- ☐ Web Layout
- ☑ Print Layout
- ☐ Outline

CHANGE THE VIEW

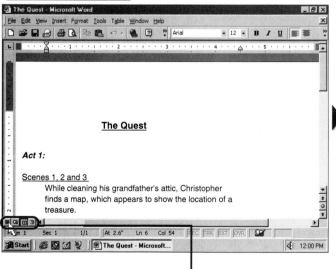

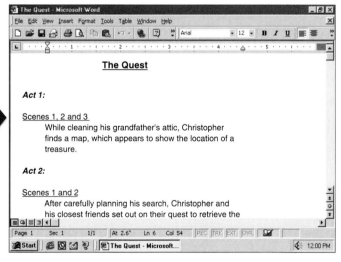

■ When you first start Word, the document appears in the Print Layout view.

**1** To change the view, click one of the following buttons.

　▤ Normal

　▣ Web Layout

　▤ Print Layout

　▤ Outline

■ The document appears in the new view.

## THE FOUR VIEWS

### Normal View

This view simplifies your document so you can quickly enter, edit and format text. The Normal view does not display margins or page numbers.

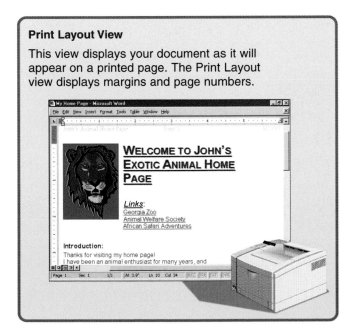

### Web Layout View

This view displays your document as it will appear on the Web. The Web Layout view is useful when you are using Word to create a Web page.

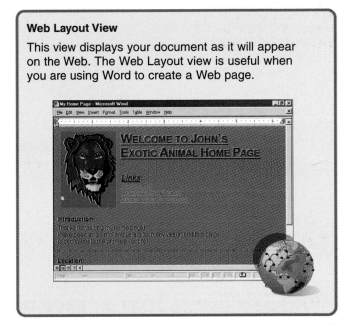

### Print Layout View

This view displays your document as it will appear on a printed page. The Print Layout view displays margins and page numbers.

### Outline View

This view helps you review and work with the structure of your document. The Outline view lets you collapse a document to see only the main headings or expand a document to see all the main headings and text. This view is useful for working with long documents.

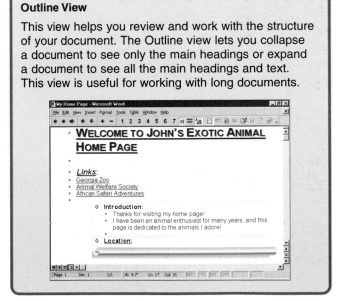

# SAVE A DOCUMENT

You can save your document to store it for future use. This allows you to later review and edit the document.

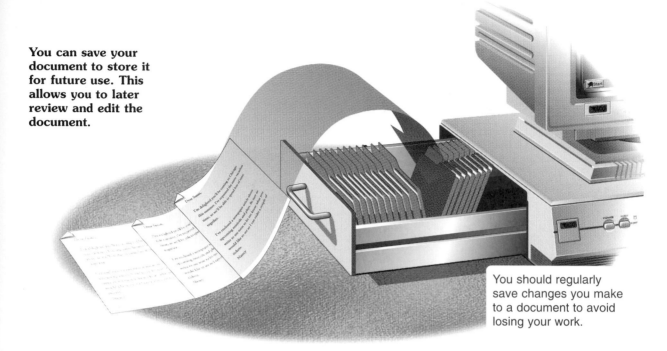

You should regularly save changes you make to a document to avoid losing your work.

## SAVE A DOCUMENT

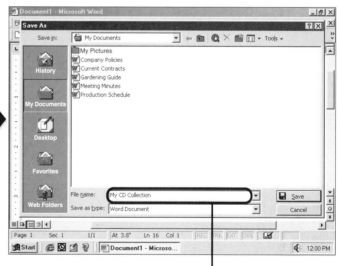

**1** Click 🖫 to save your document.

*Note: If 🖫 is not displayed, click 🔽 on the Standard toolbar to display all the buttons.*

■ The Save As dialog box appears.

*Note: If you previously saved your document, the Save As dialog box will not appear since you have already named the document.*

**2** Type a name for the document.

## What are the commonly used folders I can access?

**History**

Provides access to folders and documents you recently used.

**My Documents**

Provides a convenient place to store a document.

**Desktop**

Lets you store a document on the Windows desktop.

**Favorites**

Provides a place to store a document you will frequently access.

**Web Folders**

Can help you store a document on the Web.

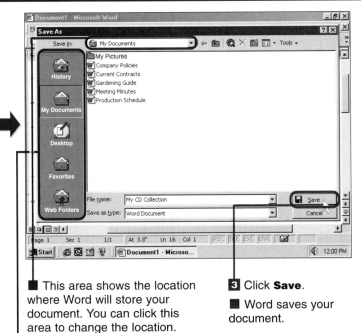

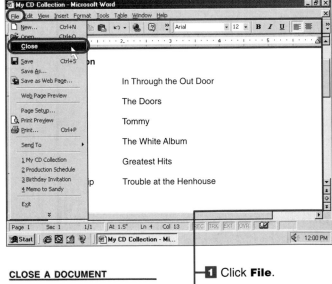

■ This area shows the location where Word will store your document. You can click this area to change the location.

■ This area allows you to access commonly used folders. To display the contents of a folder, click the folder.

**3** Click **Save**.

■ Word saves your document.

### CLOSE A DOCUMENT

When you finish working with a document, you can close the document to remove it from your screen.

**1** Click **File**.

**2** Click **Close** to close the document.

# OPEN A DOCUMENT

You can open a saved
document and display
it on your screen. This
allows you to review
and make changes to
the document.

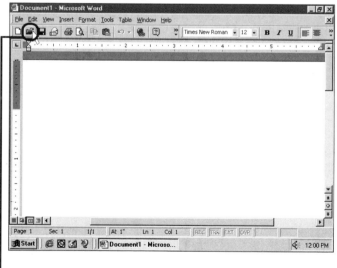

**1** Click 📷 to open
a document.

*Note: If 📷 is not displayed,
click 🔽 on the Standard toolbar
to display all the buttons.*

■ The Open dialog
box appears.

■ This area shows the
location of the displayed
documents. You can click
this area to change the
location.

■ This area allows you
to access commonly
used folders. To display
the contents of a folder,
click the folder.

*Note: For information on the
commonly used folders, see
the top of page 29.*

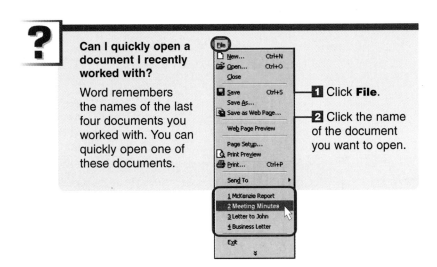

**Can I quickly open a document I recently worked with?**

Word remembers the names of the last four documents you worked with. You can quickly open one of these documents.

**1** Click **File**.

**2** Click the name of the document you want to open.

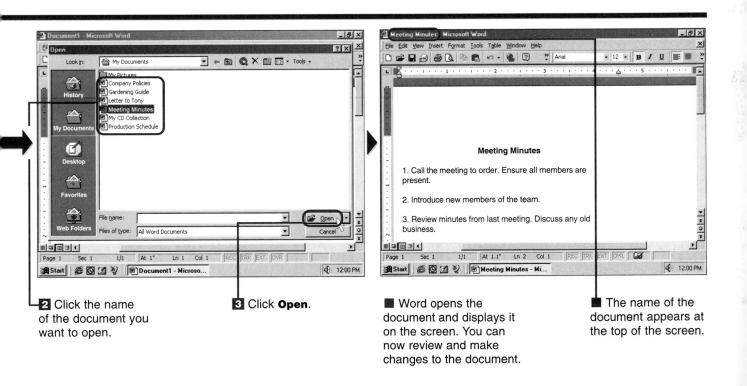

**2** Click the name of the document you want to open.

**3** Click **Open**.

■ Word opens the document and displays it on the screen. You can now review and make changes to the document.

■ The name of the document appears at the top of the screen.

# PREVIEW A DOCUMENT

You can use the Print Preview feature to see how your document will look when printed. This lets you confirm that the document will print the way you want.

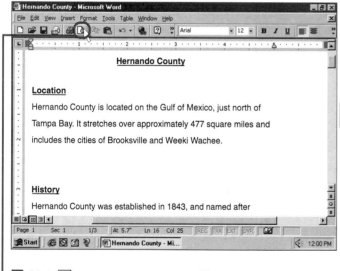

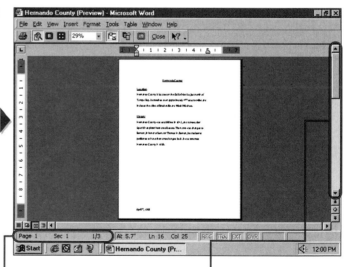

**1** Click 🔍 to preview your document.

*Note: If 🔍 is not displayed, click ⤨ on the Standard toolbar to display all the buttons.*

■ The Print Preview window appears.

■ This area indicates which page is displayed and the total number of pages in your document.

■ If your document contains more than one page, you can use the scroll bar to view the other pages.

## 2 SAVE, OPEN AND PRINT A DOCUMENT

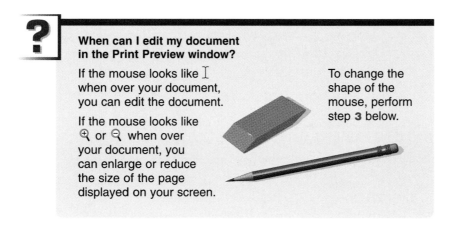

**When can I edit my document in the Print Preview window?**

If the mouse looks like I when over your document, you can edit the document.

If the mouse looks like ⊕ or ⊖ when over your document, you can enlarge or reduce the size of the page displayed on your screen.

To change the shape of the mouse, perform step **3** below.

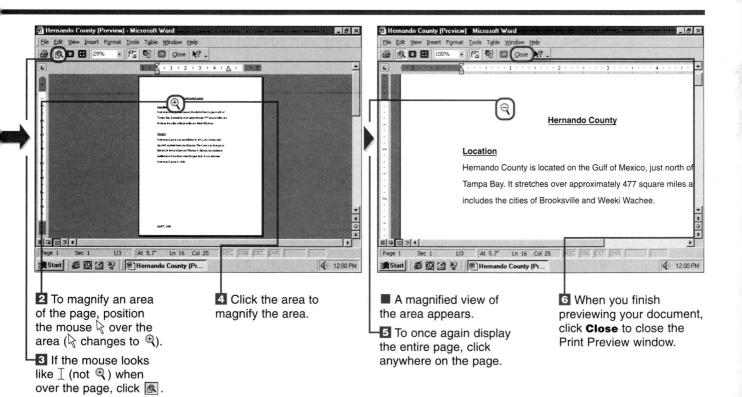

**2** To magnify an area of the page, position the mouse �ᐟ over the area (ᐟ changes to ⊕).

**3** If the mouse looks like I (not ⊕) when over the page, click 🔍.

**4** Click the area to magnify the area.

■ A magnified view of the area appears.

**5** To once again display the entire page, click anywhere on the page.

**6** When you finish previewing your document, click **Close** to close the Print Preview window.

# PRINT A DOCUMENT

You can produce a
paper copy of the
document displayed
on your screen.

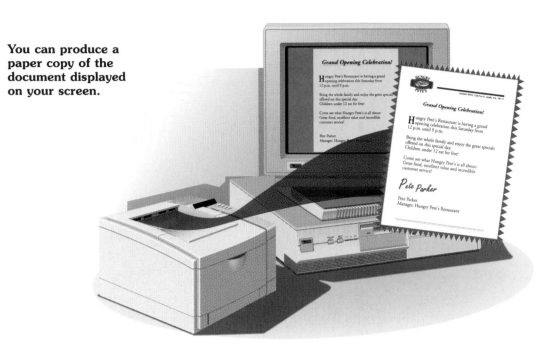

Before printing your
document, make sure
the printer is turned
on and contains an
adequate supply of
paper.

## PRINT A DOCUMENT

**1** Click anywhere in
the document or page
you want to print.

■ To print only some of
the text in the document,
select the text you want
to print. To select text,
see page 22.

**2** Click **File**.

**3** Click **Print**.

■ The Print dialog box
appears.

## ? Which print option should I use?

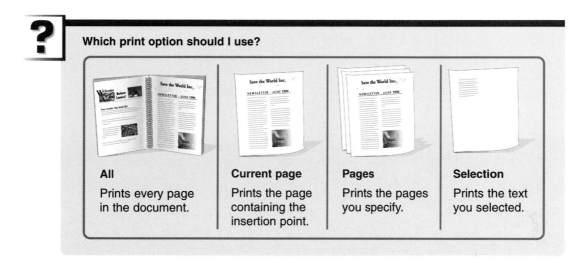

**All**
Prints every page in the document.

**Current page**
Prints the page containing the insertion point.

**Pages**
Prints the pages you specify.

**Selection**
Prints the text you selected.

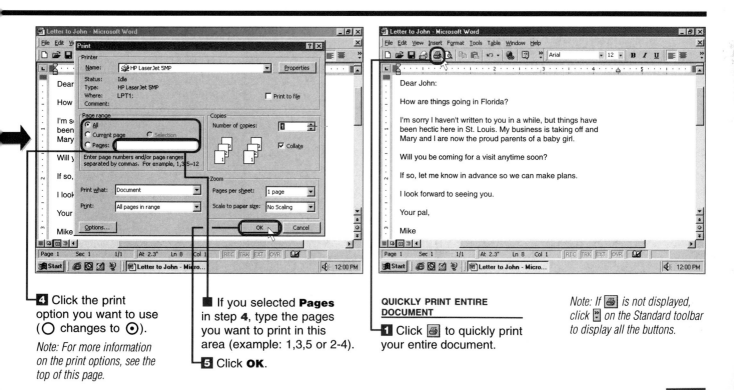

**4** Click the print option you want to use (○ changes to ⊙).

*Note: For more information on the print options, see the top of this page.*

■ If you selected **Pages** in step **4**, type the pages you want to print in this area (example: 1,3,5 or 2-4).

**5** Click **OK**.

**QUICKLY PRINT ENTIRE DOCUMENT**

**1** Click 🖨 to quickly print your entire document.

*Note: If 🖨 is not displayed, click 🔽 on the Standard toolbar to display all the buttons.*

# CREATE A NEW DOCUMENT

You can create a new
document to start
writing a letter,
memo or report.

Think of each document
as a separate piece of
paper. Creating a new
document is like placing
a new piece of paper on
your screen.

## CREATE A NEW DOCUMENT

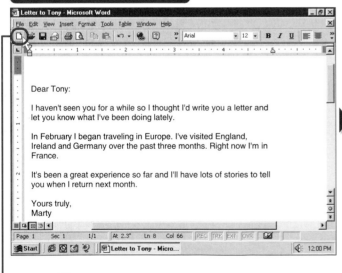

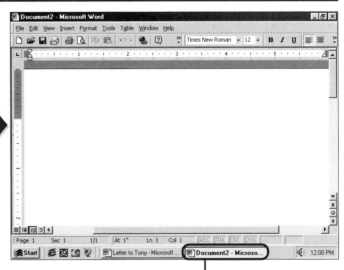

**1** Click ▢ to create
a new document.

*Note: If ▢ is not displayed,
click ⯮ on the Standard toolbar
to display all the buttons.*

■ A new document
appears. The previous
document is now hidden
behind the new document.

■ A button for the new
document appears on
the taskbar.

# SWITCH BETWEEN DOCUMENTS

Word lets you have many documents open at once. You can easily switch from one open document to another.

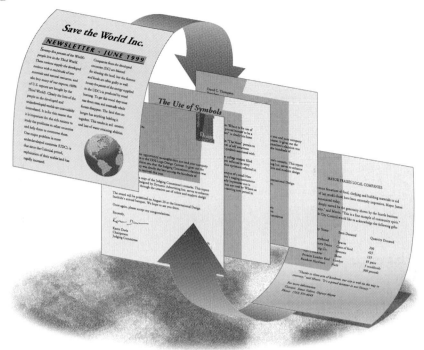

## SWITCH BETWEEN DOCUMENTS

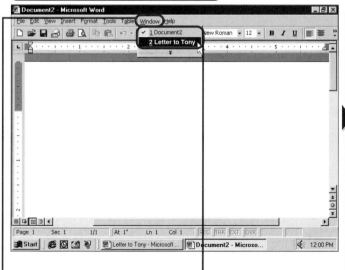

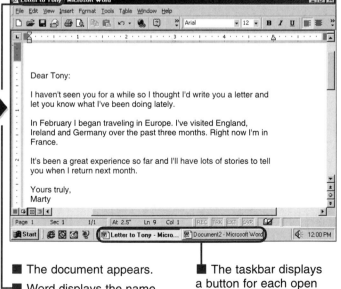

**1** Click **Window** to display a list of all the documents you have open.

**2** Click the name of the document you want to switch to.

■ The document appears.

■ Word displays the name of the current document at the top of your screen.

■ The taskbar displays a button for each open document. You can also switch to a document by clicking its button on the taskbar.

# E-MAIL A DOCUMENT

You can e-mail the
document displayed
on your screen to a
friend, family member
or colleague.

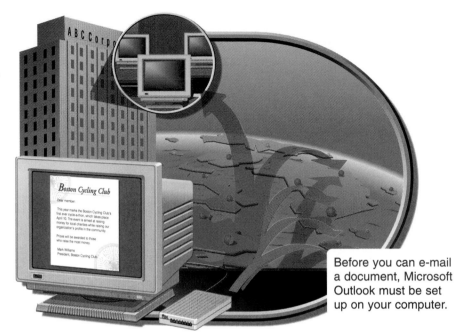

Before you can e-mail
a document, Microsoft
Outlook must be set
up on your computer.

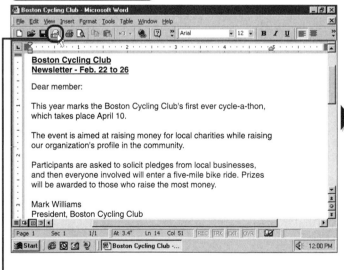

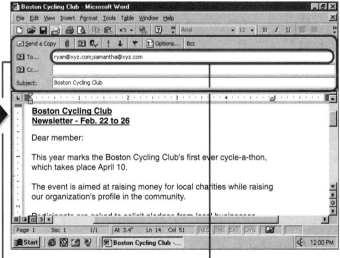

**1** Click 🖃 to e-mail the
displayed document.

*Note: If 🖃 is not displayed,
click 🔽 on the Standard toolbar
to display all the buttons.*

■ An area appears for you
to address the message.

**2** Click this area and
type the e-mail address
of each person you want
to receive the message.
Separate each address
with a semicolon (;).

38

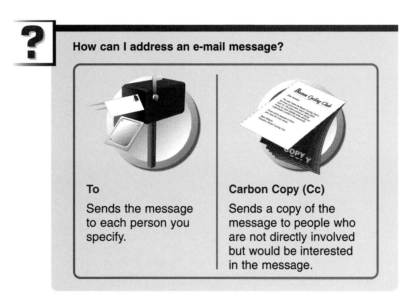

**How can I address an e-mail message?**

**To**

Sends the message to each person you specify.

**Carbon Copy (Cc)**

Sends a copy of the message to people who are not directly involved but would be interested in the message.

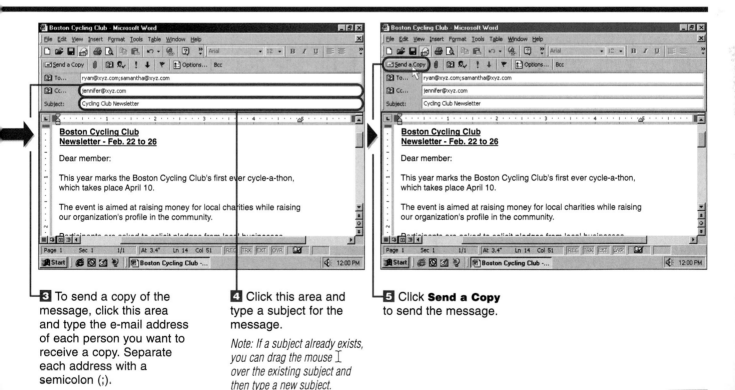

**3** To send a copy of the message, click this area and type the e-mail address of each person you want to receive a copy. Separate each address with a semicolon (;).

**4** Click this area and type a subject for the message.

*Note: If a subject already exists, you can drag the mouse I over the existing subject and then type a new subject.*

**5** Click **Send a Copy** to send the message.

# INSERT AND DELETE TEXT

Word lets you add new text to your document and remove text you no longer need.

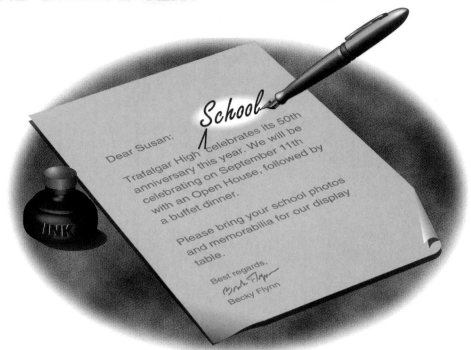

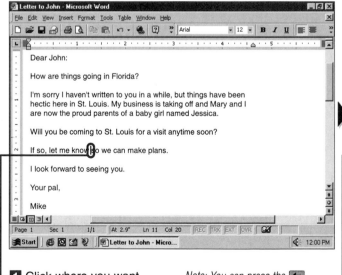

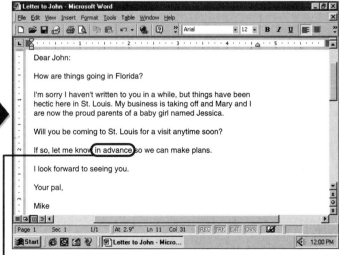

**1** Click where you want to insert the new text.

■ The text you type will appear where the insertion point flashes on the screen.

*Note: You can press the ←, →, ↑ or ↓ key to move the insertion point.*

**2** Type the text you want to insert. To insert a blank space, press the **Spacebar**.

■ The words to the right of the new text move forward.

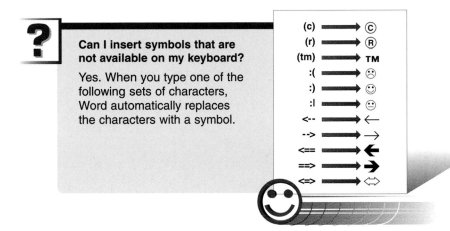

**Can I insert symbols that are not available on my keyboard?**

Yes. When you type one of the following sets of characters, Word automatically replaces the characters with a symbol.

## DELETE TEXT

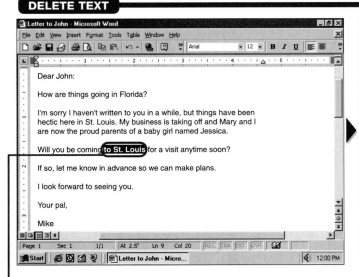

**1** Select the text you want to delete. To select text, see page 22.

**2** Press the Delete key to remove the text.

■ The text disappears. The remaining text moves to fill any empty spaces.

■ To delete a single character, click to the right of the character you want to delete and then press the ◆Backspace key. Word deletes the character to the left of the flashing insertion point.

# MOVE OR COPY TEXT

**You can move or copy text to a new location in your document.**

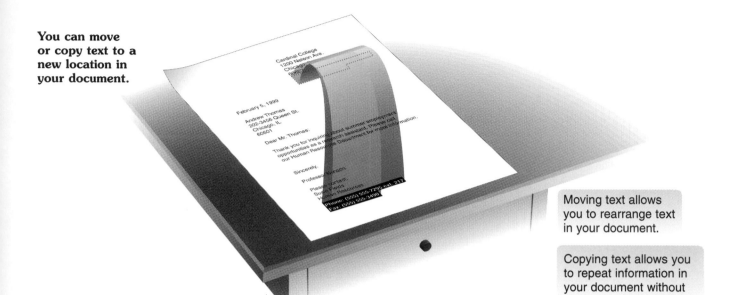

Moving text allows you to rearrange text in your document.

Copying text allows you to repeat information in your document without having to retype the text.

## MOVE OR COPY TEXT

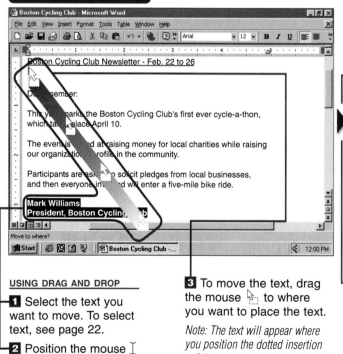

**USING DRAG AND DROP**

**1** Select the text you want to move. To select text, see page 22.

**2** Position the mouse I over the selected text ( I changes to ⌖).

**3** To move the text, drag the mouse ⌖ to where you want to place the text.

*Note: The text will appear where you position the dotted insertion point on your screen.*

■ The text moves to the new location.

■ To copy text, perform steps **1** to **3**, except press and hold down the `Ctrl` key as you perform step **3**.

**?**

**Why does the Clipboard toolbar appear when I move or copy text?**

The Clipboard toolbar may appear when you move or copy text using the toolbar buttons. Each icon on the Clipboard toolbar represents text you have selected to move or copy.

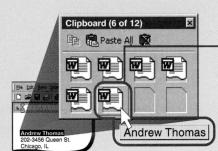

■ To see the text an icon represents, position the mouse ⌖ over the icon. A yellow box appears, displaying the first few words. You can click the icon to place the text in your document.

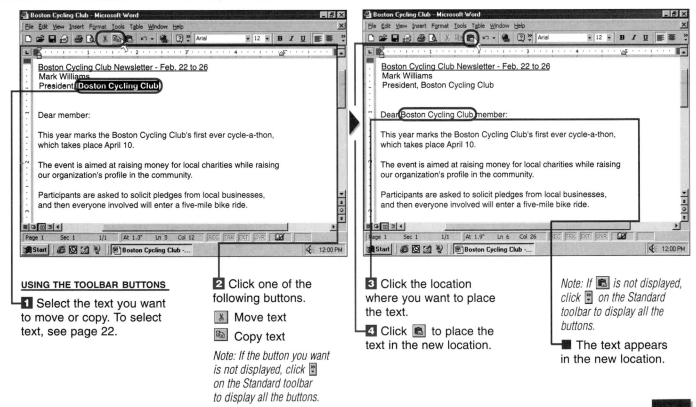

**USING THE TOOLBAR BUTTONS**

**1** Select the text you want to move or copy. To select text, see page 22.

**2** Click one of the following buttons.

✂ Move text

▤ Copy text

*Note: If the button you want is not displayed, click* ⏵ *on the Standard toolbar to display all the buttons.*

**3** Click the location where you want to place the text.

**4** Click ▤ to place the text in the new location.

*Note: If* ▤ *is not displayed, click* ⏵ *on the Standard toolbar to display all the buttons.*

■ The text appears in the new location.

# UNDO CHANGES

Word remembers the last changes you made to your document. If you regret these changes, you can cancel them by using the Undo feature.

The Undo feature can cancel your last editing and formatting changes.

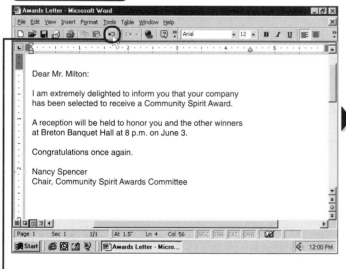

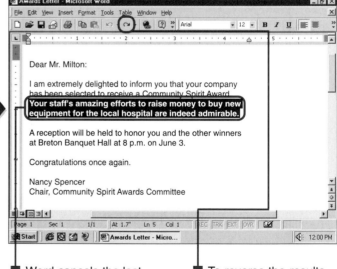

**1** Click 🔙 to undo the last change you made to your document.

*Note: If 🔙 is not displayed, click ⏬ on the Standard toolbar to display all the buttons.*

■ Word cancels the last change you made to your document.

■ You can repeat step **1** to cancel previous changes you made.

■ To reverse the results of using the Undo feature, click 🔜.

*Note: If 🔜 is not displayed, click ⏬ on the Standard toolbar to display all the buttons.*

# COUNT WORDS IN A DOCUMENT

**You can quickly determine the number of words in your document.**

Dear Susan:

Trafalgar High School celebrates its 50th anniversary this year. We will be celebrating on September 11th with an Open House, followed by a buffet dinner.

Please bring your school photos and memorabilia for our display table.

**Word Count**

When you count the number of words in your document, Word also displays the number of pages, characters, paragraphs and lines in the document.

## COUNT WORDS IN A DOCUMENT

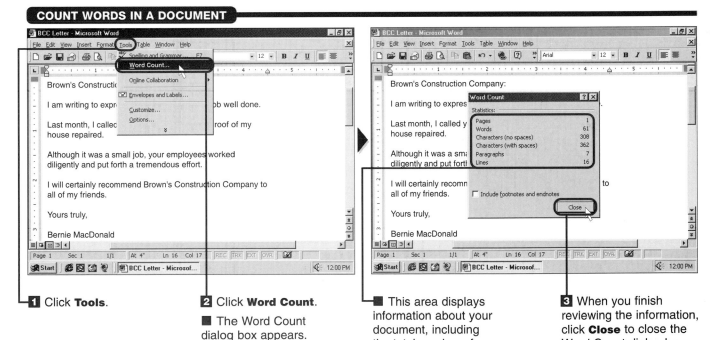

**1** Click **Tools**.

**2** Click **Word Count**.

■ The Word Count dialog box appears.

■ This area displays information about your document, including the total number of words in the document.

**3** When you finish reviewing the information, click **Close** to close the Word Count dialog box.

# FIND AND REPLACE TEXT

**The Find and Replace feature can locate and replace every occurrence of a word or phrase in your document. This is useful if you have frequently misspelled a name.**

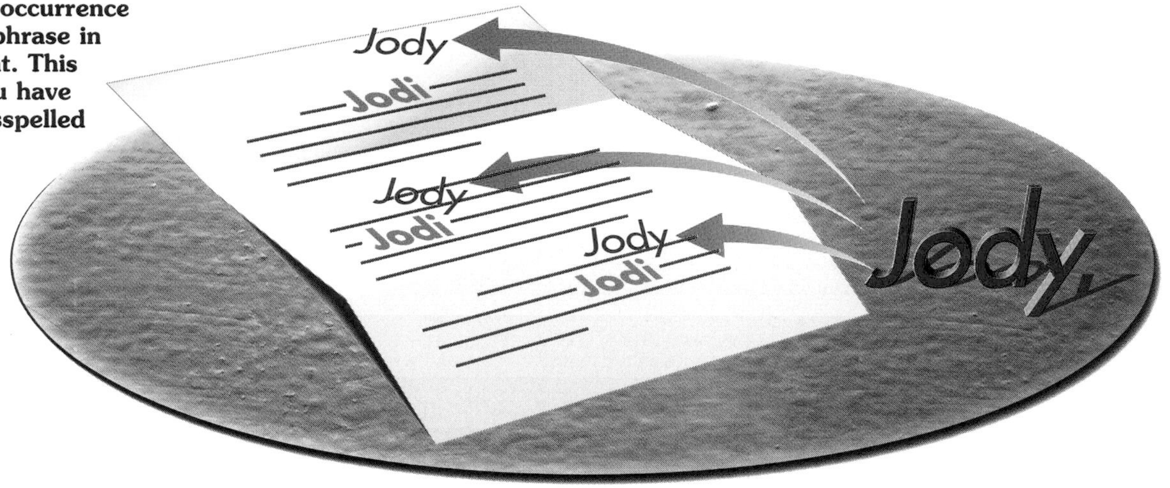


## FIND AND REPLACE TEXT

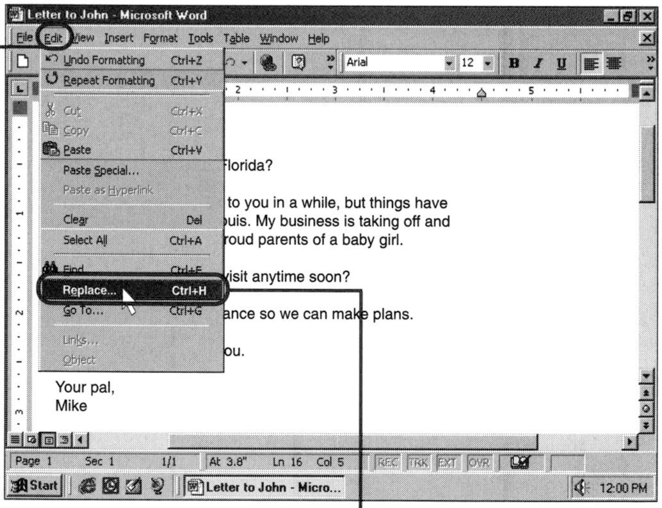


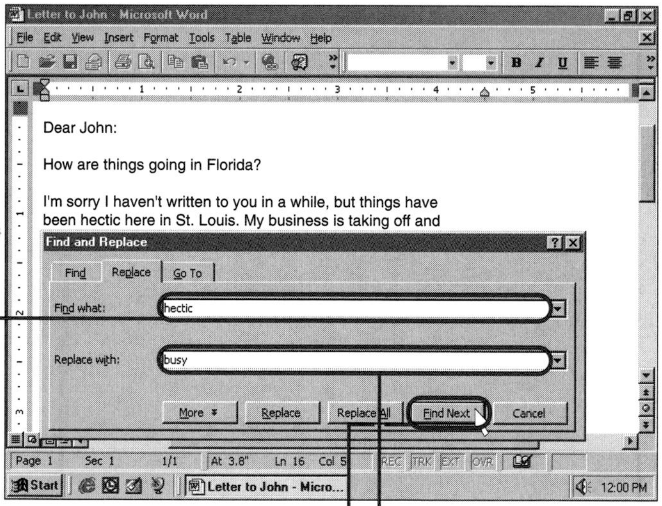


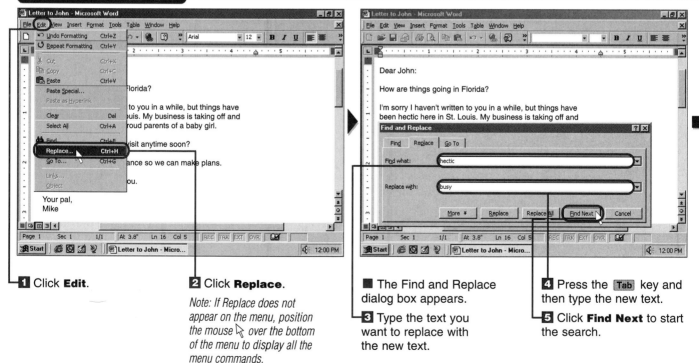

**1** Click **Edit**.

**2** Click **Replace**.

*Note: If Replace does not appear on the menu, position the mouse over the bottom of the menu to display all the menu commands.*

■ The Find and Replace dialog box appears.

**3** Type the text you want to replace with the new text.

**4** Press the Tab key and then type the new text.

**5** Click **Find Next** to start the search.

**Can I find text in my document without replacing the text?**

Yes. You can use the Find and Replace feature to locate a word or phrase in your document. Perform steps **1** to **3** below, typing the text you want to find in step **3**. Then perform step **5** until you find the text in your document.

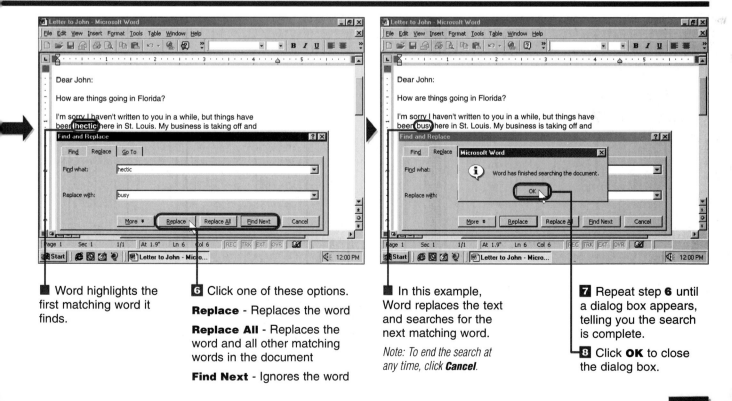

■ Word highlights the first matching word it finds.

**6** Click one of these options.

**Replace** - Replaces the word

**Replace All** - Replaces the word and all other matching words in the document

**Find Next** - Ignores the word

■ In this example, Word replaces the text and searches for the next matching word.

*Note: To end the search at any time, click **Cancel**.*

**7** Repeat step **6** until a dialog box appears, telling you the search is complete.

**8** Click **OK** to close the dialog box.

# CHECK SPELLING AND GRAMMAR

You can find and correct all the misspelled words and grammar errors in your document.

Word compares every word in your document to words in its dictionary. If a word in your document does not exist in the dictionary, Word considers the word misspelled.

## CHECK SPELLING AND GRAMMAR

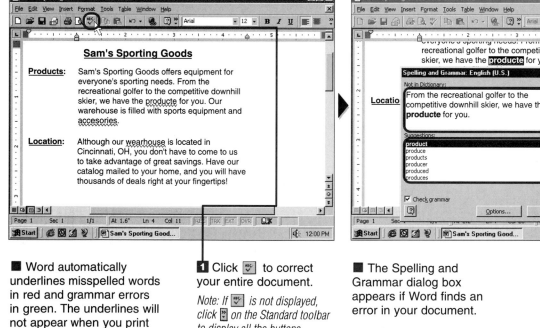

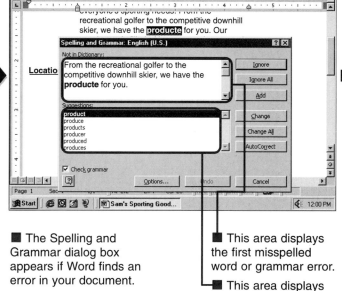

■ Word automatically underlines misspelled words in red and grammar errors in green. The underlines will not appear when you print your document.

**1** Click 📝 to correct your entire document.

*Note: If 📝 is not displayed, click 🔽 on the Standard toolbar to display all the buttons.*

■ The Spelling and Grammar dialog box appears if Word finds an error in your document.

■ This area displays the first misspelled word or grammar error.

■ This area displays suggestions for correcting the text.

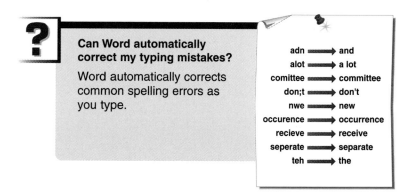

**?**

**Can Word automatically correct my typing mistakes?**

Word automatically corrects common spelling errors as you type.

| | | |
|---|---|---|
| adn | ⟶ | and |
| alot | ⟶ | a lot |
| comittee | ⟶ | committee |
| don;t | ⟶ | don't |
| nwe | ⟶ | new |
| occurence | ⟶ | occurrence |
| recieve | ⟶ | receive |
| seperate | ⟶ | separate |
| teh | ⟶ | the |

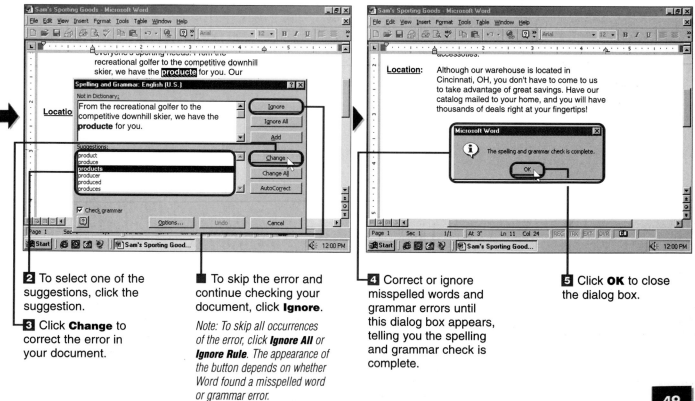

**2** To select one of the suggestions, click the suggestion.

**3** Click **Change** to correct the error in your document.

■ To skip the error and continue checking your document, click **Ignore**.

*Note: To skip all occurrences of the error, click **Ignore All** or **Ignore Rule**. The appearance of the button depends on whether Word found a misspelled word or grammar error.*

**4** Correct or ignore misspelled words and grammar errors until this dialog box appears, telling you the spelling and grammar check is complete.

**5** Click **OK** to close the dialog box.

# USING THE THESAURUS

You can use the Thesaurus feature to replace a word in your document with one that is more suitable.

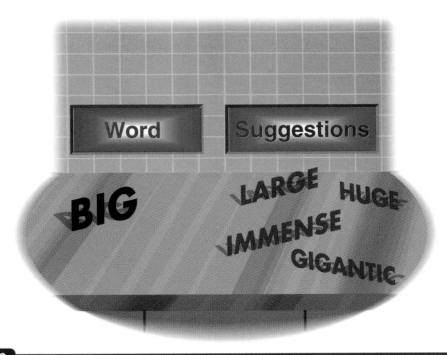

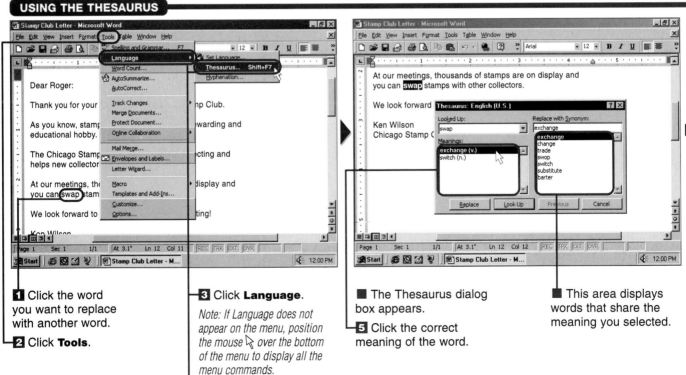

**1** Click the word you want to replace with another word.

**2** Click **Tools**.

**3** Click **Language**.

*Note: If Language does not appear on the menu, position the mouse ⤶ over the bottom of the menu to display all the menu commands.*

**4** Click **Thesaurus**.

■ The Thesaurus dialog box appears.

**5** Click the correct meaning of the word.

■ This area displays words that share the meaning you selected.

50

**?**

**How can the thesaurus help me?**

Many people use the thesaurus to replace a word that appears repeatedly in a document. Replacing repeatedly used words can help add variety to your writing. Using the thesaurus included with Word is faster and more convenient than searching through a printed thesaurus.

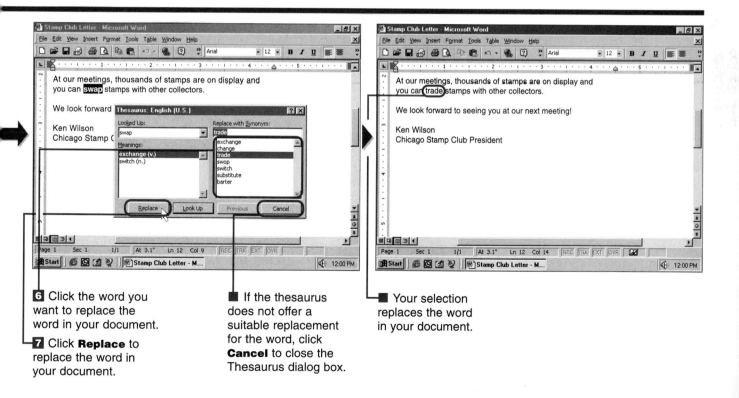

**6** Click the word you want to replace the word in your document.

**7** Click **Replace** to replace the word in your document.

■ If the thesaurus does not offer a suitable replacement for the word, click **Cancel** to close the Thesaurus dialog box.

■ Your selection replaces the word in your document.

# CHANGE FONT OF TEXT

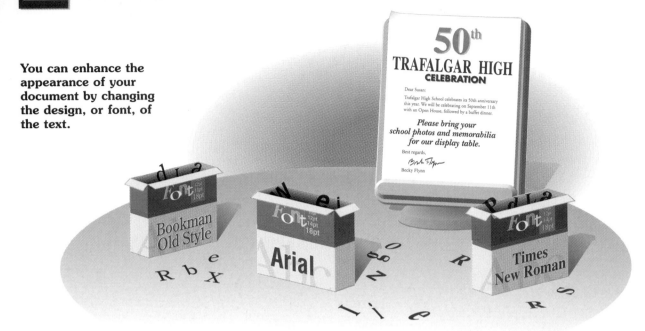

You can enhance the appearance of your document by changing the design, or font, of the text.

CHANGE FONT OF TEXT

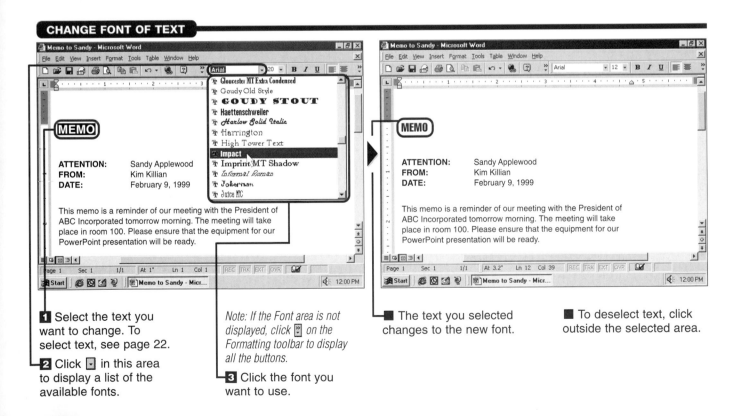

**1** Select the text you want to change. To select text, see page 22.

**2** Click ⬇ in this area to display a list of the available fonts.

*Note: If the Font area is not displayed, click ⁑ on the Formatting toolbar to display all the buttons.*

**3** Click the font you want to use.

■ The text you selected changes to the new font.

■ To deselect text, click outside the selected area.

# CHANGE SIZE OF TEXT

You can increase or decrease the size of text in your document.

Word measures the size of text in points. There are approximately 72 points in one inch.

Larger text is easier to read, but smaller text allows you to fit more information on a page.

## CHANGE SIZE OF TEXT

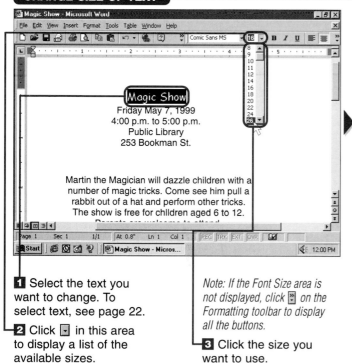

**1** Select the text you want to change. To select text, see page 22.

**2** Click ⏷ in this area to display a list of the available sizes.

*Note: If the Font Size area is not displayed, click ⏷ on the Formatting toolbar to display all the buttons.*

**3** Click the size you want to use.

■ The text you selected changes to the new size.

■ To deselect text, click outside the selected area.

# CHANGE TEXT COLOR

You can change the color of text to draw attention to headings or important information in your document.

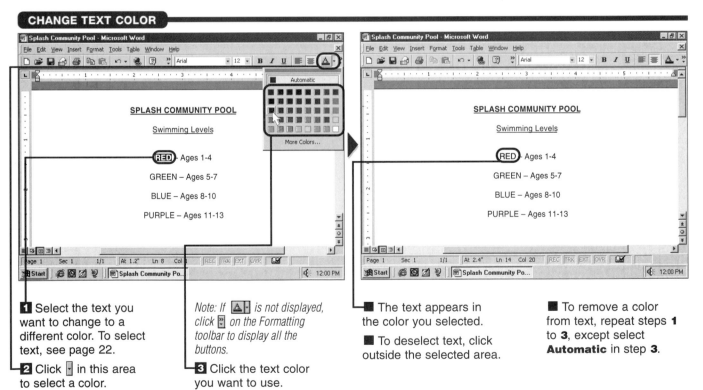

**1** Select the text you want to change to a different color. To select text, see page 22.

**2** Click ⏷ in this area to select a color.

*Note: If ⏷ is not displayed, click ⏵ on the Formatting toolbar to display all the buttons.*

**3** Click the text color you want to use.

■ The text appears in the color you selected.

■ To deselect text, click outside the selected area.

■ To remove a color from text, repeat steps **1** to **3**, except select **Automatic** in step **3**.

54

# HIGHLIGHT TEXT

You can highlight text you want to stand out in your document. Highlighting text is useful for marking information you want to review or verify later.

## HIGHLIGHT TEXT

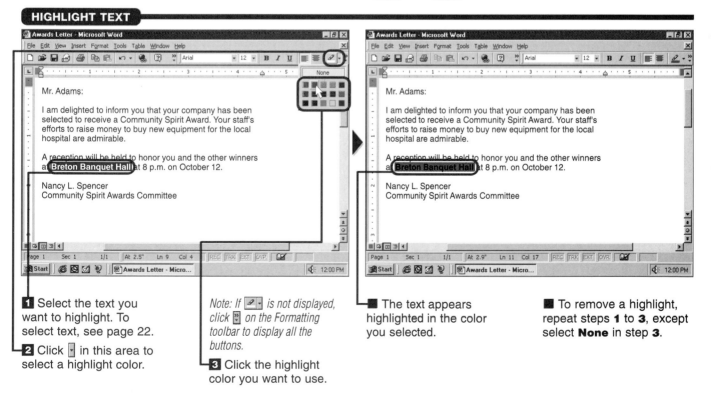

**1** Select the text you want to highlight. To select text, see page 22.

**2** Click ⋅ in this area to select a highlight color.

*Note: If ✎⋅ is not displayed, click » on the Formatting toolbar to display all the buttons.*

**3** Click the highlight color you want to use.

■ The text appears highlighted in the color you selected.

■ To remove a highlight, repeat steps **1** to **3**, except select **None** in step **3**.

# BOLD, ITALIC AND UNDERLINE

You can use the Bold, Italic and Underline features to emphasize text in your document.

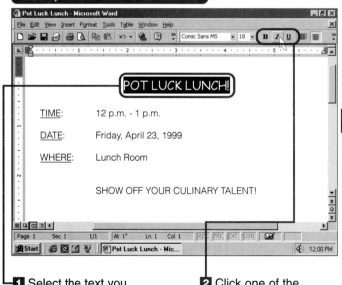

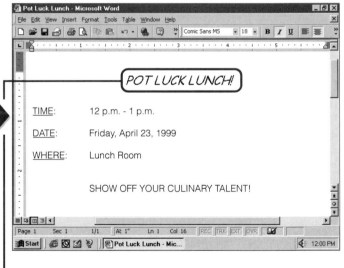

**1** Select the text you want to change. To select text, see page 22.

**2** Click one of the following buttons.

**B** Bold

**I** Italic

**U** Underline

*Note: If the button you want is not displayed, click* ⁚ *on the Formatting toolbar to display all the buttons.*

■ The text you selected appears in the new style.

■ To deselect text, click outside the selected area.

■ To remove a bold, italic or underline style, repeat steps **1** and **2**.

# COPY FORMATTING

**You can make one area of text in your document look exactly like another.**

You may want to copy the formatting of text to make all the headings or important words in your document look the same.

## COPY FORMATTING

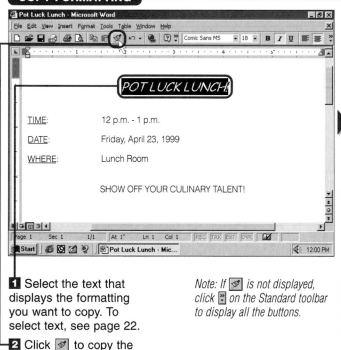

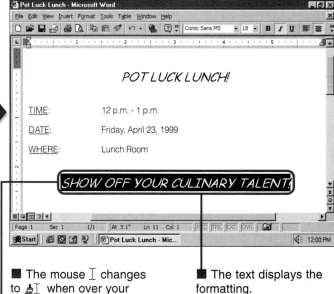

**1** Select the text that displays the formatting you want to copy. To select text, see page 22.

**2** Click 🖌 to copy the formatting.

*Note: If 🖌 is not displayed, click ⏩ on the Standard toolbar to display all the buttons.*

■ The mouse I changes to 🖌I when over your document.

**3** Select the text you want to display the same formatting.

■ The text displays the formatting.

■ To deselect text, click outside the selected area.

# CHANGE ALIGNMENT OF TEXT

You can enhance
the appearance
of your document
by aligning text
in different ways.

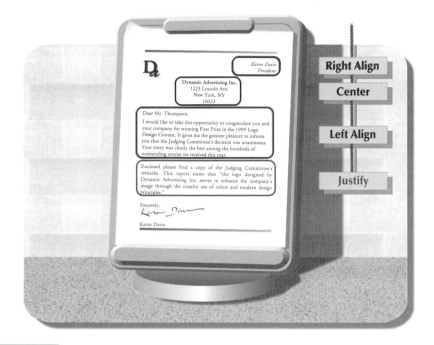

Right Align

Center

Left Align

Justify

## CHANGE ALIGNMENT OF TEXT

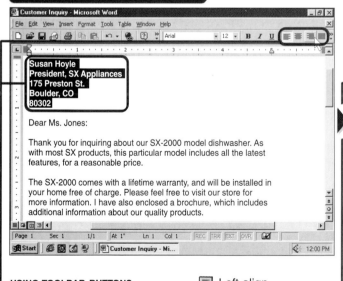

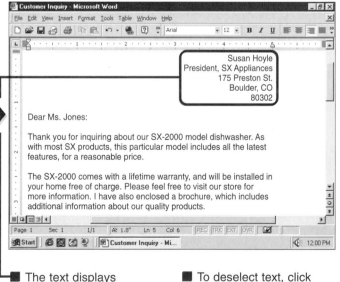

**USING TOOLBAR BUTTONS**

**1** Select the text you want
to align differently. To select
text, see page 22.

**2** Click one of the
following buttons.

🔲 Left align

🔲 Center

🔲 Right align

🔲 Justify

*Note: If the button you want
is not displayed, click* 🔲
*on the Formatting toolbar
to display all the buttons.*

■ The text displays
the new alignment.

■ To deselect text, click
outside the selected area.

**?**

**Can I use different alignments within a single line of text?**

You can use the Click and Type feature to vary the alignment within a line of text. For example, you can left align your name and right align the date on the same line.

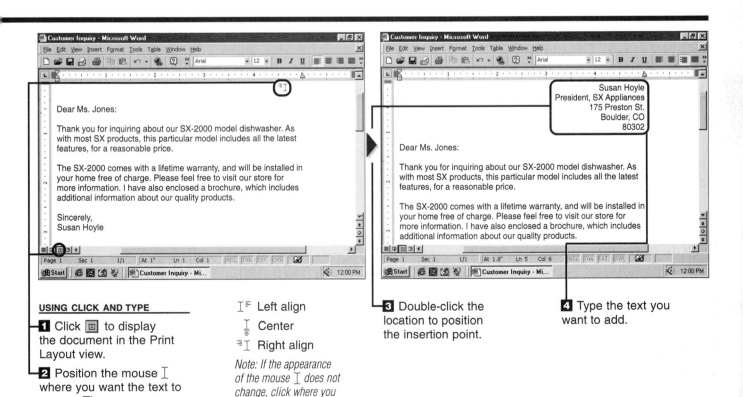

**USING CLICK AND TYPE**

**1** Click 🔲 to display the document in the Print Layout view.

**2** Position the mouse ⌶ where you want the text to appear. The appearance of the mouse ⌶ indicates how Word will align the text.

⌶⁼ Left align

⌶ Center

⁼⌶ Right align

*Note: If the appearance of the mouse ⌶ does not change, click where you want to add text.*

**3** Double-click the location to position the insertion point.

**4** Type the text you want to add.

# INDENT PARAGRAPHS

You can use the Indent feature to make paragraphs in your document stand out.

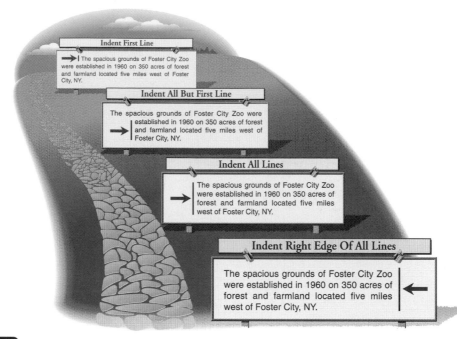

**Indent First Line**

The spacious grounds of Foster City Zoo were established in 1960 on 350 acres of forest and farmland located five miles west of Foster City, NY.

**Indent All But First Line**

The spacious grounds of Foster City Zoo were established in 1960 on 350 acres of forest and farmland located five miles west of Foster City, NY.

**Indent All Lines**

The spacious grounds of Foster City Zoo were established in 1960 on 350 acres of forest and farmland located five miles west of Foster City, NY.

**Indent Right Edge Of All Lines**

The spacious grounds of Foster City Zoo were established in 1960 on 350 acres of forest and farmland located five miles west of Foster City, NY.

## INDENT PARAGRAPHS

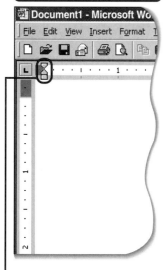

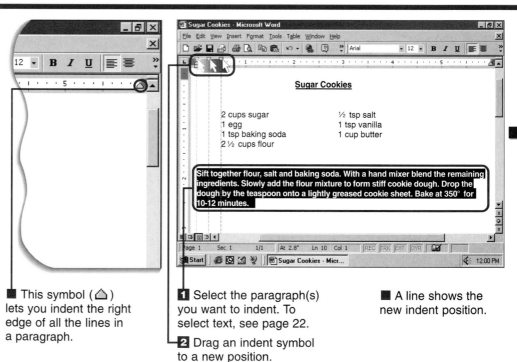

■ These symbols let you indent the left edge of a paragraph.

▽ Indent first line

△ Indent all but first line

▢ Indent all lines

■ This symbol (△) lets you indent the right edge of all the lines in a paragraph.

**1** Select the paragraph(s) you want to indent. To select text, see page 22.

**2** Drag an indent symbol to a new position.

■ A line shows the new indent position.

## What is a hanging indent?

A hanging indent moves all but the first line of a paragraph to the right. Hanging indents are useful when you are creating a résumé, glossary or bibliography.

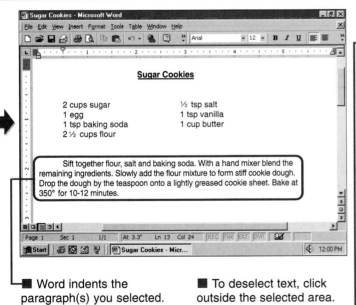

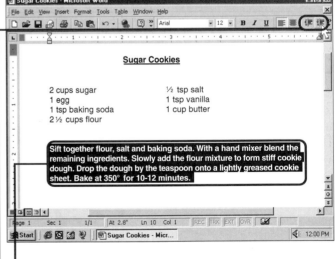

**QUICKLY INDENT ALL LINES IN A PARAGRAPH**

■ Word indents the paragraph(s) you selected.

■ To deselect text, click outside the selected area.

**1** Select the paragraph you want to indent. To select text, see page 22.

**2** Click one of the following buttons.

🔳 Move paragraph left

🔳 Move paragraph right

*Note: If the button you want is not displayed, click ⯮ on the Formatting toolbar to display all the buttons.*

# CHANGE TAB SETTINGS

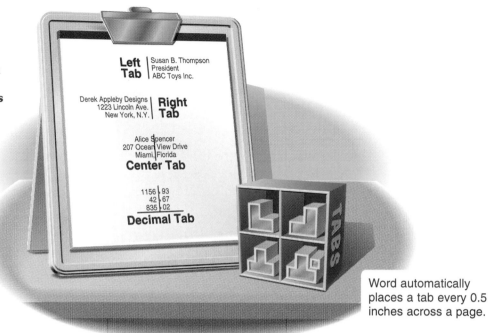

You can use tabs to line up columns of information in your document. Word offers several types of tabs for you to choose from.

Left Tab | Susan B. Thompson
President
ABC Toys Inc.

Derek Appleby Designs
1223 Lincoln Ave.
New York, N.Y. | Right Tab

Alice Spencer
207 Ocean View Drive
Miami, Florida
Center Tab

1156 | 93
42 | 67
835 | 02
Decimal Tab

Word automatically places a tab every 0.5 inches across a page.

## CHANGE TAB SETTINGS

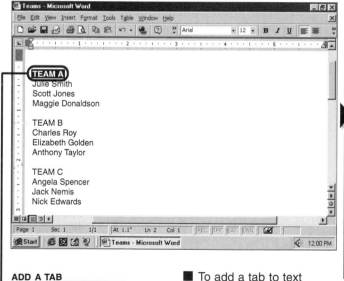

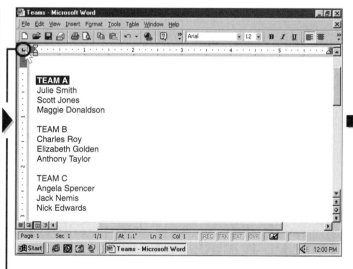

### ADD A TAB

■1 Select the text you want to contain the new tab. To select text, see page 22.

■ To add a tab to text you are about to type, click where you want to type the text.

■2 Click this area until the type of tab you want to add appears.

⌐ Left Tab

⊥ Center Tab

⌐ Right Tab

⊥ Decimal Tab

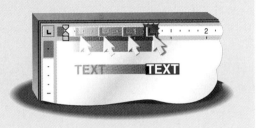

**How can I move a tab?**

To move a tab, select the text containing the tab you want to move. To select text, see page 22. Position the mouse ⤢ over the tab you want to move and then drag the tab to a new location on the ruler.

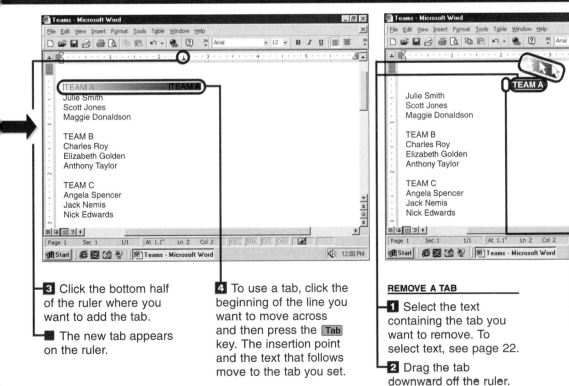

**3** Click the bottom half of the ruler where you want to add the tab.

■ The new tab appears on the ruler.

**4** To use a tab, click the beginning of the line you want to move across and then press the `Tab` key. The insertion point and the text that follows move to the tab you set.

**REMOVE A TAB**

**1** Select the text containing the tab you want to remove. To select text, see page 22.

**2** Drag the tab downward off the ruler.

■ The tab disappears from the ruler.

■ To move text back to the left margin, click to the left of the first character. Then press the `Backspace` key.

# CHANGE LINE SPACING

You can change the
amount of space between
the lines of text in your
document. Changing the
line spacing can help
make your document
easier to review and edit.

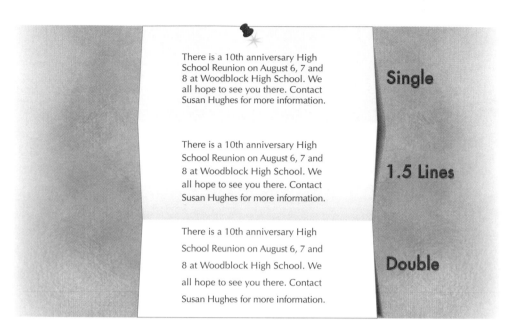

There is a 10th anniversary High
School Reunion on August 6, 7 and
8 at Woodblock High School. We
all hope to see you there. Contact
Susan Hughes for more information.

**Single**

There is a 10th anniversary High
School Reunion on August 6, 7 and
8 at Woodblock High School. We
all hope to see you there. Contact
Susan Hughes for more information.

**1.5 Lines**

There is a 10th anniversary High
School Reunion on August 6, 7 and
8 at Woodblock High School. We
all hope to see you there. Contact
Susan Hughes for more information.

**Double**

## CHANGE LINE SPACING

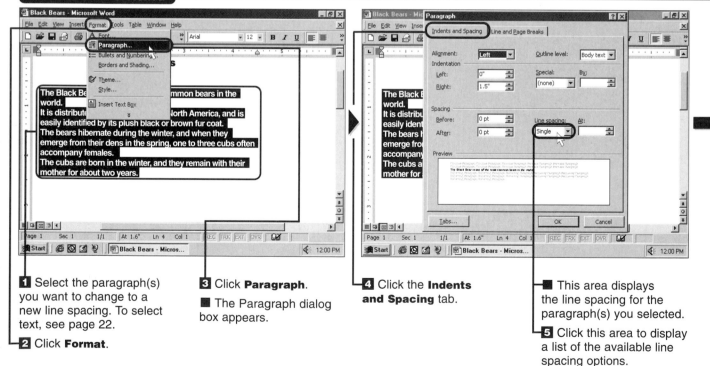

**1** Select the paragraph(s)
you want to change to a
new line spacing. To select
text, see page 22.

**2** Click **Format**.

**3** Click **Paragraph**.

■ The Paragraph dialog
box appears.

**4** Click the **Indents
and Spacing** tab.

■ This area displays
the line spacing for the
paragraph(s) you selected.

**5** Click this area to display
a list of the available line
spacing options.

**?**

**Does Word ever automatically adjust the line spacing?**

Word automatically increases the spacing of lines that contain large characters.

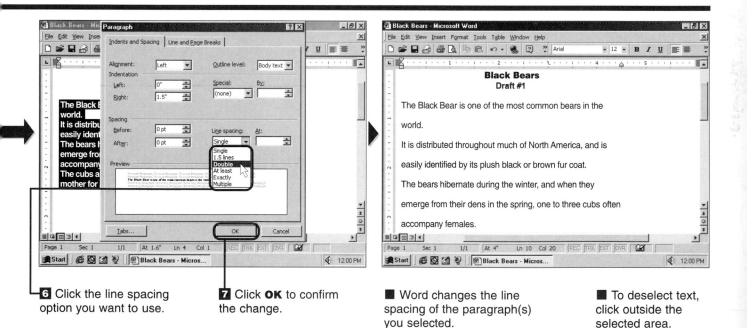

**6** Click the line spacing option you want to use.

**7** Click **OK** to confirm the change.

■ Word changes the line spacing of the paragraph(s) you selected.

■ To deselect text, click outside the selected area.

# ADD BULLETS OR NUMBERS

You can separate items in a list by beginning each item with a bullet or number.

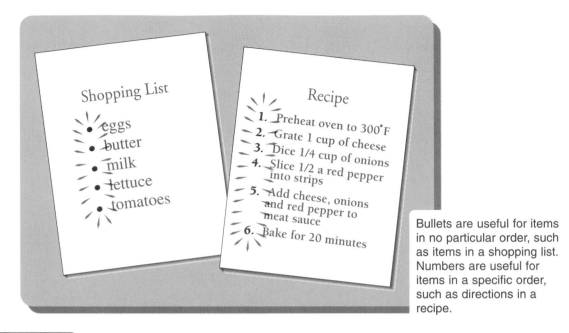

Bullets are useful for items in no particular order, such as items in a shopping list. Numbers are useful for items in a specific order, such as directions in a recipe.

## ADD BULLETS OR NUMBERS

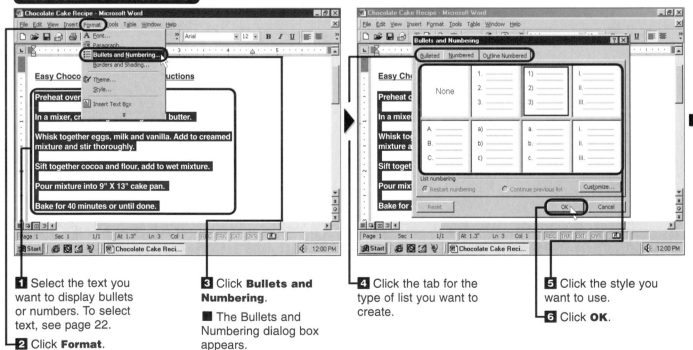

**1** Select the text you want to display bullets or numbers. To select text, see page 22.

**2** Click **Format**.

**3** Click **Bullets and Numbering**.

■ The Bullets and Numbering dialog box appears.

**4** Click the tab for the type of list you want to create.

**5** Click the style you want to use.

**6** Click **OK**.

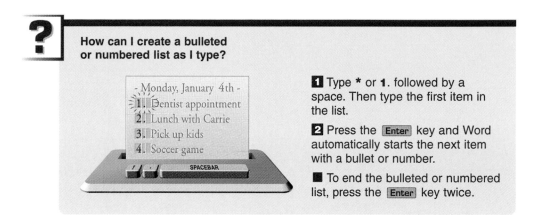

**How can I create a bulleted or numbered list as I type?**

- Monday, January 4th -
1. Dentist appointment
2. Lunch with Carrie
3. Pick up kids
4. Soccer game

SPACEBAR

**1** Type * or **1**. followed by a space. Then type the first item in the list.

**2** Press the Enter key and Word automatically starts the next item with a bullet or number.

■ To end the bulleted or numbered list, press the Enter key twice.

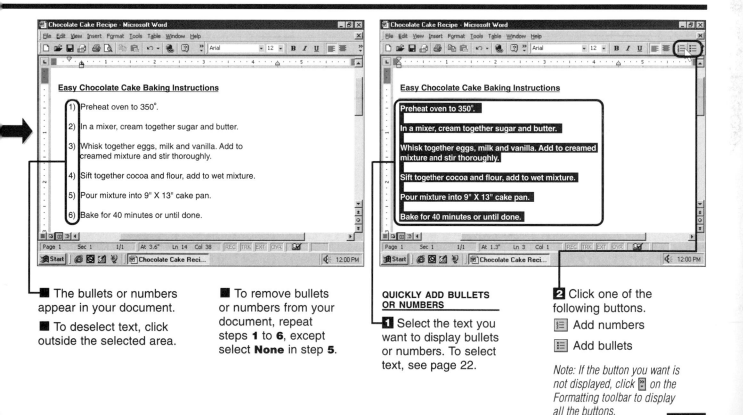

■ The bullets or numbers appear in your document.

■ To deselect text, click outside the selected area.

■ To remove bullets or numbers from your document, repeat steps **1** to **6**, except select **None** in step **5**.

**QUICKLY ADD BULLETS OR NUMBERS**

**1** Select the text you want to display bullets or numbers. To select text, see page 22.

**2** Click one of the following buttons.

Add numbers

Add bullets

Note: If the button you want is not displayed, click on the Formatting toolbar to display all the buttons.

# INSERT A PAGE BREAK

If you want to start a new page at a specific place in your document, you can insert a page break. A page break indicates where one page ends and another begins.

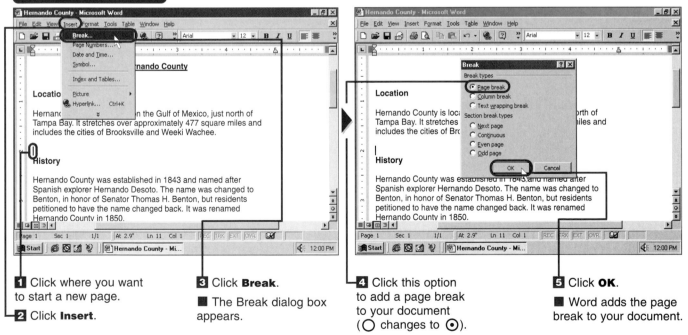

**1** Click where you want to start a new page.

**2** Click **Insert**.

**3** Click **Break**.

■ The Break dialog box appears.

**4** Click this option to add a page break to your document (○ changes to ⊙).

**5** Click **OK**.

■ Word adds the page break to your document.

68

**?**

**Will Word ever insert page breaks automatically?**

When you fill a page with text, Word automatically starts a new page by inserting a page break for you.

## DELETE A PAGE BREAK

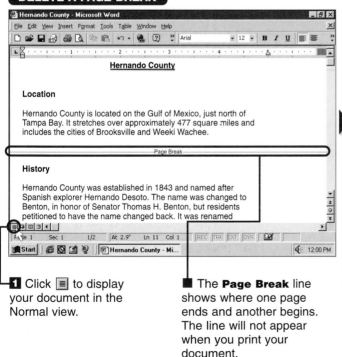

**1** Click ▤ to display your document in the Normal view.

■ The **Page Break** line shows where one page ends and another begins. The line will not appear when you print your document.

*Note: You may need to scroll through your document to view the line.*

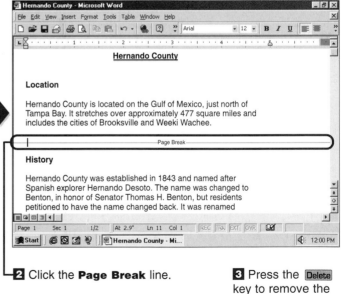

**2** Click the **Page Break** line.

**3** Press the Delete key to remove the page break.

# INSERT A SECTION BREAK

You can divide your document into sections so you can format each section separately.

Dividing your document into sections allows you to apply formatting to only part of your document. For example, you may want to vertically center text on a page or change the margins for only part of your document.

## INSERT A SECTION BREAK

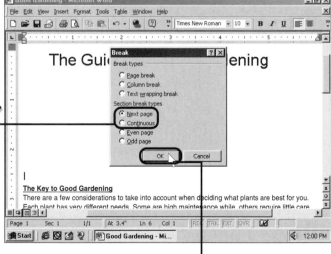

**1** Click where you want to start a new section.

**2** Click **Insert**.

**3** Click **Break**.

■ The Break dialog box appears.

**4** Click the type of section break you want to add (○ changes to ⊙).

**Next page** - Create a new section on a new page

**Continuous** - Create a new section on the current page

**5** Click **OK** to confirm your selection.

■ Word adds the section break to your document.

70

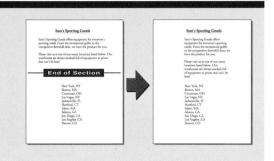

**Will the appearance of my document change when I delete a section break?**

When you delete a section break, the text above the break assumes the appearance of the text below the break. For example, if you changed the margins for the text below the section break, the text above the break will also display the new margins when you delete the break.

## DELETE A SECTION BREAK

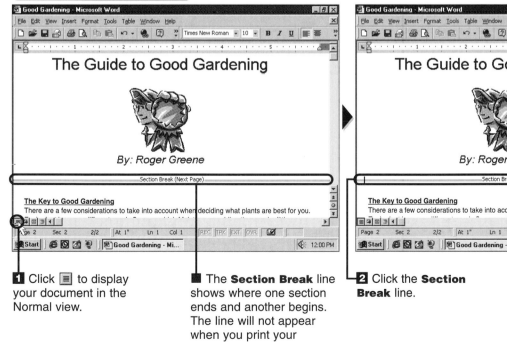

**1** Click ▤ to display your document in the Normal view.

■ The **Section Break** line shows where one section ends and another begins. The line will not appear when you print your document.

*Note: You may need to scroll through your document to view the line.*

**2** Click the **Section Break** line.

**3** Press the Delete key to remove the section break.

# CHANGE MARGINS

A margin is the amount of space between the text in your document and the edge of your paper. You can change the margins to suit your needs.

Changing margins lets you accommodate letterhead and other specialty paper.

Word automatically sets the top and bottom margins to 1 inch and the left and right margins to 1.25 inches.

## CHANGE MARGINS

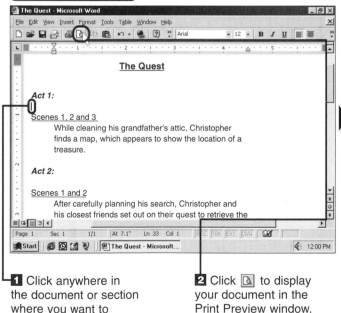

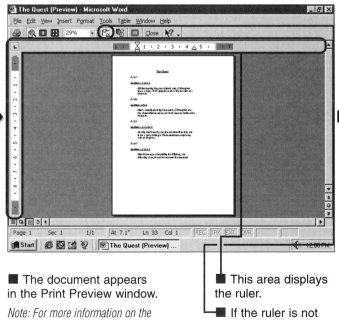

**1** Click anywhere in the document or section where you want to change the margins.

*Note: To change the margins for part of a document, you must divide the document into sections. See page 70.*

**2** Click 🔍 to display your document in the Print Preview window.

*Note: If 🔍 is not displayed, click ⯈ on the Standard toolbar to display all the buttons.*

■ The document appears in the Print Preview window.

*Note: For more information on the Print Preview feature, see page 32.*

■ This area displays the ruler.

■ If the ruler is not displayed, click 🔍.

**How can I quickly change the left and right margins for only part of my document?**

You can change the indentation of paragraphs to quickly change the left and right margins for only part of your document. To indent paragraphs, see page 60.

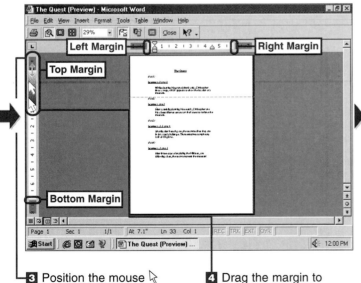

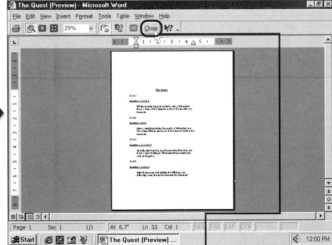

**3** Position the mouse ⤢ over a margin you want to change (⤢ changes to ↕ or ↔).

**4** Drag the margin to a new location. A line shows the new location.

*Note: To view the exact measurement of a margin, press and hold down the* Alt *key as you drag the margin.*

■ The margin moves to the new location.

**5** Repeat steps **3** and **4** for each margin you want to change.

**6** When you finish changing the margins, click **Close** to close the Print Preview window.

# ADD PAGE NUMBERS

You can have Word number the pages in your document.

Page numbers are only displayed on your screen in the Print Layout view. For information on the views, see page 26.

## ADD PAGE NUMBERS

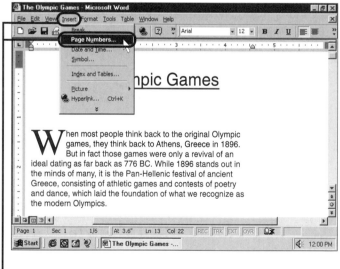

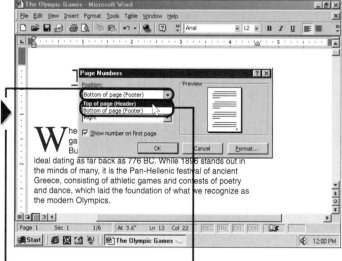

**1** Click **Insert**.

**2** Click **Page Numbers**.

■ The Page Numbers dialog box appears.

**3** Click this area to select a position for the page numbers.

**4** Click the position where you want the page numbers to appear.

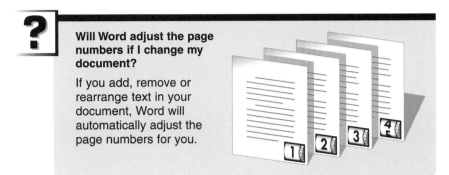

**Will Word adjust the page numbers if I change my document?**

If you add, remove or rearrange text in your document, Word will automatically adjust the page numbers for you.

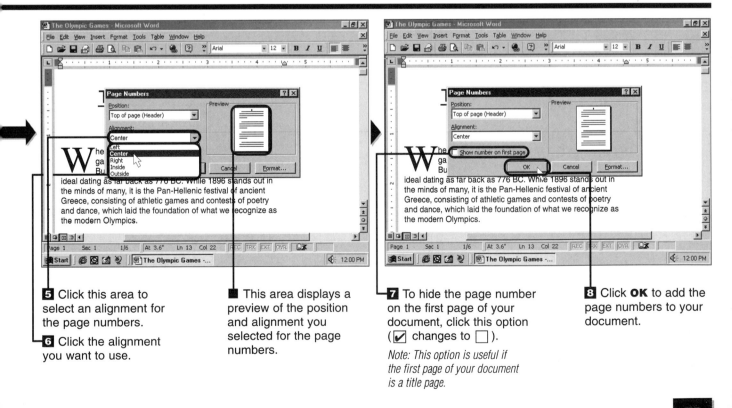

**5** Click this area to select an alignment for the page numbers.

**6** Click the alignment you want to use.

■ This area displays a preview of the position and alignment you selected for the page numbers.

**7** To hide the page number on the first page of your document, click this option (☑ changes to ☐).

*Note: This option is useful if the first page of your document is a title page.*

**8** Click **OK** to add the page numbers to your document.

# CENTER TEXT ON A PAGE

You can vertically center text on each page of your document. This is useful for creating title pages and short memos.

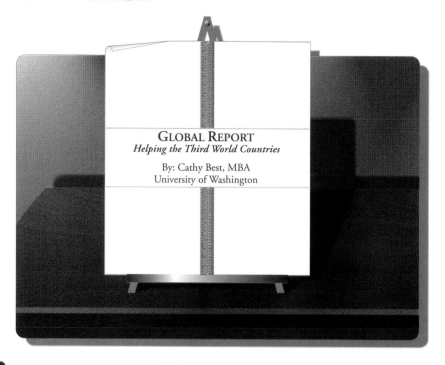

GLOBAL REPORT
*Helping the Third World Countries*

By: Cathy Best, MBA
University of Washington

**CENTER TEXT ON A PAGE**

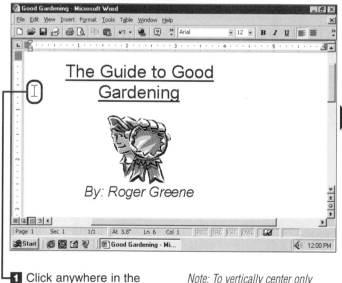

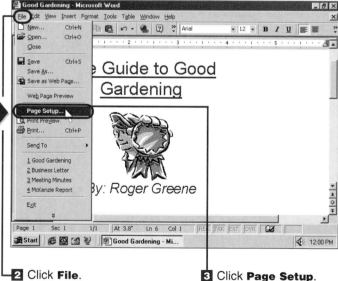

**1** Click anywhere in the document or section you want to vertically center.

*Note: To vertically center only some of the text in a document, you must divide the document into sections. To divide a document into sections, see page 70.*

**2** Click **File**.

**3** Click **Page Setup**.

■ The Page Setup dialog box appears.

**?** How can I display the entire page on my screen so I can clearly view the centered text?

You can use the Print Preview feature to display the entire page on your screen. This lets you see how the centered text will appear on a printed page. For information on using Print Preview, see page 32.

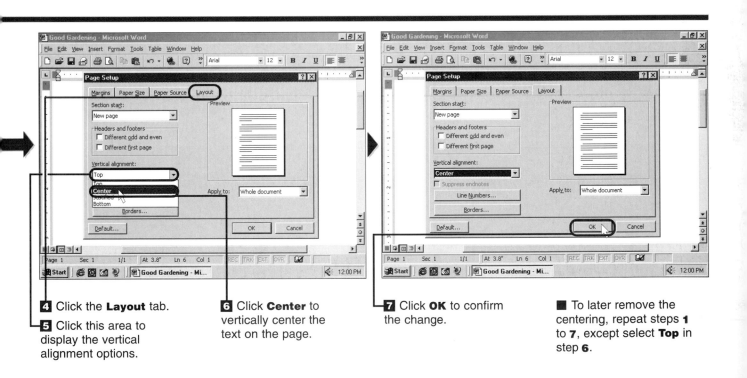

**4** Click the **Layout** tab.

**5** Click this area to display the vertical alignment options.

**6** Click **Center** to vertically center the text on the page.

**7** Click **OK** to confirm the change.

■ To later remove the centering, repeat steps **1** to **7**, except select **Top** in step **6**.

# CREATE A TABLE

You can create
a table to neatly
display information
in your document.

## CREATE A TABLE

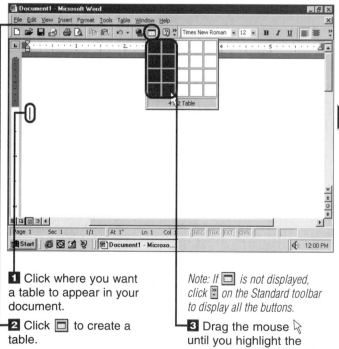

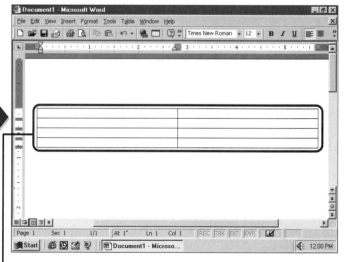

**1** Click where you want
a table to appear in your
document.

**2** Click 🔲 to create a
table.

*Note: If 🔲 is not displayed,
click 》 on the Standard toolbar
to display all the buttons.*

**3** Drag the mouse ⟍
until you highlight the
number of columns and
rows you want the table
to contain.

■ The table appears
in your document.

**?**

**What are columns, rows and cells in a table?**

■ A column is a vertical line of boxes.

■ A row is a horizontal line of boxes.

■ A cell is one box.

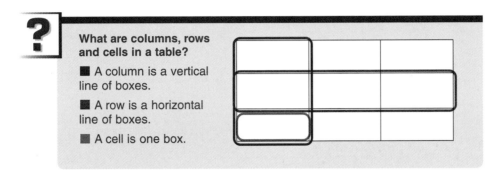

## DELETE A TABLE

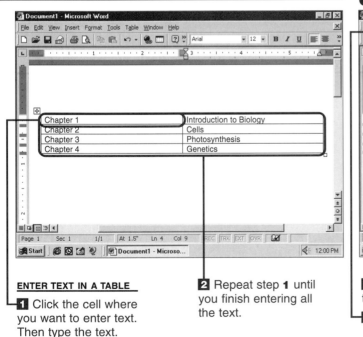

**ENTER TEXT IN A TABLE**

**1** Click the cell where you want to enter text. Then type the text.

**2** Repeat step **1** until you finish entering all the text.

**1** Click anywhere in the table you want to delete.

**2** Click **Table**.

**3** Click **Delete**.

**4** Click **Table**.

# CHANGE COLUMN WIDTH OR ROW HEIGHT

After you have created a table, you can change the width of columns and the height of rows.

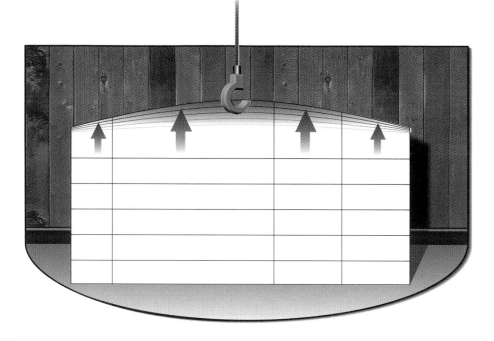

## CHANGE COLUMN WIDTH

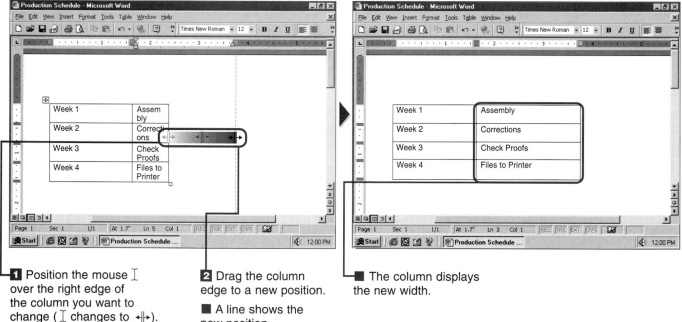

**1** Position the mouse I over the right edge of the column you want to change ( I changes to ↔).

**2** Drag the column edge to a new position.

■ A line shows the new position.

■ The column displays the new width.

**Does Word ever automatically adjust the column width or row height?**

When you enter text in a table, Word may automatically increase the width of a column or the height of a row to accommodate the text you type.

## CHANGE ROW HEIGHT

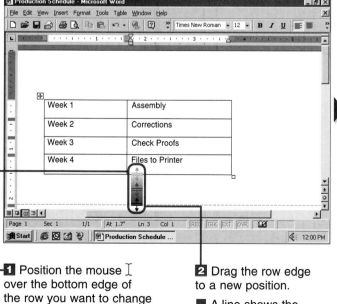

**1** Position the mouse ⌶ over the bottom edge of the row you want to change (⌶ changes to ↕).

**2** Drag the row edge to a new position.

■ A line shows the new position.

■ The row displays the new height.

*Note: You cannot change the row height in the Normal or Outline view. For information on the views, see page 26.*

# ADD A ROW OR COLUMN

You can add a row or column to your table when you want to insert additional information.

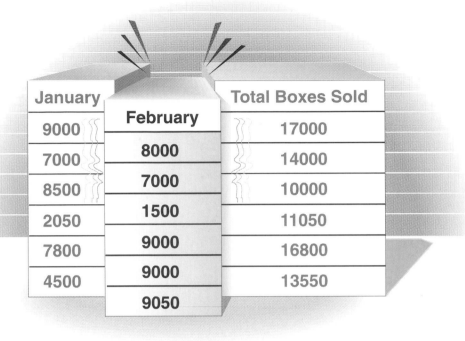

| January | February | Total Boxes Sold |
|---------|----------|------------------|
| 9000 | | 17000 |
| 7000 | 8000 | 14000 |
| 8500 | 7000 | 10000 |
| 2050 | 1500 | 11050 |
| 7800 | 9000 | 16800 |
| 4500 | 9000 | 13550 |
| | 9050 | |

## ADD A ROW

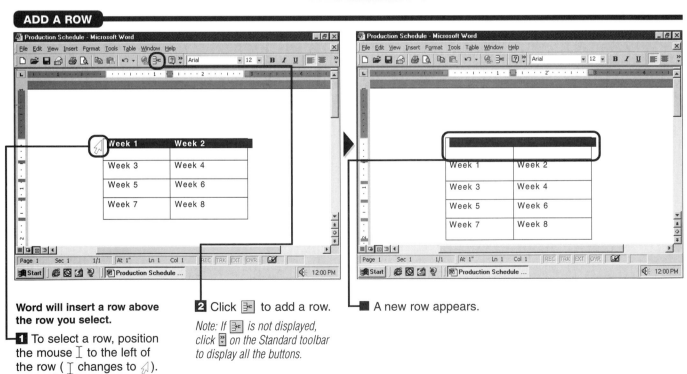

**Word will insert a row above the row you select.**

**1** To select a row, position the mouse I to the left of the row ( I changes to ⤏). Then click the left mouse button.

**2** Click ⧉ to add a row.

*Note: If ⧉ is not displayed, click ⧉ on the Standard toolbar to display all the buttons.*

■ A new row appears.

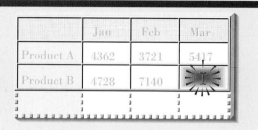

**Can I add a row to the bottom of a table?**

Yes. To add a row to the bottom of a table, click the bottom right cell in the table and then press the **Tab** key.

## ADD A COLUMN

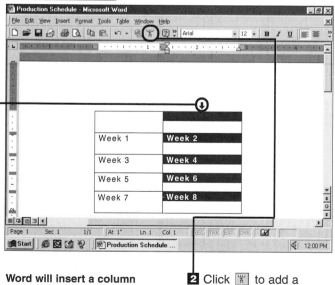

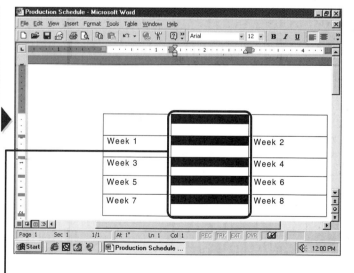

Word will insert a column to the left of the column you select.

**1** To select a column, position the mouse I over the top of the column ( I changes to ↓ ). Then click the left mouse button.

**2** Click  to add a column.

*Note: If ⊞ is not displayed, click ⊞ on the Standard toolbar to display all the buttons.*

■ A new column appears.

# DELETE A ROW OR COLUMN

You can delete a
row or column you
no longer need.

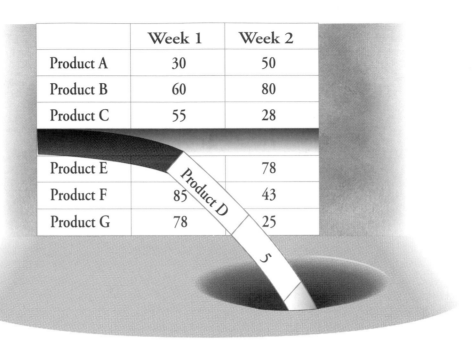

| | Week 1 | Week 2 |
|---|---|---|
| Product A | 30 | 50 |
| Product B | 60 | 80 |
| Product C | 55 | 28 |
| Product E | | 78 |
| Product F | 85 | 43 |
| Product G | 78 | 25 |

## DELETE A ROW OR COLUMN

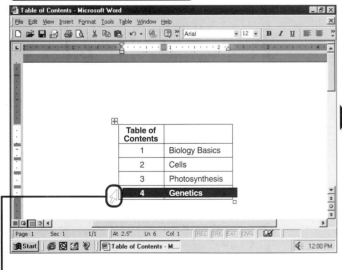

**1** To select the row you
want to delete, position the
mouse I to the left of the
row ( I changes to ⇗).
Then click the left mouse
button.

■ To select the column
you want to delete,
position the mouse I
over the top of the column
( I changes to ↓). Then
click the left mouse button.

**2** Click ✂ to delete
the row or column.

*Note: If ✂ is not displayed,
click ⯮ on the Standard
toolbar to display all the
buttons.*

■ The row or column
disappears.

# MERGE CELLS

You can combine two or
more cells in your table
to create one large cell.
Merging cells is useful
when you want to
display a title across
the top of your table.

## MERGE CELLS

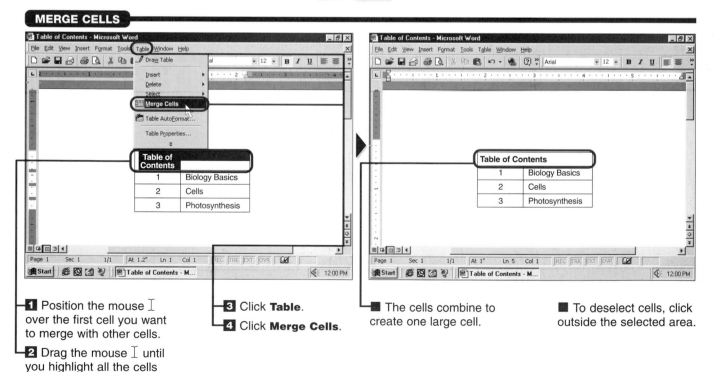

**1** Position the mouse I over the first cell you want to merge with other cells.

**2** Drag the mouse I until you highlight all the cells you want to merge.

**3** Click **Table**.

**4** Click **Merge Cells**.

■ The cells combine to create one large cell.

■ To deselect cells, click outside the selected area.

# MOVE A TABLE

You can move a
table from one
location in your
document to
another.

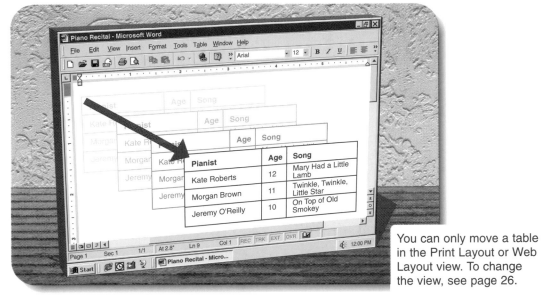

You can only move a table
in the Print Layout or Web
Layout view. To change
the view, see page 26.

## MOVE A TABLE

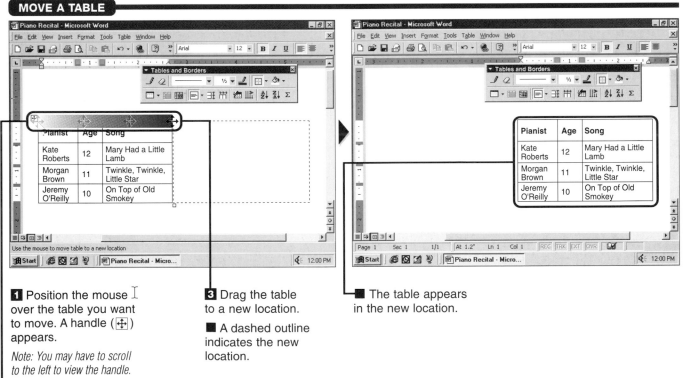

**1** Position the mouse I
over the table you want
to move. A handle (⊞)
appears.

*Note: You may have to scroll
to the left to view the handle.*

**2** Position the mouse I
over the handle
( I changes to ⁺⧉).

**3** Drag the table
to a new location.

■ A dashed outline
indicates the new
location.

■ The table appears
in the new location.

86

# SIZE A TABLE

You can change
the size of a table
to improve the
layout of the table.

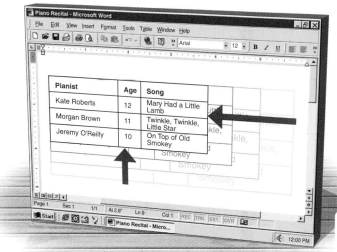

You can only size a table
in the Print Layout or Web
Layout view. To change
the view, see page 26.

## SIZE A TABLE

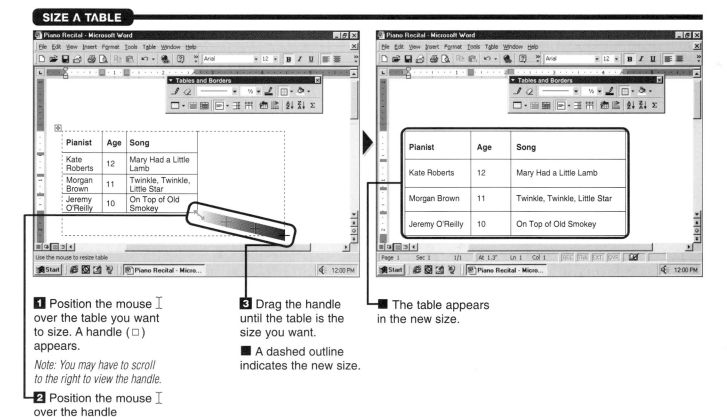

**1** Position the mouse I
over the table you want
to size. A handle (□)
appears.

*Note: You may have to scroll
to the right to view the handle.*

**2** Position the mouse I
over the handle
( I changes to ↖ ).

**3** Drag the handle
until the table is the
size you want.

■ A dashed outline
indicates the new size.

■ The table appears
in the new size.

# FORMAT A TABLE

Word offers many
ready-to-use designs
that you can choose
from to give your table
a new appearance.

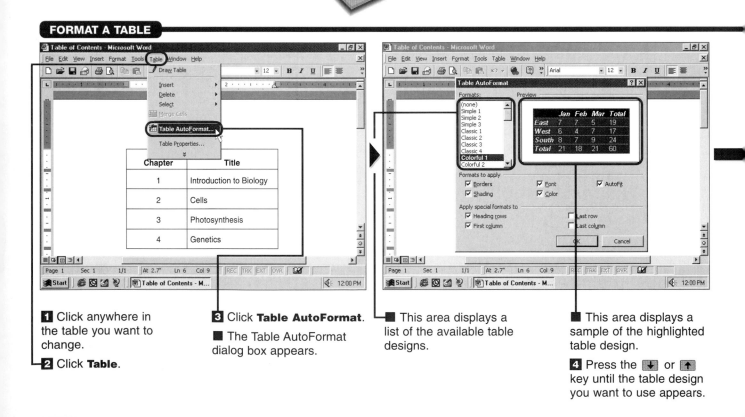

## FORMAT A TABLE

**1** Click anywhere in
the table you want to
change.

**2** Click **Table**.

**3** Click **Table AutoFormat**.

■ The Table AutoFormat
dialog box appears.

■ This area displays a
list of the available table
designs.

■ This area displays a
sample of the highlighted
table design.

**4** Press the ⬇ or ⬆
key until the table design
you want to use appears.

## What is the AutoFit option used for?

The AutoFit option changes the size of your table based on the amount of text in the table. If you do not want Word to change the size of your table, you can turn off the AutoFit option in step **5** below ( ☑ changes to ☐ ).

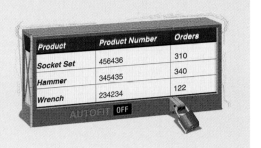

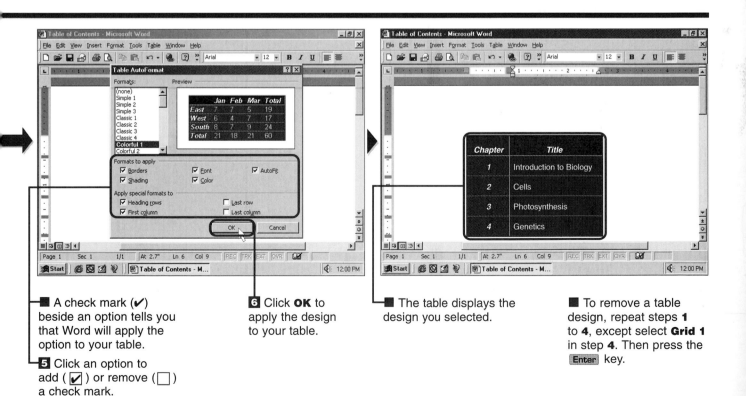

■ A check mark (✔) beside an option tells you that Word will apply the option to your table.

**5** Click an option to add ( ☑ ) or remove ( ☐ ) a check mark.

**6** Click **OK** to apply the design to your table.

■ The table displays the design you selected.

■ To remove a table design, repeat steps **1** to **4**, except select **Grid 1** in step **4**. Then press the **Enter** key.

| Team B | | | |
|---|---|---|---|
| Player | Goals | Assists | Points |
| B. Laird | 5 | 1 | 6 |
| A. Tan | 2 | 5 | 7 |
| P. Phillips | 3 | 2 | 5 |
| R. Westman | 7 | 1 | 8 |
| L. Porter | 1 | 4 | 5 |
| H. Roberts | 0 | 3 | 3 |
| S. Desert | 6 | 2 | 8 |
| M. Lee | 4 | 4 | 8 |
| C. Collins | 2 | 5 | 7 |
| K. Davids | 9 | 0 | 9 |
| | | | |
| Team C | | | |
| Player | Goals | Assists | Points |
| S. Toner | 6 | 1 | 7 |
| J. Cane | 5 | 2 | 7 |

| | | | | |
|---|---|---|---|---|
| L. Samson | 2 | 3 | 5 | |
| R. Kinnear | | 2 | 2 | 11 |
| T. Lappen | 6 | | 4 | |
| A. Coster | 3 | | 8 | |
| D. Saire | | | 5 | |
| B. Miller | | | | |
| E. Pelham | | | | |
| G. Cross | | | | |

**Workbook**

REVENUE

Payroll

Jan

# Using Excel

# INTRODUCTION TO EXCEL

Excel is a spreadsheet program you can use to organize, analyze and attractively present data, such as a budget or sales report.

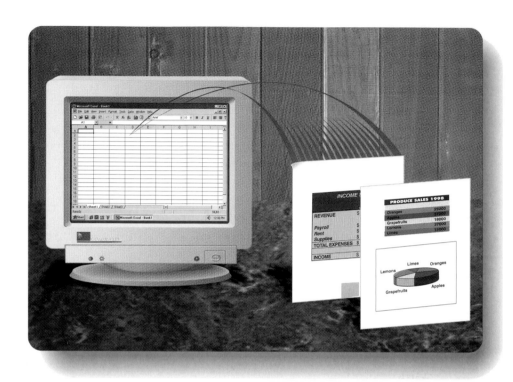

## Editing and Formatting

Excel lets you efficiently enter, edit and format data in a worksheet. You can quickly enter a series of numbers, change the width of columns or insert new rows. You can also emphasize data by changing the font, color and style of data.

## Using Formulas and Functions

Formulas and functions allow you to perform calculations and analyze data in a worksheet. Common calculations include finding the sum, average or total number of items in a list.

## Creating Charts

Excel helps you create colorful charts from your worksheet data. If you change the data in your worksheet, Excel will automatically update the chart to display the changes. You can move and size a chart to suit your needs.

# START EXCEL

When you start
Excel, a blank
worksheet appears
on your screen. You
can enter data into
this worksheet.

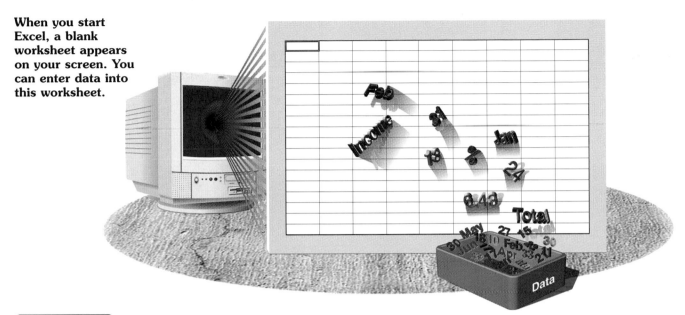

## START EXCEL

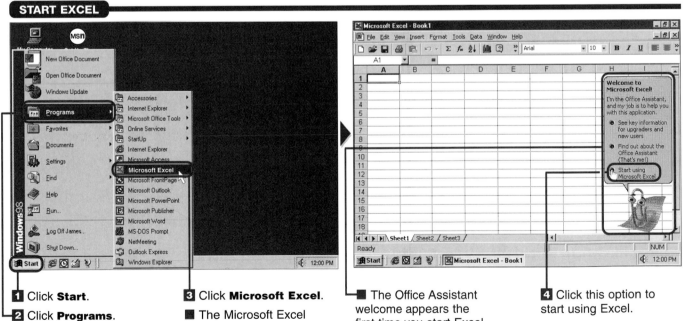

**1** Click **Start**.

**2** Click **Programs**.

**3** Click **Microsoft Excel**.

■ The Microsoft Excel
window appears, displaying
a blank worksheet.

■ The Office Assistant
welcome appears the
first time you start Excel.

**4** Click this option to
start using Excel.

*Note: For information on the
Office Assistant, see page 14.*

93

# THE EXCEL SCREEN

The Excel screen displays several items to help you perform tasks efficiently.

**Menu Bar**

Provides access to lists of commands available in Excel.

**Formatting Toolbar**

Contains buttons to help you select formatting commands, such as Bold and Underline.

**Standard Toolbar**

Contains buttons to help you select common commands, such as Save and Print.

**Formula Bar**

Displays the cell reference and contents of the active cell. A cell reference identifies the location of a cell in a worksheet and consists of a column letter followed by a row number, such as **A1**.

**Active Cell**

Displays a thick border. You enter data into the active cell.

**Cell**

The area where a row and column intersect.

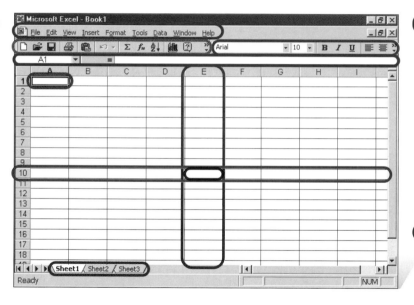

**Row**

A horizontal line of cells. A number identifies each row.

**Worksheet Tabs**

An Excel file is called a workbook. Each workbook is divided into several worksheets. Excel displays a tab for each worksheet.

A workbook is similar to a three-ring binder that contains several sheets of paper.

**Column**

A vertical line of cells. A letter identifies each column.

# CHANGE THE ACTIVE CELL

You can make any cell
in your worksheet the
active cell. You enter
data into the active cell.

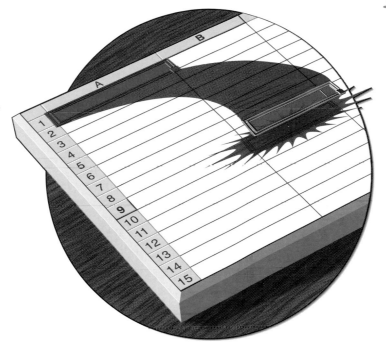

## CHANGE THE ACTIVE CELL

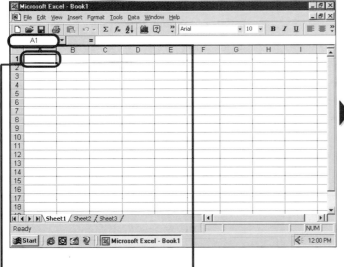

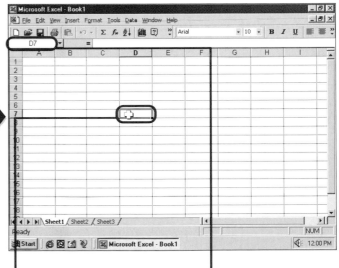

■ The active cell
displays a thick border.

■ The cell reference for
the active cell appears in
this area. A cell reference
identifies the location of
each cell in a worksheet
and consists of a column
letter followed by a row
number (example: **A1**).

**1** Click the cell you want
to make the active cell.

*Note: You can also press the*
*←, →, ↑ or ↓ key*
*to change the active cell.*

■ The cell reference
for the new active cell
appears in this area.

**95**

# ENTER DATA

You can enter data into your worksheet quickly and easily.

**SALES REPORT IN UNITS**

| | 1995 | 1996 | 1997 | 1998 |
|---|---|---|---|---|
| January | 10500 | 8850 | 9000 | 10400 |
| February | 9400 | 9750 | 9500 | 9850 |
| March | 6450 | 8450 | 8950 | 9900 |
| April | 7890 | 9000 | 9400 | 10850 |
| May | 8920 | 7359 | 8700 | 11500 |

## ENTER DATA

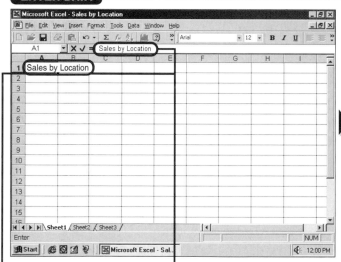

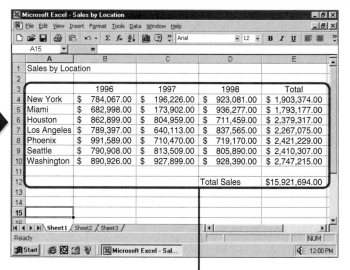

**1** Click the cell where you want to enter data. Then type the data.

*Note: In this example, the size of data was changed from 10 point to 12 point to make the data easier to read.*

■ If you make a typing mistake, press the ◄Backspace key to remove the incorrect data. Then type the correct data.

■ The data you type appears in the active cell and the formula bar.

**2** Press the Enter key to enter the data and move down one cell.

*Note: To enter the data and move one cell in any direction, press the ←, →, ↓ or ↑ key.*

**3** Repeat steps **1** and **2** until you finish entering all your data.

**?**

**How do I use the number keys on the right side of my keyboard?**

When **NUM** appears at the bottom of your screen, you can use the number keys on the right side of your keyboard to enter numbers.

■ To turn the display of **NUM** on or off, press the [Num Lock] key.

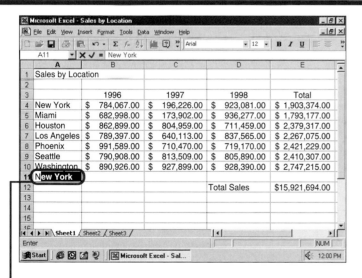

| 4 | TOTAL EXPENSES | |
| 5 | | |
| 6 | | |

| 4 | TOTAL EX | 227 |
| 5 | | |
| 6 | | |

**Long Words**

If text is too long to fit in a cell, the text will spill into the neighboring cell.

If the neighboring cell contains data, Excel will display as much of the text as the column width will allow. To change the column width to display all the text, see page 142.

| 4 | 1.22E+10 | |
| 5 | | |
| 6 | | |

| 4 | ##### | |
| 5 | | |
| 6 | | |

**Long Numbers**

If a number is too long to fit in a cell, Excel will display the number in scientific form or as number signs (#). To change the column width to display the number, see page 142.

**AUTOCOMPLETE**

■ If the first few letters you type match another cell in the column, Excel may complete the text for you.

**1** To enter the text Excel provides, press the [Enter] key.

■ To enter different text, continue typing.

# SELECT CELLS

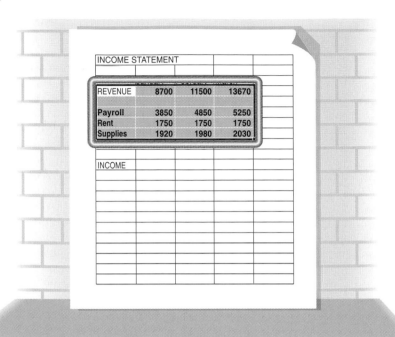

Before performing many tasks in Excel, you must select the cells you want to work with. Selected cells appear highlighted on your screen.

INCOME STATEMENT

| REVENUE | 8700 | 11500 | 13670 |
|---------|------|-------|-------|
| Payroll | 3850 | 4850 | 5250 |
| Rent | 1750 | 1750 | 1750 |
| Supplies | 1920 | 1980 | 2030 |

INCOME

## SELECT CELLS

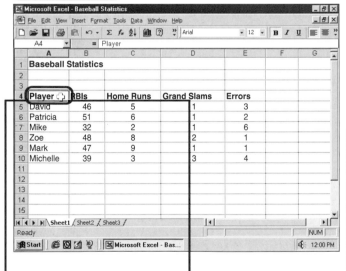

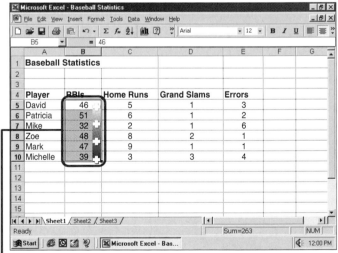

### SELECT A CELL

**1** Click the cell you want to select.

■ The cell becomes the active cell and displays a thick border.

### SELECT A GROUP OF CELLS

**1** Position the mouse ⇧ over the first cell you want to select.

**2** Drag the mouse ⇧ until you highlight all the cells you want to select.

■ To select multiple groups of cells, press and hold down the **Ctrl** key as you repeat steps **1** and **2** for each group.

■ To deselect cells, click any cell.

**?**

**How do I select all the cells in my worksheet?**

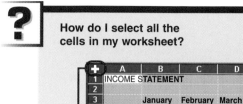

■ To select all the cells in your worksheet, click the box (☐) at the top left corner of your worksheet where the row and column headings meet.

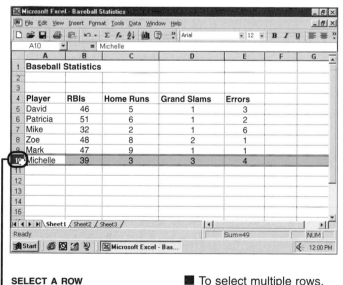

**SELECT A ROW**

**1** Click the number of the row you want to select.

■ To select multiple rows, position the mouse ✥ over the number of the first row you want to select. Then drag the mouse ✥ until you highlight all the rows you want to select.

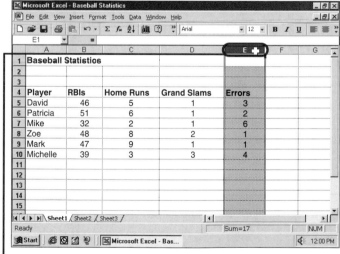

**SELECT A COLUMN**

**1** Click the letter of the column you want to select.

■ To select multiple columns, position the mouse ✥ over the letter of the first column you want to select. Then drag the mouse ✥ until you highlight all the columns you want to select.

# COMPLETE A SERIES

Excel can save you time by completing a text or number series for you.

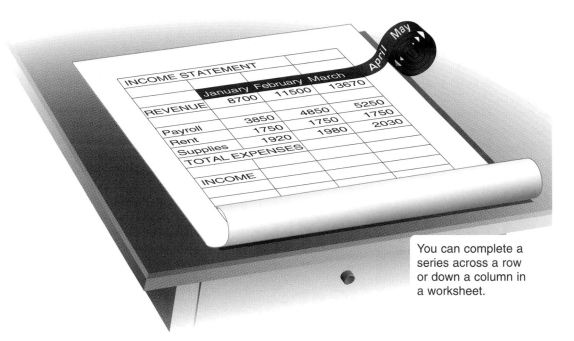

You can complete a series across a row or down a column in a worksheet.

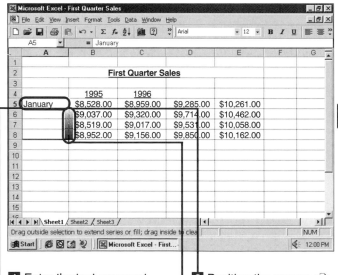

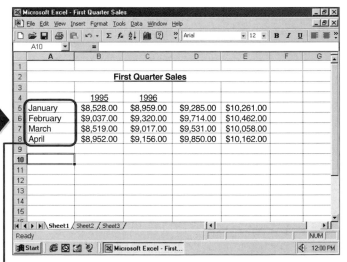

**1** Enter the text you want to start the series.

**2** Click the cell containing the text you entered.

**3** Position the mouse ⏚ over the bottom right corner of the cell (⏚ changes to +).

**4** Drag the mouse + over the cells you want to include in the series.

■ The cells display the text series.

*Note: If Excel cannot determine the text series you want to complete, it will copy the text in the first cell to the cells you select.*

■ To deselect cells, click any cell.

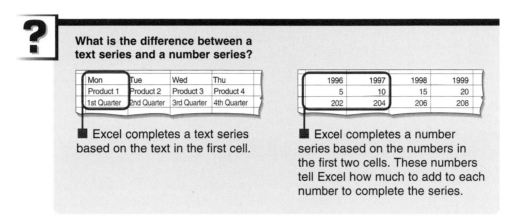

**What is the difference between a text series and a number series?**

| Mon | Tue | Wed | Thu |
|---|---|---|---|
| Product 1 | Product 2 | Product 3 | Product 4 |
| 1st Quarter | 2nd Quarter | 3rd Quarter | 4th Quarter |

■ Excel completes a text series based on the text in the first cell.

| 1996 | 1997 | 1998 | 1999 |
|---|---|---|---|
| 5 | 10 | 15 | 20 |
| 202 | 204 | 206 | 208 |

■ Excel completes a number series based on the numbers in the first two cells. These numbers tell Excel how much to add to each number to complete the series.

## COMPLETE A NUMBER SERIES

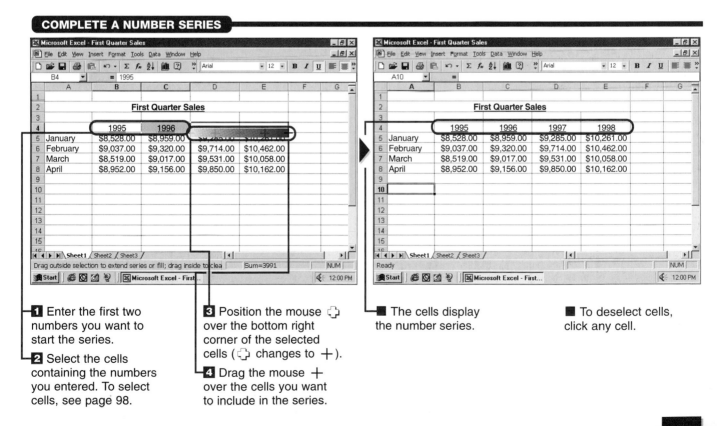

**1** Enter the first two numbers you want to start the series.

**2** Select the cells containing the numbers you entered. To select cells, see page 98.

**3** Position the mouse over the bottom right corner of the selected cells (changes to +).

**4** Drag the mouse + over the cells you want to include in the series.

■ The cells display the number series.

■ To deselect cells, click any cell.

# SCROLL THROUGH A WORKSHEET

If your worksheet contains a lot of data, your computer screen may not be able to display all the data at once. You must scroll through your worksheet to view other areas of the worksheet.

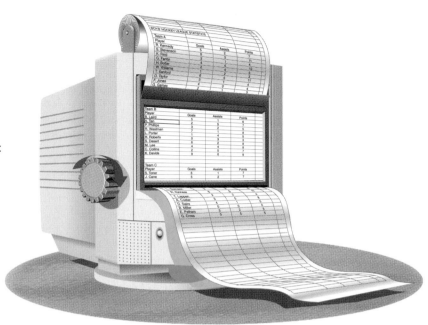

## SCROLL THROUGH A WORKSHEET

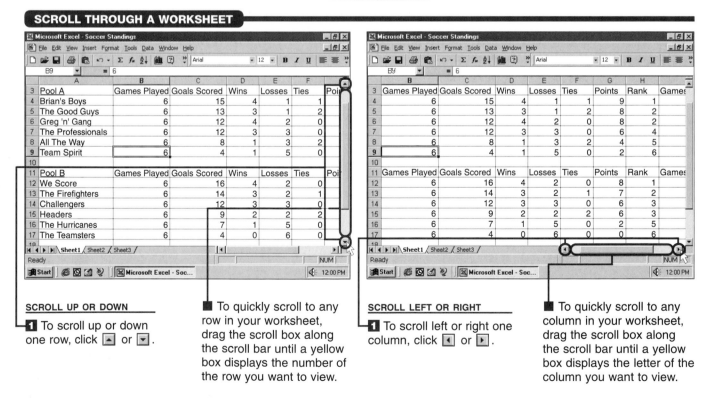

**SCROLL UP OR DOWN**

**1** To scroll up or down one row, click ▲ or ▼.

■ To quickly scroll to any row in your worksheet, drag the scroll box along the scroll bar until a yellow box displays the number of the row you want to view.

**SCROLL LEFT OR RIGHT**

**1** To scroll left or right one column, click ◄ or ►.

■ To quickly scroll to any column in your worksheet, drag the scroll box along the scroll bar until a yellow box displays the letter of the column you want to view.

# SWITCH BETWEEN WORKSHEETS

The worksheet displayed on your screen is one of several worksheets in your workbook. You can easily switch from one worksheet to another.

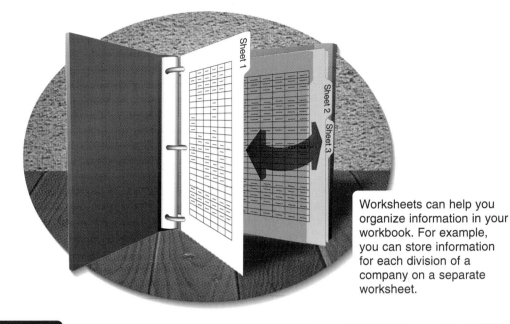

Worksheets can help you organize information in your workbook. For example, you can store information for each division of a company on a separate worksheet.

## SWITCH BETWEEN WORKSHEETS

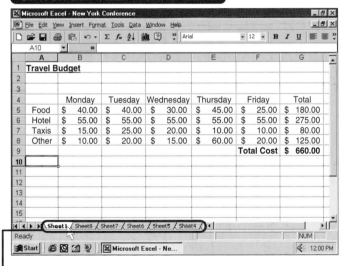

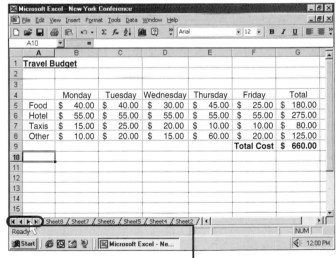

**1** To display the contents of a worksheet, click the tab of the worksheet.

■ The worksheet you selected displays a white tab.

■ The contents of the worksheet appear. The contents of the other worksheets in your workbook are hidden.

### BROWSE THROUGH WORKSHEET TABS

■ If you have many worksheets in your workbook, you may not be able to see all the tabs.

*Note: To insert additional worksheets, see page 104.*

**1** Click one of the following buttons to browse through the tabs.

| ⏮ | Display first tab |
| ◀ | Display tab to the left |
| ▶ | Display tab to the right |
| ⏭ | Display last tab |

# INSERT A WORKSHEET

You can insert a
new worksheet
to add related
information to
your workbook.

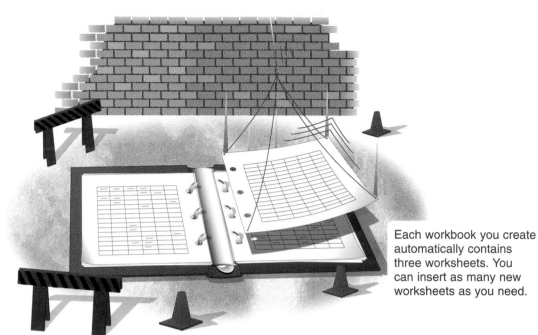

Each workbook you create
automatically contains
three worksheets. You
can insert as many new
worksheets as you need.

## INSERT A WORKSHEET

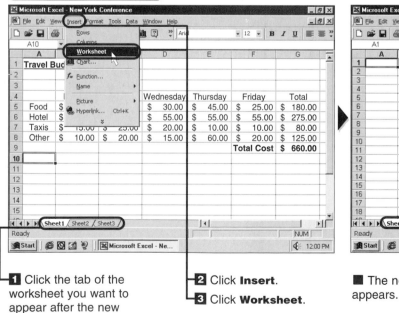

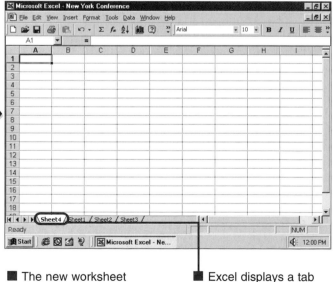

**1** Click the tab of the
worksheet you want to
appear after the new
worksheet.

**2** Click **Insert**.

**3** Click **Worksheet**.

■ The new worksheet
appears.

■ Excel displays a tab
for the new worksheet.

# DELETE A WORKSHEET

You can permanently remove a worksheet you no longer need from your workbook.

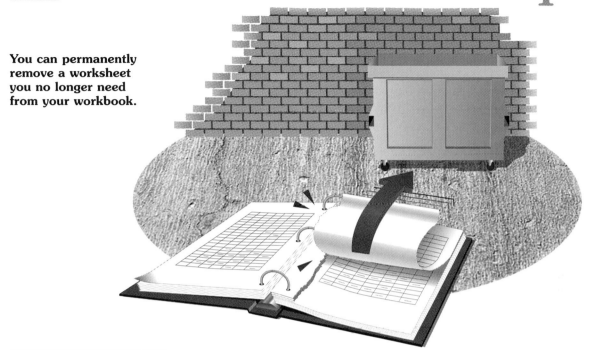

## DELETE A WORKSHEET

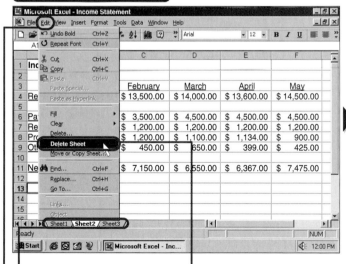

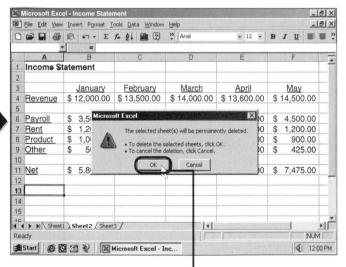

**1** Click the tab of the worksheet you want to delete.

**2** Click **Edit**.

**3** Click **Delete Sheet**.

*Note: If Delete Sheet does not appear on the menu, position the mouse ⤳ over the bottom of the menu to display all the menu commands.*

■ A warning dialog box appears.

**4** Click **OK** to permanently delete the worksheet.

# RENAME A WORKSHEET

You can give each worksheet in your workbook a descriptive name. Descriptive names can help you locate information of interest.

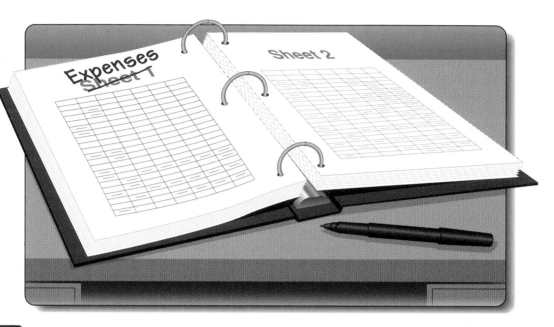

**RENAME A WORKSHEET**

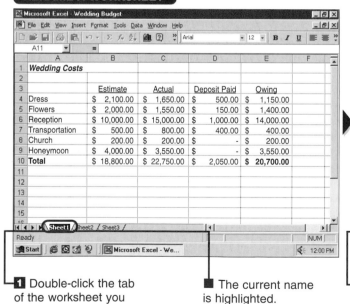

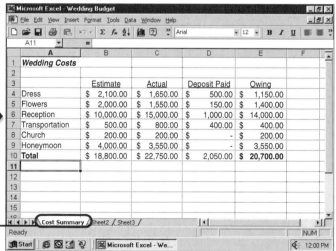

**1** Double-click the tab of the worksheet you want to rename.

■ The current name is highlighted.

**2** Type a new name and then press the Enter key.

*Note: A worksheet name can contain up to 31 characters, including spaces.*

# MOVE A WORKSHEET

You can reorganize
data by moving a
worksheet to a
new location in
your workbook.

## MOVE A WORKSHEET

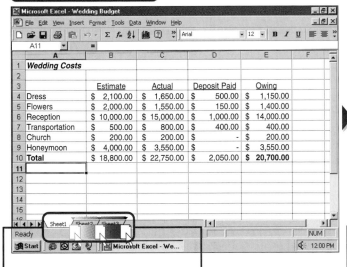

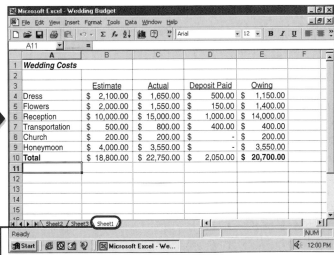

**1** Position the mouse ⌖ over the tab of the worksheet you want to move.

**2** Drag the worksheet to a new location.

■ An arrow ( ▼ ) shows where the worksheet will appear.

■ The worksheet appears in the new location.

# SAVE A WORKBOOK

You can save your workbook to store it for future use. This lets you later review and make changes to the workbook.

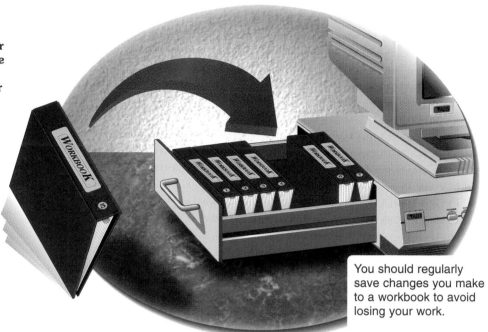

You should regularly save changes you make to a workbook to avoid losing your work.

## SAVE A WORKBOOK

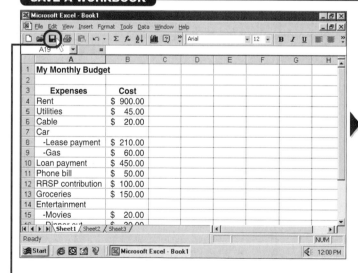

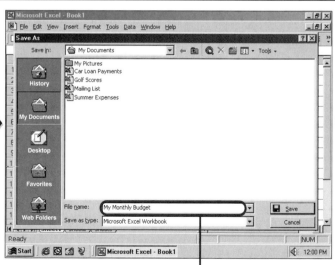

**1** Click 🖫 to save your workbook.

*Note: If 🖫 is not displayed, click ⏵ on the Standard toolbar to display all the buttons.*

■ The Save As dialog box appears.

*Note: If you previously saved your workbook, the Save As dialog box will not appear since you have already named the workbook.*

**2** Type a name for the workbook.

**What are the commonly used folders I can access?**

**History**

Provides access to folders and workbooks you recently used.

**My Documents**

Provides a convenient place to store a workbook.

**Desktop**

Lets you store a workbook on the Windows desktop.

**Favorites**

Provides a place to store a workbook you will frequently access.

**Web Folders**

Can help you store a workbook on the Web.

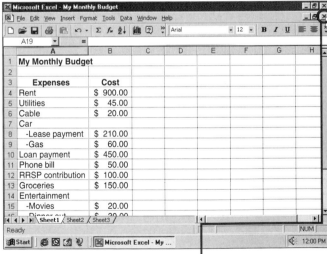

■ This area shows the location where Excel will store your workbook. You can click this area to change the location.

■ This area allows you to access commonly used folders. To display the contents of a folder, click the folder.

**3** Click **Save**.

■ Excel saves your workbook.

**CLOSE A WORKBOOK**

When you finish using a workbook, you can close the workbook to remove it from your screen.

**1** Click ⊠ to close the workbook.

# CREATE A NEW WORKBOOK

You can easily create another workbook to store new data.

## CREATE A NEW WORKBOOK

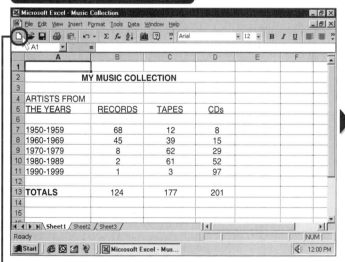

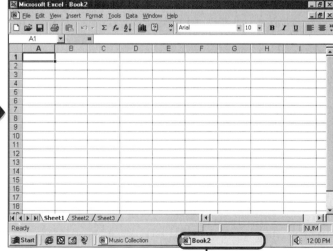

**1** Click 🗋 to create a new workbook.

*Note: If 🗋 is not displayed, click 🔽 on the Standard toolbar to display all the buttons.*

■ A new workbook appears. The previous workbook is now hidden behind the new workbook.

■ A button for the new workbook appears on the taskbar.

# SWITCH BETWEEN WORKBOOKS

Excel lets you have many workbooks open at once. You can easily switch from one open workbook to another.

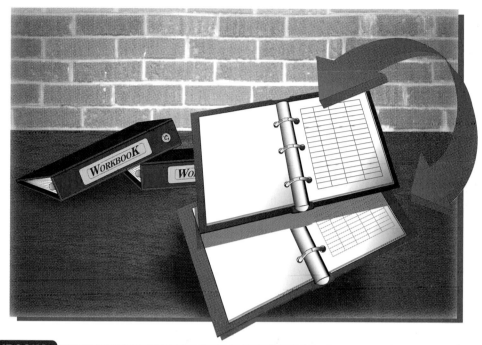

## SWITCH BETWEEN WORKBOOKS

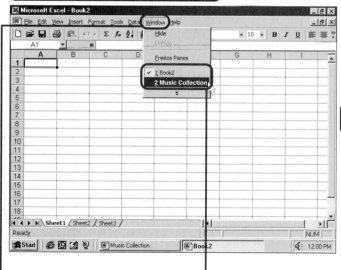

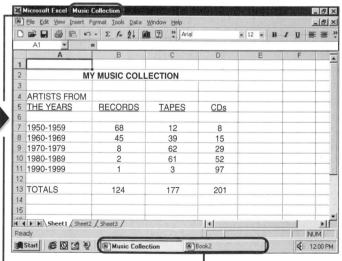

**1** Click **Window** to display a list of all the workbooks you have open.

**2** Click the name of the workbook you want to switch to.

■ The workbook appears.

■ Excel displays the name of the current workbook at the top of your screen.

■ The taskbar displays a button for each open workbook. You can also switch to a workbook by clicking its button on the taskbar.

# E-MAIL A WORKSHEET

You can e-mail a worksheet to a friend, family member or colleague.

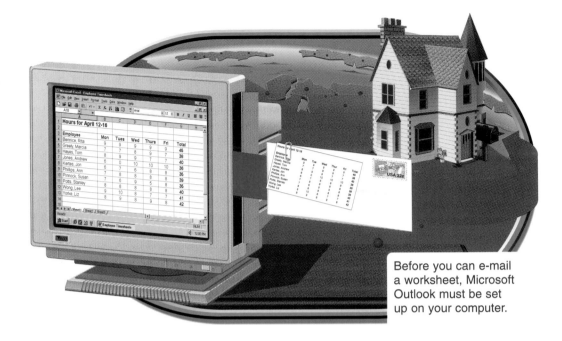

Before you can e-mail a worksheet, Microsoft Outlook must be set up on your computer.

## E-MAIL A WORKSHEET

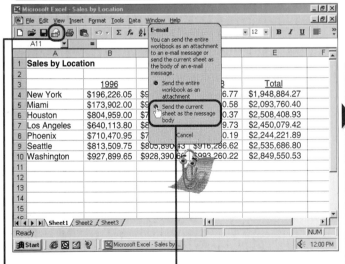

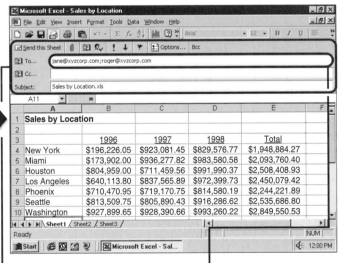

**1** Click 🖃 to e-mail the current worksheet.

*Note: If 🖃 is not displayed, click 🖹 on the Standard toolbar to display all the buttons.*

■ If the workbook contains data in more than one worksheet, a message appears, asking if you want to send the entire workbook or just the current worksheet.

**2** Click this option to send the current worksheet.

■ An area appears for you to address the message.

**3** Click this area and type the e-mail address of each person you want to receive the message. Separate each address with a semicolon (;).

**?** **How do I e-mail an entire workbook?**

To e-mail an entire workbook, perform steps **1** to **5** below, except select **Send the entire workbook as an attachment** in step **2**. Then click **Send** to send the message. When you e-mail an entire workbook, the workbook appears as an icon in the message.

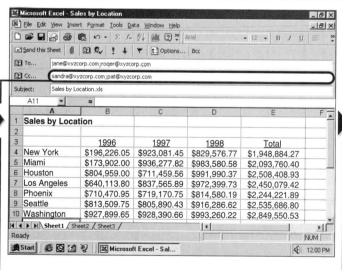

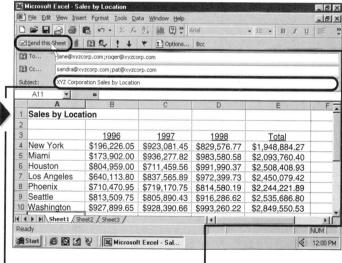

**4** To send a copy of the message, click this area and type the e-mail address of each person you want to receive a copy. Separate each address with a semicolon (;).

*Note: You may want to send a copy of the message to people who are not directly involved but would be interested in the message.*

**5** Click this area and type a subject for the message.

*Note: If a subject already exists, you can drag the mouse I over the existing subject and then type a new subject.*

**6** Click **Send this Sheet** to send the message.

# EDIT DATA

You can edit data in your worksheet to correct a mistake, remove data you no longer need or update data.

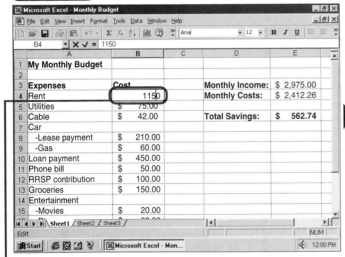

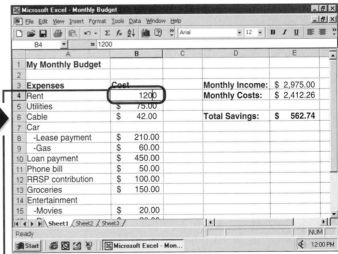

**1** Double-click the cell containing the data you want to edit.

■ A flashing insertion point appears in the cell.

**2** Press the ← or → key to move the insertion point to where you want to remove or add characters.

**3** To remove the character to the left of the insertion point, press the ◆Backspace key.

**4** To add data where the insertion point flashes on your screen, type the data.

**5** When you finish making changes to the data, press the Enter key.

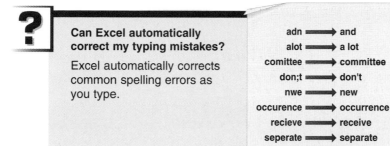

**?** **Can Excel automatically correct my typing mistakes?**

Excel automatically corrects common spelling errors as you type.

| | | |
|---|---|---|
| adn | ➡ | and |
| alot | ➡ | a lot |
| comittee | ➡ | committee |
| don;t | ➡ | don't |
| nwe | ➡ | new |
| occurence | ➡ | occurrence |
| recieve | ➡ | receive |
| seperate | ➡ | separate |
| teh | ➡ | the |

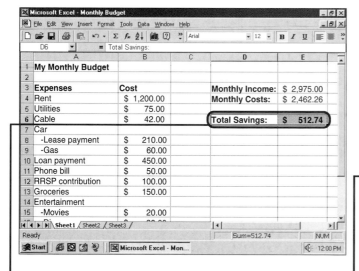

**DELETE DATA**

**1** Select the cells containing the data you want to delete. To select cells, see page 98.

**2** Press the Delete key.

■ The data in the cells you selected disappears.

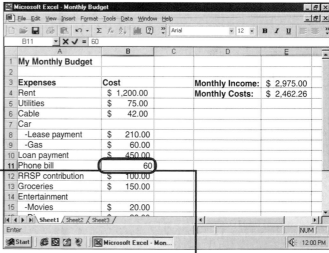

**REPLACE ALL DATA IN A CELL**

**1** Click the cell containing the data you want to replace with new data.

**2** Type the new data and then press the Enter key.

# MOVE OR COPY DATA

You can move or copy data to a new location in your worksheet.

Moving data allows you to reorganize data in your worksheet.

Copying data allows you to repeat data in your worksheet without having to retype the data.

## MOVE OR COPY DATA

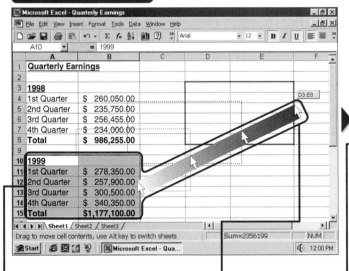

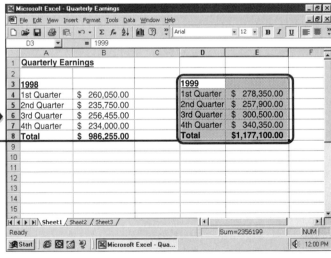

### USING DRAG AND DROP

**1** Select the cells containing the data you want to move. To select cells, see page 98.

**2** Position the mouse ⇩ over a border of the selected cells (⇩ changes to ↖).

**3** To move the data, drag the mouse ↖ to where you want to place the data.

*Note: A gray box indicates where the data will appear.*

■ The data moves to the new location.

■ To copy data, perform steps **1** to **3**, except press and hold down the `Ctrl` key as you perform step **3**.

118

**Why does the Clipboard toolbar appear when I move or copy data?**

The Clipboard toolbar may appear when you move or copy data using the toolbar buttons. Each icon on the Clipboard toolbar represents data you have selected to move or copy.

Clipboard (5 of 12)

Paste All

Games Played

■ To see the data an icon represents, position the mouse over the icon. A yellow box appears, displaying the data. You can click the icon to place the data in your worksheet.

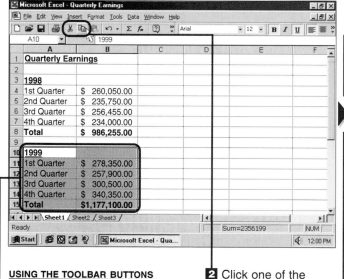

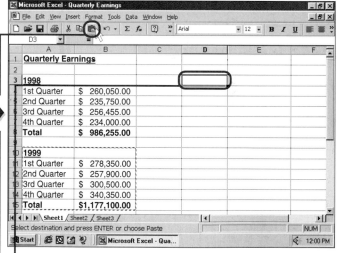

**USING THE TOOLBAR BUTTONS**

**1** Select the cells containing the data you want to move or copy. To select cells, see page 98.

**2** Click one of the following buttons.

✂ Move data

📋 Copy data

*Note: If the button you want is not displayed, click on the Standard toolbar to display all the buttons.*

**3** Click the cell where you want to place the data. This cell will become the top left cell of the new location.

**4** Click 📋 to place the data in the new location.

*Note: If 📋 is not displayed, click on the Standard toolbar to display all the buttons.*

■ The data appears in the new location.

# INSERT A ROW OR COLUMN

You can add a row
or column to your
worksheet when
you want to insert
additional data.

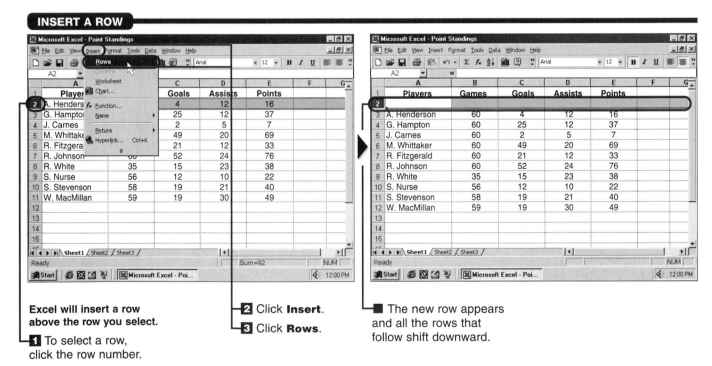

**Excel will insert a row
above the row you select.**

**1** To select a row,
click the row number.

**2** Click **Insert**.

**3** Click **Rows**.

■ The new row appears
and all the rows that
follow shift downward.

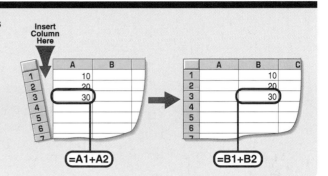

**?**

**Do I need to adjust my formulas when I insert a row or column?**

When you insert a row or column, Excel automatically updates any formulas affected by the insertion. For information on formulas, see page 126.

Insert
Column
Here

=A1+A2 → =B1+B2

## INSERT A COLUMN

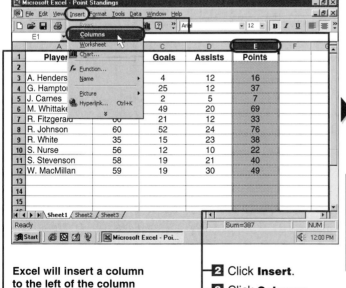

**Excel will insert a column to the left of the column you select.**

**1** To select a column, click the column letter.

**2** Click **Insert**.

**3** Click **Columns**.

**■** The new column appears and all the columns that follow shift to the right.

# DELETE A ROW OR COLUMN

You can delete a row
or column from your
worksheet to remove
cells and data you no
longer need.

## DELETE A ROW

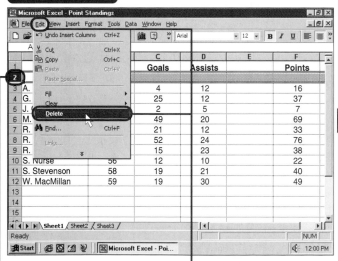

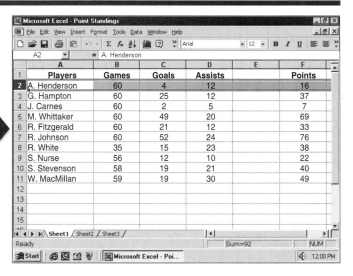

**1** To select the row
you want to delete,
click the row number.

**2** Click **Edit**.

**3** Click **Delete**.

■ The row disappears
and all the rows that
follow shift upward.

**Why did #REF! appear in a cell after I deleted a row or column?**

If #REF! appears in a cell in your worksheet, you deleted data needed to calculate a formula. Before you delete a row or column, make sure the row or column does not contain data that is used in a formula. For information on formulas, see page 126.

## DELETE A COLUMN

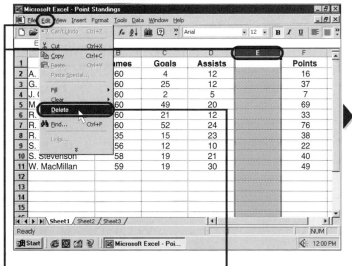

**1** To select the column you want to delete, click the column letter.

**2** Click **Edit**.

**3** Click **Delete**.

■ The column disappears and all the columns that follow shift to the left.

# ZOOM IN OR OUT

**Excel allows you to enlarge or reduce the display of data on your screen.**

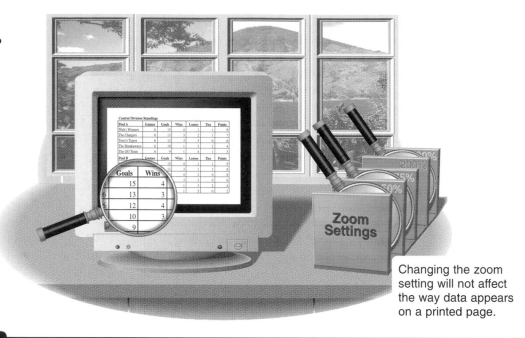

Changing the zoom setting will not affect the way data appears on a printed page.

**ZOOM IN OR OUT**

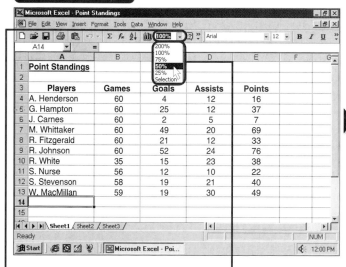

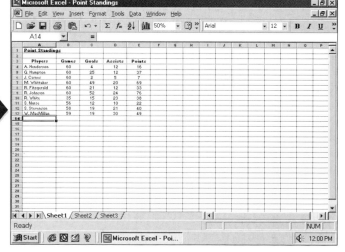

**1** Click ▾ in this area to display a list of zoom settings.

*Note: If the Zoom area is not displayed, click ⏵ on the Standard toolbar to display all the buttons.*

**2** Click the zoom setting you want to use.

■ The worksheet appears in the new zoom setting. You can edit the worksheet as usual.

■ To return to the normal zoom setting, repeat steps **1** and **2**, except select **100%** in step **2**.

124

# UNDO CHANGES

Excel remembers the last changes you made to your worksheet. If you regret these changes, you can cancel them by using the Undo feature.

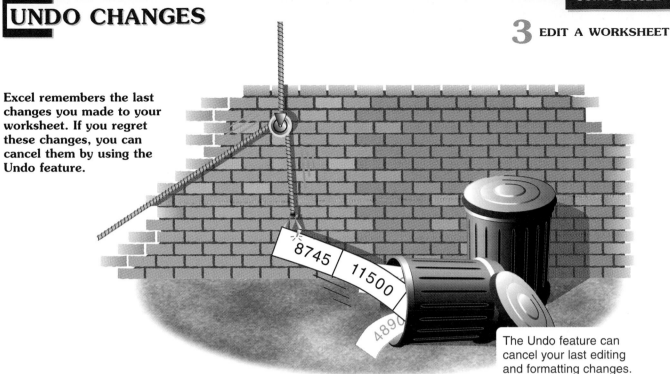

The Undo feature can cancel your last editing and formatting changes.

## UNDO CHANGES

**1** Click ↰ to undo the last change you made to your worksheet.

*Note: If ↰ is not displayed, click ▸ on the Standard toolbar to display all the buttons.*

■ Excel cancels the last change you made to your worksheet.

■ You can repeat step **1** to cancel previous changes you made.

■ To reverse the results of using the Undo feature, click ↱.

*Note: If ↱ is not displayed, click ▸ on the Standard toolbar to display all the buttons.*

# INTRODUCTION TO FORMULAS

A formula allows you to calculate and analyze data in your worksheet.

A formula always begins with an equal sign (=).

## INTRODUCTION TO FORMULAS

| | A | |
|---|---|---|
| 1 | 10 | |
| 2 | 20 | |
| 3 | 30 | |
| 4 | 40 | |
| 5 | | |
| 6 | | |

=A1+A2+A3*A4
=10+20+30*40 = 1230

=A1+(A2+A3)*A4
=10+(20+30)*40 = 2010

=A1*(A3-A2)+A4
=10*(30-20)+40 = 140

=A3/(A1+A2)+A4
=30/(10+20)+40 = 41

### Order of Calculations

Excel performs calculations in the following order:

1 Exponents (^)

2 Multiplication (*) and Division (/)

3 Addition (+) and Subtraction (-)

You can use parentheses ( ) to change the order in which Excel performs calculations. Excel will perform the calculations inside the parentheses first.

### Cell References

When entering formulas, use cell references instead of actual data whenever possible. For example, enter the formula **=A1+A2** instead of **=10+20**.

When you use cell references and you change a number used in a formula, Excel will automatically redo the calculation for you.

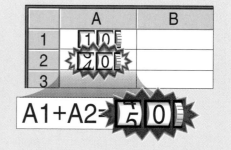

A1+A2=

126

## ERRORS IN FORMULAS

**An error message appears when Excel cannot properly calculate or display the result of a formula.**

Errors in formulas are often the result of typing mistakes. You can correct an error by editing the formula. To edit a formula, see page 129.

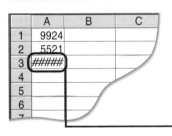

### #####

The column is too narrow to display the result of the calculation. You can change the column width to display the result. To change the column width, see page 142.

■ This cell contains the formula:

=A1*A2

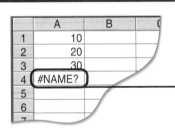

### #NAME?

The formula contains a cell reference Excel does not recognize.

■ This cell contains the formula:

=AQ+A2+A3

In this example, the cell reference A1 was typed incorrectly.

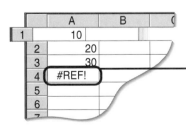

### #REF!

The formula refers to a cell that is not valid.

■ This cell contains the formula:

=A1+A2+A3

In this example, a row containing a cell used in the formula was deleted.

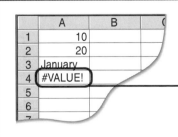

### #VALUE!

The formula refers to a cell that Excel cannot use in a calculation.

■ This cell contains the formula:

=A1+A2+A3

In this example, a cell used in the formula contains text.

# ENTER A FORMULA

You can enter a
formula into any cell
in your worksheet.
A formula helps
you calculate and
analyze data in
your worksheet.

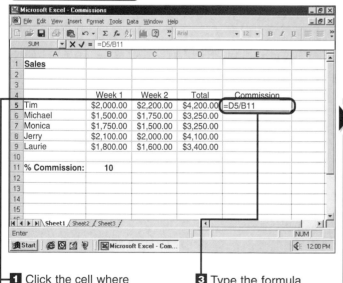

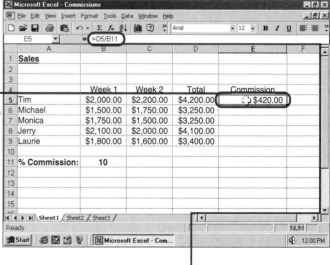

**1** Click the cell where
you want to enter a
formula.

**2** Type an equal sign (=)
to begin the formula.

**3** Type the formula
and then press the
Enter key.

■ The result of the
calculation appears
in the cell.

**4** To view the formula
you entered, click the cell
containing the formula.

■ The formula for the cell
appears in the formula bar.

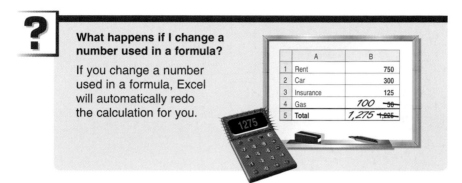

**What happens if I change a number used in a formula?**

If you change a number used in a formula, Excel will automatically redo the calculation for you.

| | A | B |
|---|---|---|
| 1 | Rent | 750 |
| 2 | Car | 300 |
| 3 | Insurance | 125 |
| 4 | Gas | *100* ~~50~~ |
| 5 | Total | *1,275* ~~1,225~~ |

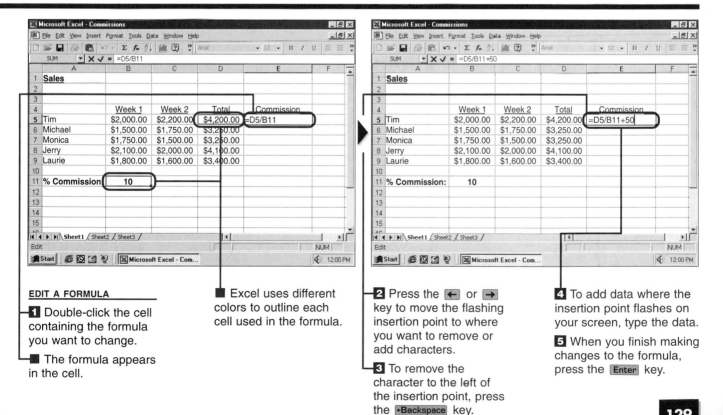

**EDIT A FORMULA**

**1** Double-click the cell containing the formula you want to change.

■ The formula appears in the cell.

■ Excel uses different colors to outline each cell used in the formula.

**2** Press the ← or → key to move the flashing insertion point to where you want to remove or add characters.

**3** To remove the character to the left of the insertion point, press the ◆Backspace key.

**4** To add data where the insertion point flashes on your screen, type the data.

**5** When you finish making changes to the formula, press the Enter key.

# INTRODUCTION TO FUNCTIONS

A function is a ready-to-use formula that you can use to perform a calculation on the data in your worksheet.

■ A function always begins with an equal sign (=).

■ The data Excel will use to calculate a function is enclosed in parentheses ( ).

```
=SUM(A1,A2,A3)

=AVERAGE(C1,C2,C3)

=MAX(B7,C7,D7,E7)

=COUNT(D12,D13,D14)
```

```
=SUM(A1:A3)

=AVERAGE(C1:C3)

=MAX(B7:E7)

=COUNT(D12:D14)
```

**Specify Individual Cells**

When a comma (,) separates cell references in a function, Excel uses each cell to perform the calculation.

For example, =SUM(A1,A2,A3) is the same as the formula =A1+A2+A3.

**Specify Group of Cells**

When a colon (:) separates cell references in a function, Excel uses the specified cells and all cells between them to perform the calculation.

For example, =SUM(A1:A3) is the same as the formula =A1+A2+A3.

## COMMON FUNCTIONS

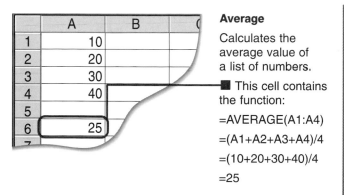

| | A | B | ( |
|---|---|---|---|
| 1 | 10 | | |
| 2 | 20 | | |
| 3 | 30 | | |
| 4 | 40 | | |
| 5 | | | |
| 6 | 25 | | |
| 7 | | | |

**Average**

Calculates the average value of a list of numbers.

■ This cell contains the function:

=AVERAGE(A1:A4)

=(A1+A2+A3+A4)/4

=(10+20+30+40)/4

=25

| | A | B | ( |
|---|---|---|---|
| 1 | 10 | | |
| 2 | 20 | | |
| 3 | 30 | | |
| 4 | 40 | | |
| 5 | | | |
| 6 | 4 | | |
| 7 | | | |

**Count**

Calculates the number of values in a list.

■ This cell contains the function:

=COUNT(A1:A4)

=4

| | A | B | ( |
|---|---|---|---|
| 1 | 10 | | |
| 2 | 20 | | |
| 3 | 30 | | |
| 4 | 40 | | |
| 5 | | | |
| 6 | 40 | | |
| 7 | | | |

**Max**

Finds the largest value in a list of numbers.

■ This cell contains the function:

=MAX(A1:A4)

=40

| | A | B | ( |
|---|---|---|---|
| 1 | 10 | | |
| 2 | 20 | | |
| 3 | 30 | | |
| 4 | 40 | | |
| 5 | | | |
| 6 | 10 | | |
| 7 | | | |

**Min**

Finds the smallest value in a list of numbers.

■ This cell contains the function:

=MIN(A1:A4)

=10

| | A | B | ( |
|---|---|---|---|
| 1 | 10 | | |
| 2 | 20 | | |
| 3 | 30 | | |
| 4 | 40 | | |
| 5 | | | |
| 6 | 100 | | |
| 7 | | | |

**Sum**

Adds a list of numbers.

■ This cell contains the function:

=SUM(A1:A4)

=A1+A2+A3+A4

=10+20+30+40

=100

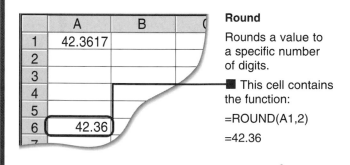

| | A | B | ( |
|---|---|---|---|
| 1 | 42.3617 | | |
| 2 | | | |
| 3 | | | |
| 4 | | | |
| 5 | | | |
| 6 | 42.36 | | |
| 7 | | | |

**Round**

Rounds a value to a specific number of digits.

■ This cell contains the function:

=ROUND(A1,2)

=42.36

# ENTER A FUNCTION

Excel helps you enter functions in your worksheet. Functions let you perform calculations without typing long, complex formulas.

=SUM(A1:A4)
=AVERAGE(A1:A4)
=ROUND(E4,2)
=COUNT(B1:B6)
=MAX(E1:E4)

## ENTER A FUNCTION

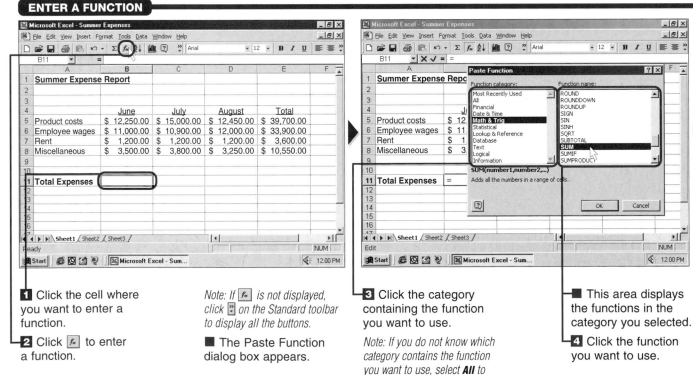

**1** Click the cell where you want to enter a function.

**2** Click ⨏ to enter a function.

*Note: If ⨏ is not displayed, click 🔽 on the Standard toolbar to display all the buttons.*

■ The Paste Function dialog box appears.

**3** Click the category containing the function you want to use.

*Note: If you do not know which category contains the function you want to use, select **All** to display a list of all the functions.*

■ This area displays the functions in the category you selected.

**4** Click the function you want to use.

**How many functions does Excel offer?**

Excel offers over 200 functions to help you analyze data in your worksheet. There are financial functions, math and trigonometry functions, date and time functions, statistical functions and many more.

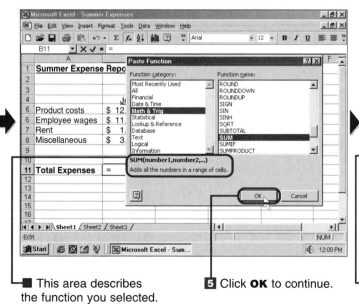

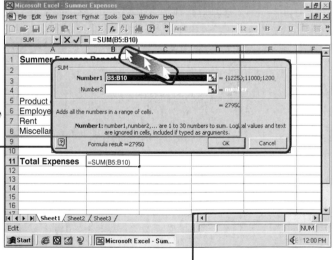

■ This area describes the function you selected.

**5** Click **OK** to continue.

■ A dialog box appears. If the dialog box covers data you want to use in the calculation, you can move the dialog box to a new location.

**6** To move the dialog box, position the mouse ⌖ over a blank area in the dialog box and then drag the dialog box to a new location.

CONTINUED ▶

# ENTER A FUNCTION

When entering a function, you must specify which numbers you want to use in the calculation.

=SUM(D1:D4)

## ENTER A FUNCTION (CONTINUED)

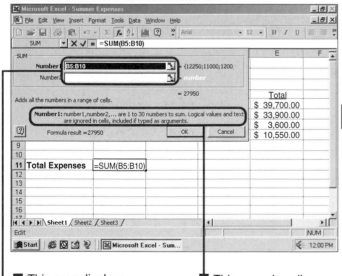

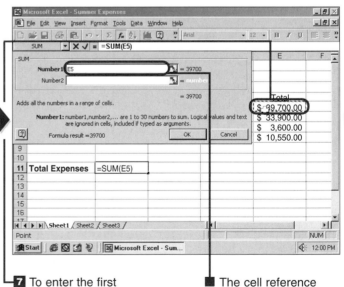

■ This area displays boxes where you enter the numbers you want to use in the calculation.

■ This area describes the numbers you need to enter.

**7** To enter the first number for the function, click the cell that contains the number.

*Note: If the number you want to use does not appear in your worksheet, type the number.*

■ The cell reference for the number appears in this area.

134

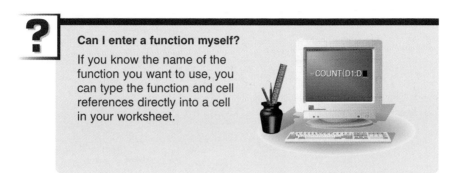

**Can I enter a function myself?**

If you know the name of the function you want to use, you can type the function and cell references directly into a cell in your worksheet.

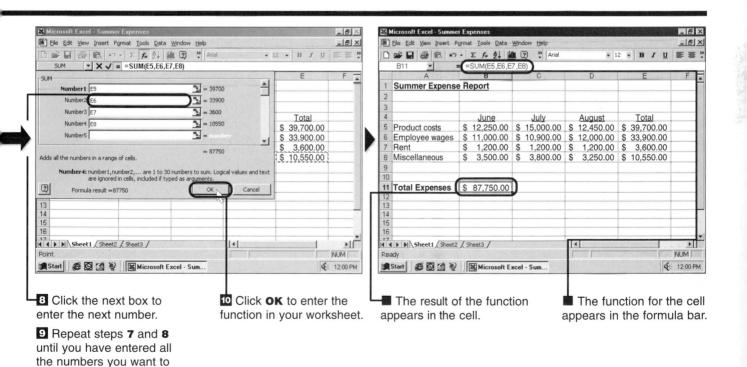

**8** Click the next box to enter the next number.

**9** Repeat steps **7** and **8** until you have entered all the numbers you want to use in the calculation.

**10** Click **OK** to enter the function in your worksheet.

■ The result of the function appears in the cell.

■ The function for the cell appears in the formula bar.

# ADD NUMBERS

You can calculate
the sum of a list
of numbers in
your worksheet.

## ADD NUMBERS

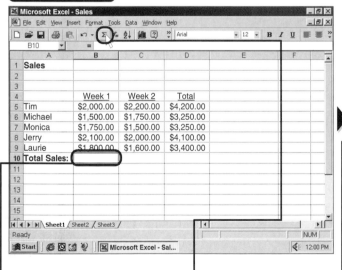

**1** Click the cell below
or to the right of the cells
containing the numbers
you want to add.

**2** Click Σ to add the
numbers.

*Note: If Σ is not displayed,
click ▸ on the Standard toolbar
to display all the buttons.*

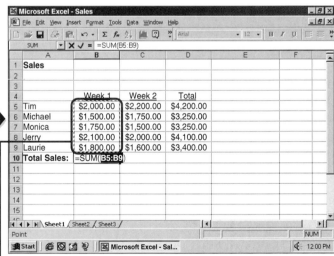

■ Excel outlines the cells
it will use in the calculation
with a dotted line.

■ If Excel does not
outline the correct cells,
select the cells containing
the numbers you want to
add. To select cells, see
page 98.

**How do I calculate the sum of rows and columns of data at the same time?**

**1** Select the cells containing the numbers you want to add and a blank row and column for the results. To select cells, see page 98.

**2** Click Σ to perform the calculations.

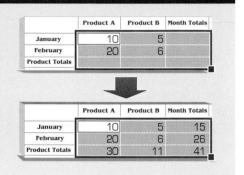

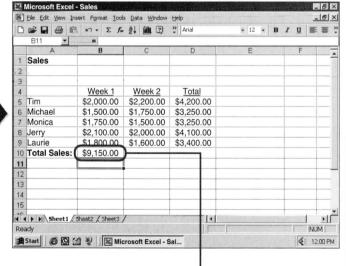

**3** Press the Enter key to perform the calculation.

■ The result of the calculation appears.

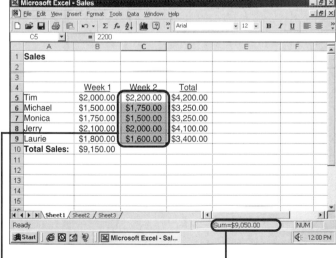

**USING AUTOCALCULATE**

You can view the sum of a list of numbers without entering a formula into your worksheet.

**1** Select the cells containing the numbers you want to include in the calculation. To select cells, see page 98.

■ This area displays the sum of the cells you selected.

# COPY A FORMULA

If you want to use the same formula several times in your worksheet, you can save time by copying the formula.

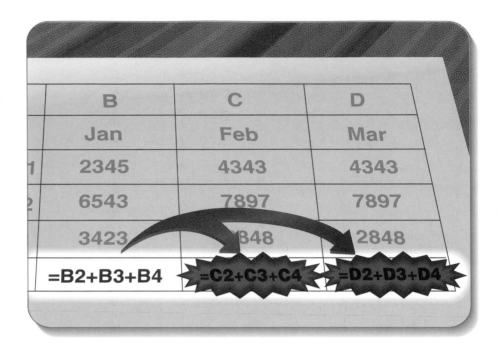

| | B | C | D |
|---|---|---|---|
| | Jan | Feb | Mar |
| 1 | 2345 | 4343 | 4343 |
| 2 | 6543 | 7897 | 7897 |
| | 3423 | 848 | 2848 |
| | =B2+B3+B4 | =C2+C3+C4 | =D2+D3+D4 |

## COPY A FORMULA—USING RELATIVE REFERENCES

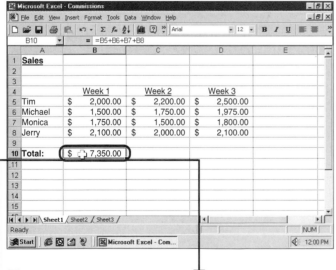

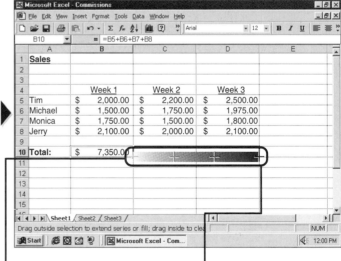

**1** Enter the formula you want to copy to other cells. To enter a formula, see page 128.

*Note: In this example, cell **B10** contains the formula =B5+B6+B7+B8.*

**2** Click the cell containing the formula you want to copy.

**3** Position the mouse ⇩ over the bottom right corner of the cell (⇩ changes to ✛).

**4** Drag the mouse ✛ over the cells you want to receive a copy of the formula.

**What is a relative reference?**

A relative reference is a cell reference that changes when you copy a formula.

| | A | B | C |
|---|---|---|---|
| 1 | 10 | 20 | 5 |
| 2 | 20 | 30 | 10 |
| 3 | 30 | 40 | 20 |
| 4 | 60 | 90 | 35 |
| 5 | | | |

=A1+A2+A3  ➡  =B1+B2+B3   =C1+C2+C3

This cell contains the formula =A1+A2+A3.

If you copy the formula to other cells in your worksheet, Excel automatically changes the cell references in the new formulas.

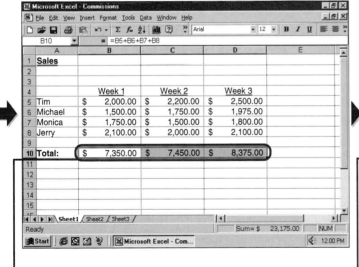

■ The results of the formulas appear.

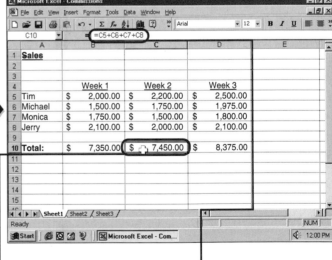

5 To see one of the new formulas, click a cell that received a copy of the formula.

■ The formula bar displays the formula with the new cell references.

# COPY A FORMULA

You can copy a formula
to other cells in your
worksheet to save time.
If you do not want
Excel to change a cell
reference when you
copy a formula, you
can use an absolute
reference.

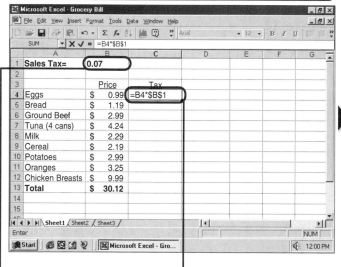

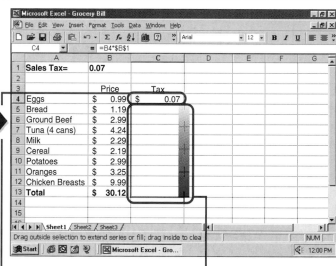

**1** Enter the data you
want to use in all the
formulas.

**2** Enter the formula you
want to copy to other
cells. To enter a formula,
see page 128.

*Note: In this example, cell **C4**
contains the formula =**B4*$B$1**.*

**3** Click the cell containing
the formula you want to copy.

**4** Position the mouse ⇦
over the bottom right corner
of the cell (⇦ changes to +).

**5** Drag the mouse +
over the cells you want
to receive a copy of the
formula.

## ? What is an absolute reference?

An absolute reference is a cell reference that does not change when you copy a formula. To make a cell reference absolute, type a dollar sign ($) before both the column letter and row number, such as $A$7.

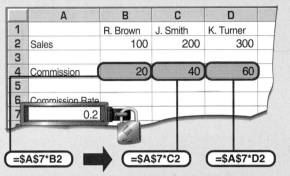

| | A | B | C | D |
|---|---|---|---|---|
| 1 | | R. Brown | J. Smith | K. Turner |
| 2 | Sales | 100 | 200 | 300 |
| 3 | | | | |
| 4 | Commission | 20 | 40 | 60 |
| 5 | | | | |
| 6 | Commission Rate | | | |
| 7 | | 0.2 | | |

=$A$7*B2   =$A$7*C2   =$A$7*D2

This cell contains the formula =$A$7*B2.

If you copy the formula to other cells in your worksheet, Excel does not change the absolute reference in the new formulas.

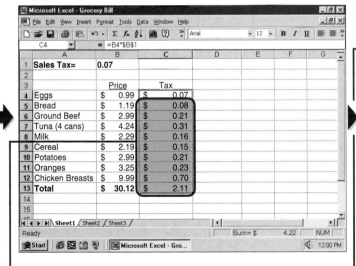

■ The results of the formulas appear.

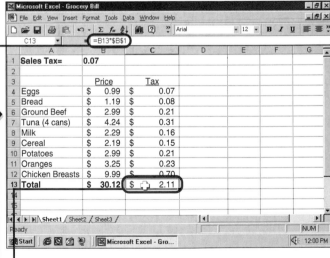

**6** To see one of the new formulas, click a cell that received a copy of the formula.

■ The formula bar displays the formula with the new cell references.

■ The absolute reference (**$B$1**) in the formula did not change. The relative reference (**B13**) in the formula did change.

# CHANGE COLUMN WIDTH

You can improve the appearance of your worksheet and display hidden data by changing the width of columns.

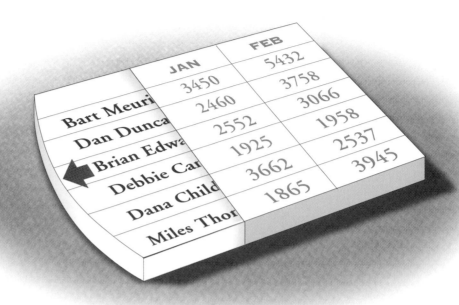

CHANGE COLUMN WIDTH

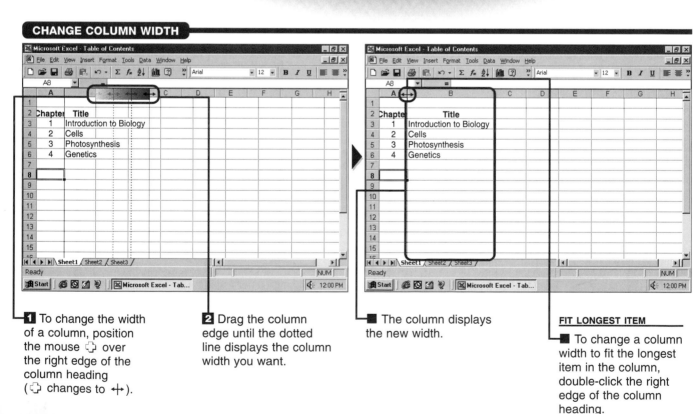

**1** To change the width of a column, position the mouse ⇩ over the right edge of the column heading (⇩ changes to ↔).

**2** Drag the column edge until the dotted line displays the column width you want.

■ The column displays the new width.

### FIT LONGEST ITEM

■ To change a column width to fit the longest item in the column, double-click the right edge of the column heading.

# CHANGE ROW HEIGHT

You can change the height of rows to add space between the rows of data in your worksheet.

## CHANGE ROW HEIGHT

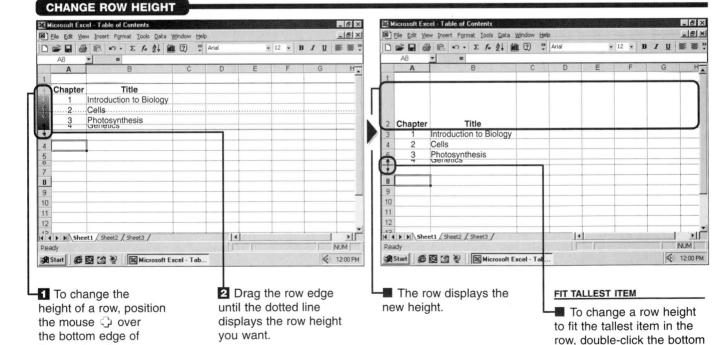

**1** To change the height of a row, position the mouse ⇩ over the bottom edge of the row heading (⇩ changes to ⭥).

**2** Drag the row edge until the dotted line displays the row height you want.

■ The row displays the new height.

**FIT TALLEST ITEM**

■ To change a row height to fit the tallest item in the row, double-click the bottom edge of the row heading.

# CHANGE FONT OF DATA

You can enhance the appearance of your worksheet by changing the font of data.

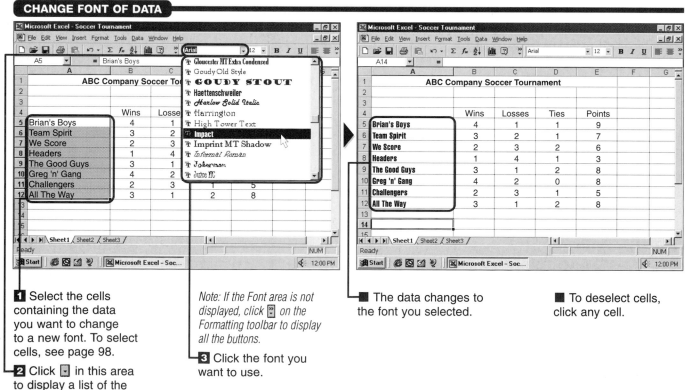

**1** Select the cells containing the data you want to change to a new font. To select cells, see page 98.

**2** Click ⬛ in this area to display a list of the available fonts.

*Note: If the Font area is not displayed, click ⬛ on the Formatting toolbar to display all the buttons.*

**3** Click the font you want to use.

■ The data changes to the font you selected.

■ To deselect cells, click any cell.

144

# CHANGE SIZE OF DATA

You can increase
or decrease the
size of data in
your worksheet.

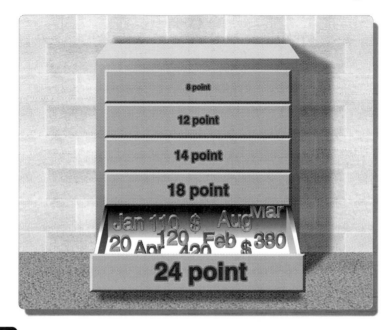

Excel measures the
size of data in points.
There are 72 points
in an inch.

## CHANGE SIZE OF DATA

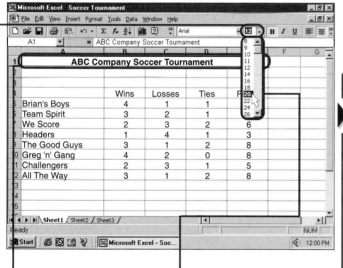

**1** Select the cells
containing the data
you want to change to
a new size. To select
cells, see page 98.

**2** Click ▪ in this area
to display a list of the
available sizes.

*Note: If the Font Size area is
not displayed, click ▪ on the
Formatting toolbar to display
all the buttons.*

**3** Click the size you
want to use.

■ The data changes to
the size you selected.

■ To deselect cells,
click any cell.

# CHANGE NUMBER FORMAT

You can quickly change
the appearance of numbers
in your worksheet without
retyping the numbers.

| SALES | | |
|---|---|---|
| Salesperson | Jan | Feb |
| Richard | 1564 | 1687 |
| Nancy | 2008 | 2114 |
| Steve | 1789 | 1487 |
| Jason | 1002 | 1298 |
| Susan | 2354 | 1809 |

| SALES | | |
|---|---|---|
| Salesperson | Jan | Feb |
| Richard | $1,564.00 | $1,687.00 |
| Nancy | $2,008.00 | $2,114.00 |
| Steve | $1,789.00 | $1,487.00 |
| Jason | $1,002.00 | $1,298.00 |
| Susan | $2,354.00 | $1,809.00 |

When you change the
format of numbers,
you do not change the
value of the numbers.

## CHANGE NUMBER FORMAT

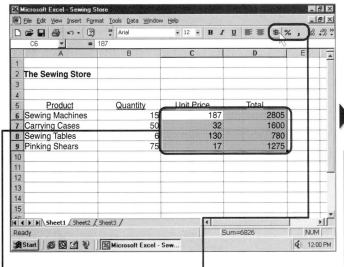

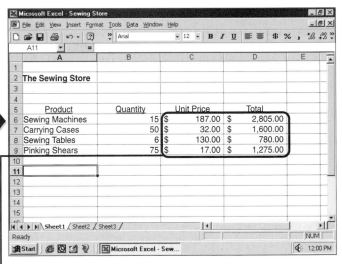

**CHANGE THE NUMBER STYLE**

**1** Select the cells
containing the numbers
you want to change. To
select cells, see page 98.

**2** Click one of the
following buttons.

$ Currency

% Percent

, Comma

*Note: If the button you want is
not displayed, click ⏵ on the
Formatting toolbar to display
all the buttons.*

■ The numbers display
the style you selected.

■ To deselect cells,
click any cell.

## How can I format the numbers in my worksheet?

| Option | | Example |
|---|---|---|
| **$** | Change to dollar value | 10 ➜ $10.00 |
| **%** | Change to percentage | 0.15 ➜ 15% |
| **,** | Add comma and display two decimal places | 1000 ➜ 1,000.00 |
| **.00** | Add decimal place | 10.13 ➜ 10.130 |
| **.00** | Remove decimal place | 10.13 ➜ 10.1 |

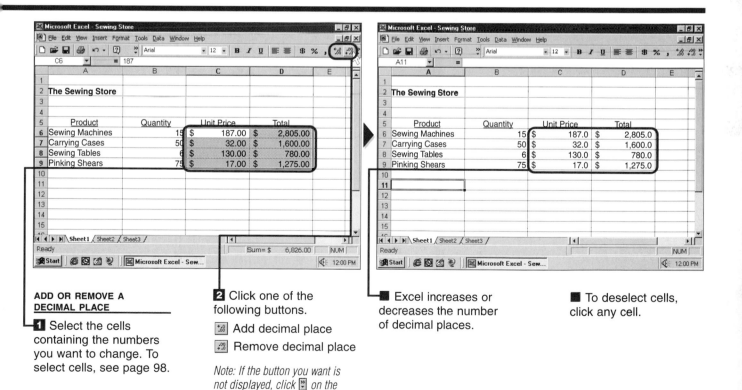

**ADD OR REMOVE A DECIMAL PLACE**

**1** Select the cells containing the numbers you want to change. To select cells, see page 98.

**2** Click one of the following buttons.

.00 Add decimal place

.00 Remove decimal place

*Note: If the button you want is not displayed, click ⟩ on the Formatting toolbar to display all the buttons.*

■ Excel increases or decreases the number of decimal places.

■ To deselect cells, click any cell.

# CHANGE CELL OR DATA COLOR

You can make your worksheet more attractive by adding color to cells or data.

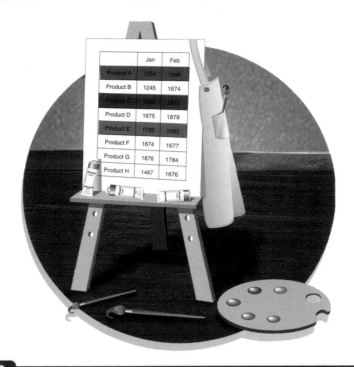

## CHANGE CELL COLOR

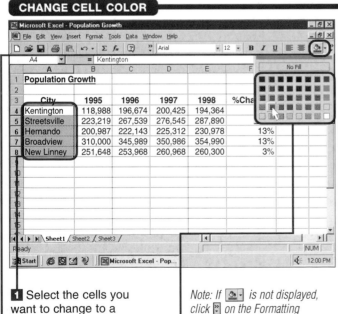

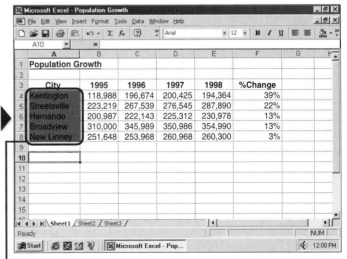

**1** Select the cells you want to change to a different color. To select cells, see page 98.

**2** Click ⬛ in this area to select a color.

*Note: If ⬛ is not displayed, click ⬛ on the Formatting toolbar to display all the buttons.*

**3** Click the cell color you want to use.

■ The cells change to the new color.

■ To deselect cells, click any cell.

■ To remove a color from cells, repeat steps **1** to **3**, except select **No Fill** in step **3**.

**?**

**What colors should I choose?**

When adding color to your worksheet, make sure you choose cell and data colors that work well together. For example, red data on a blue background is difficult to read.

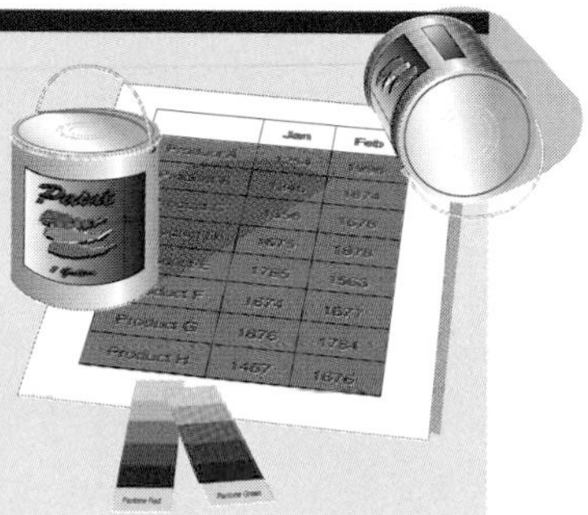

## CHANGE DATA COLOR

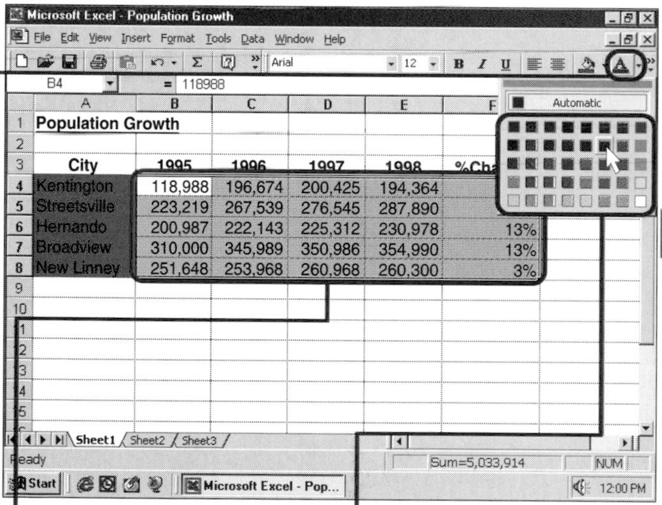


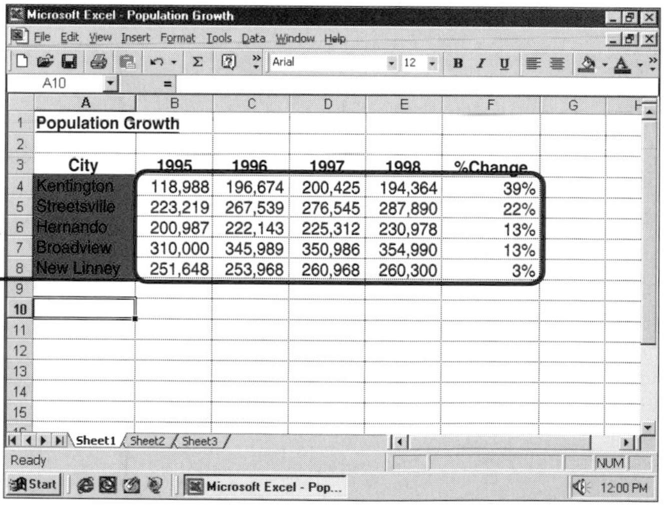


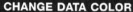

**1** Select the cells containing the data you want to change to a different color. To select cells, see page 98.

**2** Click ▾ in this area to select a color.

*Note: If* [A▾] *is not displayed, click* [»] *on the Formatting toolbar to display all the buttons.*

**3** Click the data color you want to use.

■ The data changes to the new color.

■ To deselect cells, click any cell.

■ To remove a color from data, repeat steps **1** to **3**, except select **Automatic** in step **3**.

# CHANGE ALIGNMENT OF DATA

You can change
the way Excel
aligns data within
cells in your
worksheet.

Excel automatically left
aligns text and right
aligns numbers and
dates you enter in cells.

## CHANGE ALIGNMENT OF DATA

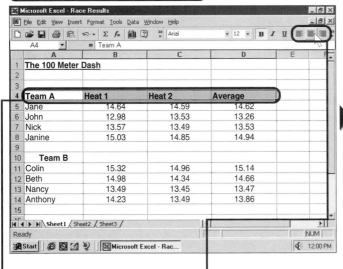

**1** Select the cells
containing the data you
want to align differently.
To select cells, see
page 98.

**2** Click one of the
following buttons.

▤ Left align

▤ Center

▤ Right align

*Note: If the button you want
is not displayed, click* ⏵
*on the Formatting toolbar
to display all the buttons.*

■ Excel aligns the data.

■ To deselect cells,
click any cell.

# CENTER DATA ACROSS COLUMNS

You can center data across several columns in your worksheet. This is useful for centering titles over your data.

## CENTER DATA ACROSS COLUMNS

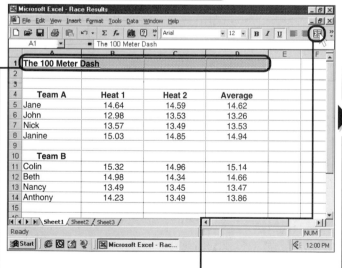

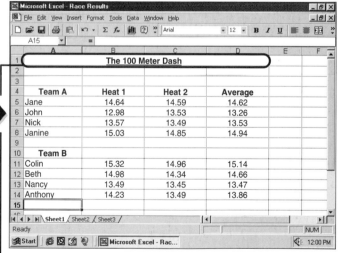

**1** Select the cells you want to center the data across. To select cells, see page 98.

*Note: The first cell you select should contain the data you want to center.*

**2** Click 🔳 to center the data.

*Note: If 🔳 is not displayed, click ⏹ on the Formatting toolbar to display all the buttons.*

■ Excel centers the data across the cells you selected.

■ To deselect cells, click any cell.

# BOLD, ITALIC AND UNDERLINE

You can use the Bold, Italic and Underline features to emphasize data in your worksheet.

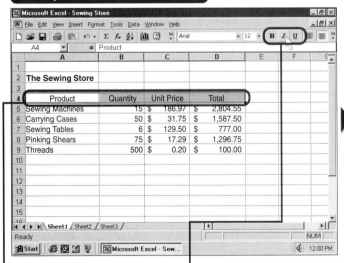

**1** Select the cells containing the data you want to change. To select cells, see page 98.

**2** Click one of the following buttons.

| **B** | Bold |
| *I* | Italic |
| U | Underline |

*Note: If the button you want is not displayed, click ⁑ on the Formatting toolbar to display all the buttons.*

■ The data displays the style you selected.

■ To deselect cells, click any cell.

■ To remove a bold, italic or underline style, repeat steps **1** and **2**.

# COPY FORMATTING

Once you format one cell to suit your needs, you can make other cells look exactly the same.

You may want to copy the formatting of cells to make all the titles in your worksheet look the same.

---

## COPY FORMATTING

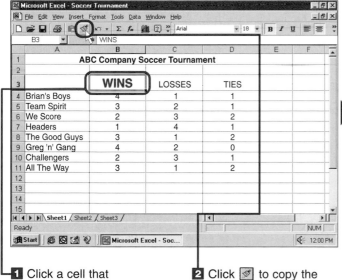

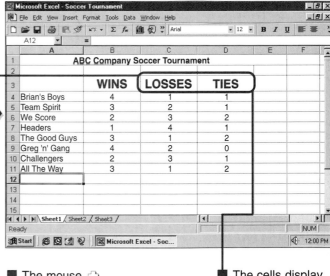

**1** Click a cell that displays the formatting you want to copy to other cells.

**2** Click ✍ to copy the formatting.

*Note: If ✍ is not displayed, click ⁑ on the Standard toolbar to display all the buttons.*

■ The mouse ⌖ changes to ⌖ᴭ when over your worksheet.

**3** Select the cells you want to display the same formatting. To select cells, see page 98.

■ The cells display the formatting.

■ To deselect cells, click any cell.

# APPLY AN AUTOFORMAT

Excel offers many
ready-to-use designs,
called AutoFormats,
that you can choose
from to give your
worksheet a new
appearance.

### APPLY AN AUTOFORMAT

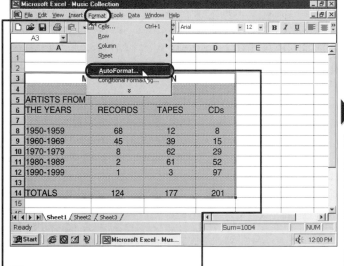

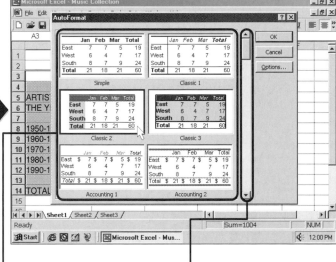

**1** Select the cells
you want to apply an
AutoFormat to. To select
cells, see page 98.

**2** Click **Format**.

**3** Click **AutoFormat**.

■ The AutoFormat
dialog box appears.

**4** Click the AutoFormat
you want to use.

■ You can use the scroll
bar to browse through the
available AutoFormats.

**What formatting does an AutoFormat include?**

Each AutoFormat includes a combination of formats, such as text and number styles, fonts, colors and borders that you can use to create a professional-looking worksheet.

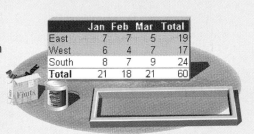

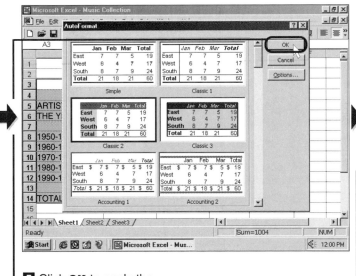

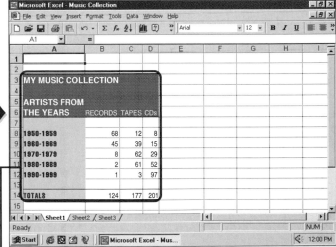

**5** Click **OK** to apply the AutoFormat to the cells you selected.

■ The cells display the AutoFormat you selected.

■ To deselect cells, click any cell.

■ To remove an AutoFormat, repeat steps **1** to **5**, except select **None** in step **4**.

# PREVIEW A WORKSHEET

You can use the Print Preview feature to see how your worksheet will look when printed. This lets you confirm that the worksheet will print the way you want.

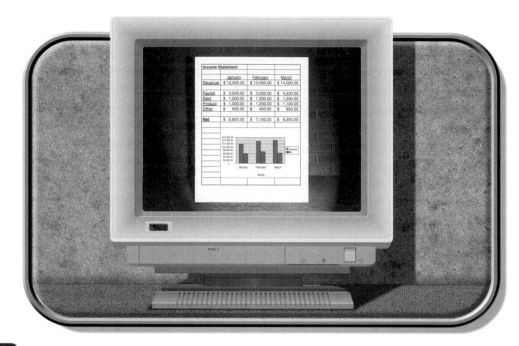

## PREVIEW A WORKSHEET

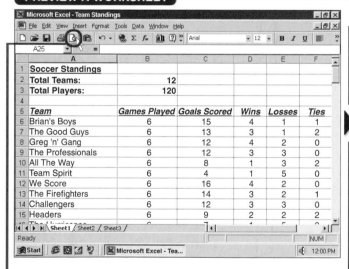

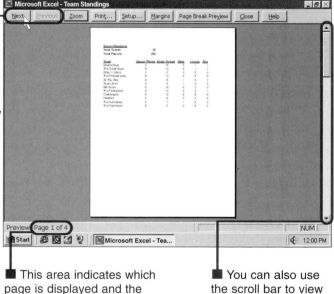

■1 Click 🔍 to preview your worksheet.

*Note: If 🔍 is not displayed, click 🔽 on the Standard toolbar to display all the buttons.*

■ The Print Preview window appears.

■ This area indicates which page is displayed and the total number of pages in your worksheet.

■2 If your worksheet contains more than one page, you can click **Next** or **Previous** to view the next or previous page.

■ You can also use the scroll bar to view other pages.

**Why does my worksheet appear in black and white in the Print Preview window?**

If you are using a black-and-white printer, your worksheet appears in black and white in the Print Preview window. If you are using a color printer, your worksheet appears in color.

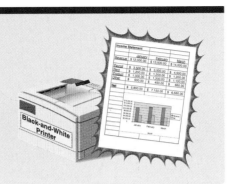

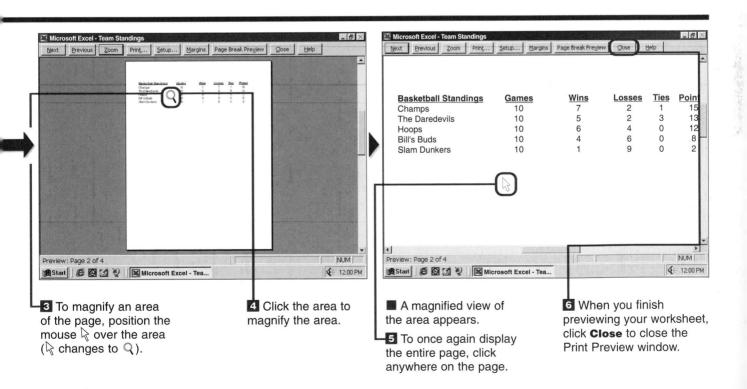

| Basketball Standings | Games | Wins | Losses | Ties | Point |
|---|---|---|---|---|---|
| Champs | 10 | 7 | 2 | 1 | 15 |
| The Daredevils | 10 | 5 | 2 | 3 | 13 |
| Hoops | 10 | 6 | 4 | 0 | 12 |
| Bill's Buds | 10 | 4 | 6 | 0 | 8 |
| Slam Dunkers | 10 | 1 | 9 | 0 | 2 |

**3** To magnify an area of the page, position the mouse over the area (changes to ).

**4** Click the area to magnify the area.

■ A magnified view of the area appears.

**5** To once again display the entire page, click anywhere on the page.

**6** When you finish previewing your worksheet, click **Close** to close the Print Preview window.

# PRINT A WORKSHEET

You can produce a
paper copy of the
worksheet displayed
on your screen.

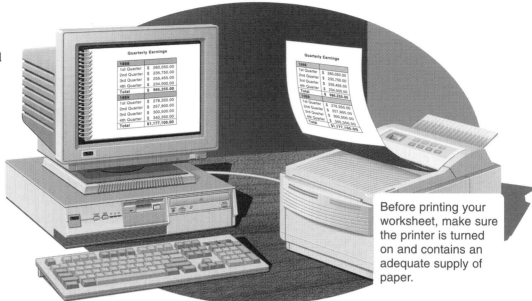

Before printing your
worksheet, make sure
the printer is turned
on and contains an
adequate supply of
paper.

## PRINT A WORKSHEET

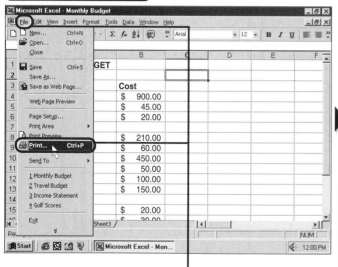

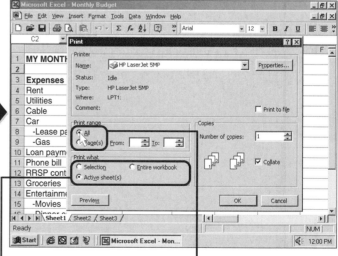

**1** Click any cell in the
worksheet you want to
print.

*Note: To print only specific
cells in a worksheet, select
the cells you want to print.
To select cells, see page 98.*

**2** Click **File**.

**3** Click **Print**.

■ The Print dialog
box appears.

**4** Click the part of the
workbook you want to
print (○ changes to ⦿).

**5** If the part of the
workbook you selected
to print contains more
than one page, click an
option to specify which
pages you want to print
(○ changes to ⦿).

158

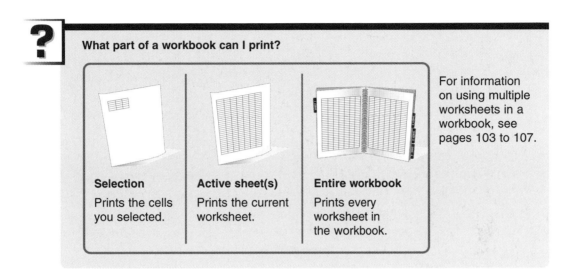

**What part of a workbook can I print?**

**Selection**
Prints the cells you selected.

**Active sheet(s)**
Prints the current worksheet.

**Entire workbook**
Prints every worksheet in the workbook.

For information on using multiple worksheets in a workbook, see pages 103 to 107.

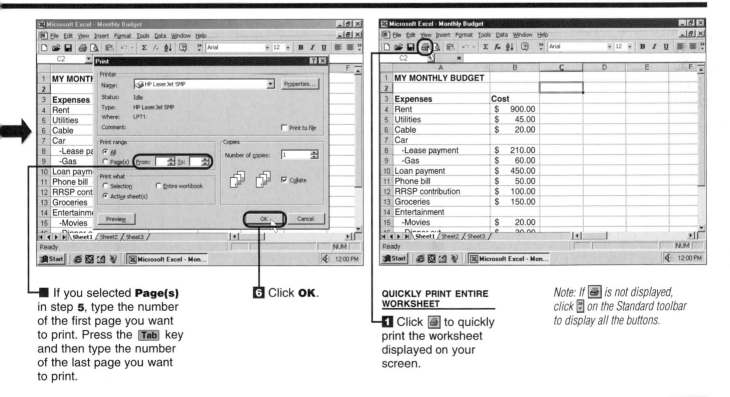

■ If you selected **Page(s)** in step **5**, type the number of the first page you want to print. Press the **Tab** key and then type the number of the last page you want to print.

**6** Click **OK**.

**QUICKLY PRINT ENTIRE WORKSHEET**

**1** Click 🖨 to quickly print the worksheet displayed on your screen.

*Note: If 🖨 is not displayed, click 🔽 on the Standard toolbar to display all the buttons.*

# CHANGE MARGINS

A margin is the amount of space between data and an edge of your paper. You can change the margins for your worksheet.

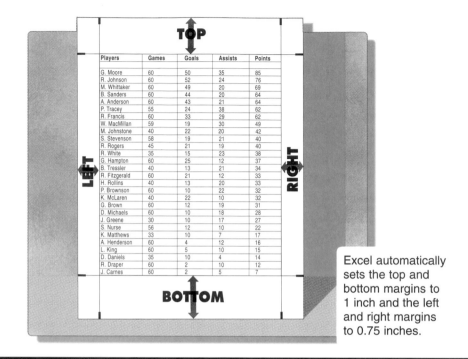

Excel automatically sets the top and bottom margins to 1 inch and the left and right margins to 0.75 inches.

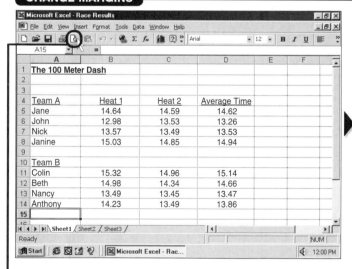

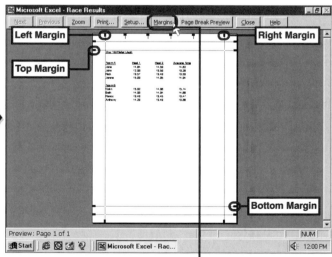

**1** Click 🔍 to display your worksheet in the Print Preview window. This window allows you to change the margins.

*Note: If 🔍 is not displayed, click ▸ on the Standard toolbar to display all the buttons.*

■ The worksheet appears in the Print Preview window.

*Note: For more information on the Print Preview feature, see page 156.*

**2** If the margins are not displayed, click **Margins**.

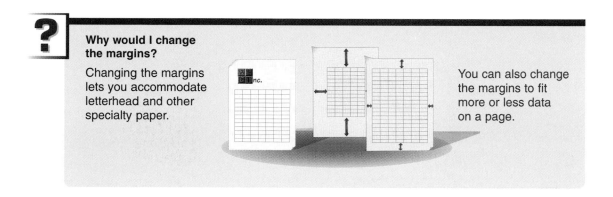

**Why would I change the margins?**

Changing the margins lets you accommodate letterhead and other specialty paper.

You can also change the margins to fit more or less data on a page.

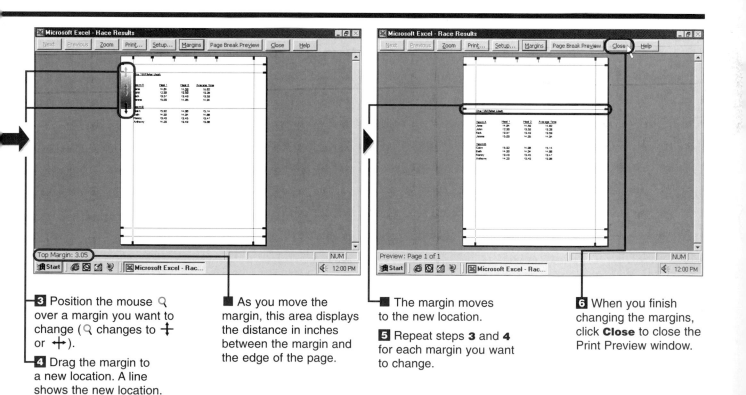

**3** Position the mouse Q over a margin you want to change (Q changes to ‡ or ‡).

**4** Drag the margin to a new location. A line shows the new location.

■ As you move the margin, this area displays the distance in inches between the margin and the edge of the page.

■ The margin moves to the new location.

**5** Repeat steps **3** and **4** for each margin you want to change.

**6** When you finish changing the margins, click **Close** to close the Print Preview window.

# CHANGE PAGE ORIENTATION

You can change the
orientation of your
printed worksheet.

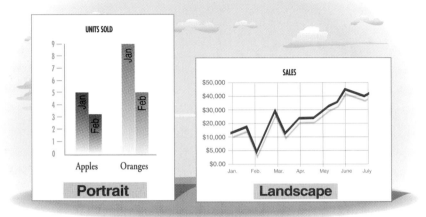

Portrait

Landscape

Excel automatically prints
worksheets in the portrait
orientation. The landscape
orientation is useful when
you want a wide worksheet
to fit on one printed page.

## CHANGE PAGE ORIENTATION

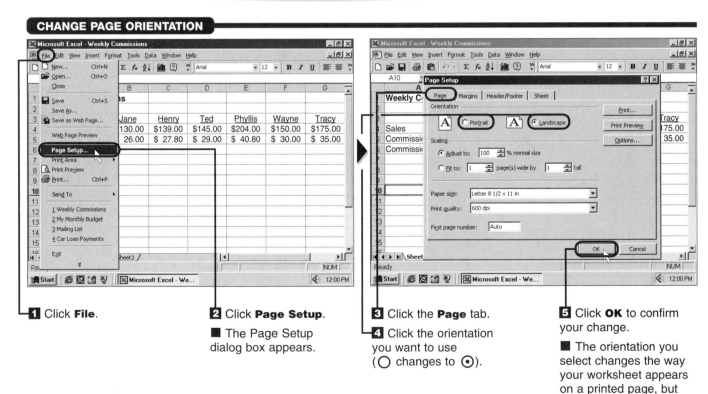

**1** Click **File**.

**2** Click **Page Setup**.

■ The Page Setup
dialog box appears.

**3** Click the **Page** tab.

**4** Click the orientation
you want to use
(○ changes to ⊙).

**5** Click **OK** to confirm
your change.

■ The orientation you
select changes the way
your worksheet appears
on a printed page, but
does not affect the way
the worksheet appears
on your screen.

# CHANGE PRINT OPTIONS

Excel offers several print options that let you change the way your worksheet appears on a printed page.

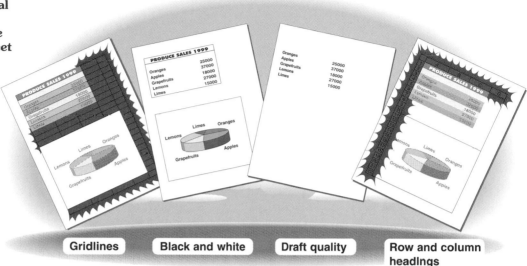

| Gridlines | Black and white | Draft quality | Row and column headings |

## CHANGE PRINT OPTIONS

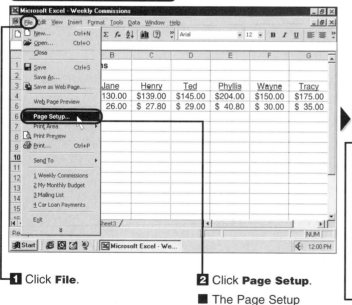

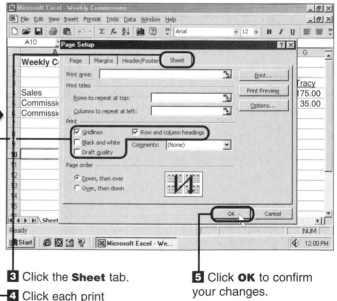

**1** Click **File**.

**2** Click **Page Setup**.

■ The Page Setup dialog box appears.

**3** Click the **Sheet** tab.

**4** Click each print option you want to use (☐ changes to ☑).

**5** Click **OK** to confirm your changes.

■ The print options you select change the way your worksheet appears on a printed page, but do not affect the way the worksheet appears on your screen.

# CREATE A CHART

You can create a chart to graphically display your worksheet data.

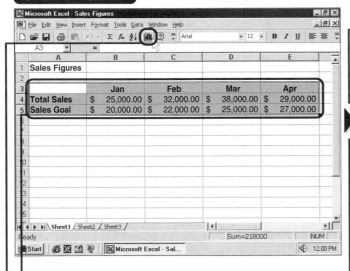

## CREATE A CHART

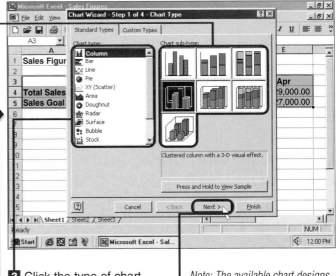

**1** Select the cells containing the data you want to display in a chart, including the row and column labels. To select cells, see page 98.

**2** Click  to create the chart.

*Note: If ▦ is not displayed, click ⁇ on the Standard toolbar to display all the buttons.*

■ The Chart Wizard appears.

**3** Click the type of chart you want to create.

**4** Click the chart design you want to use.

*Note: The available chart designs depend on the type of chart you selected in step 3.*

**5** Click **Next** to continue.

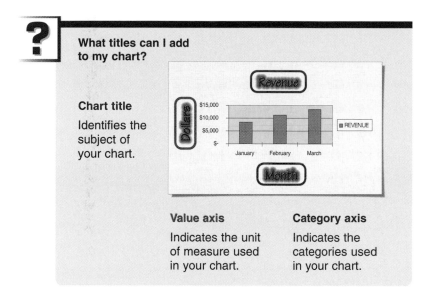

**What titles can I add to my chart?**

**Chart title**

Identifies the subject of your chart.

**Value axis**

Indicates the unit of measure used in your chart.

**Category axis**

Indicates the categories used in your chart.

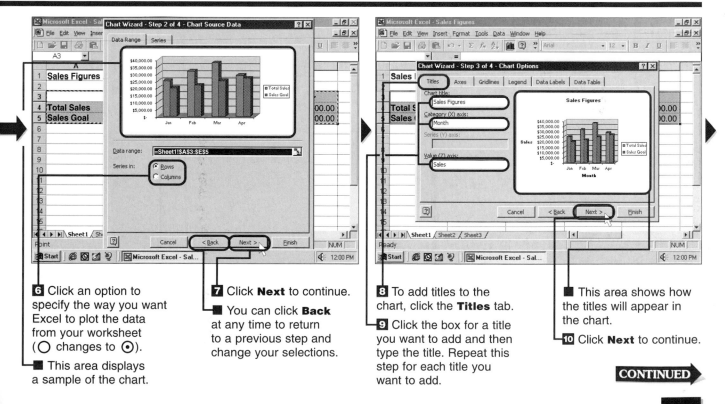

**6** Click an option to specify the way you want Excel to plot the data from your worksheet (○ changes to ⊙).

■ This area displays a sample of the chart.

**7** Click **Next** to continue.

■ You can click **Back** at any time to return to a previous step and change your selections.

**8** To add titles to the chart, click the **Titles** tab.

**9** Click the box for a title you want to add and then type the title. Repeat this step for each title you want to add.

■ This area shows how the titles will appear in the chart.

**10** Click **Next** to continue.

CONTINUED

# CREATE A CHART

When creating
a chart, you can
choose to display
the chart on the
same worksheet
as the data or
on its own sheet,
called a chart
sheet.

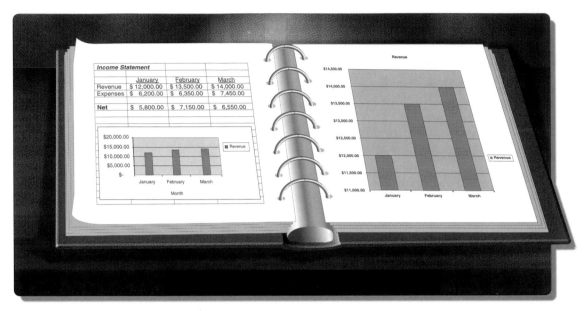

## CREATE A CHART (CONTINUED)

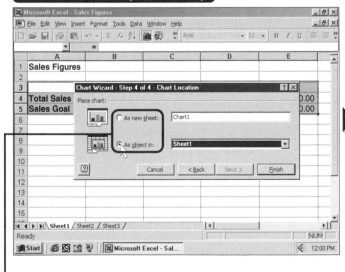

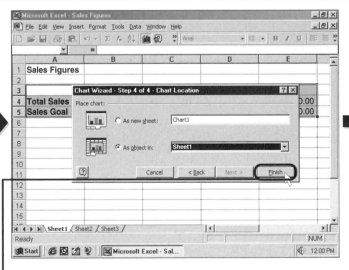

**11** Click an option to
specify where you want
to display the chart
(○ changes to ⊙).

**As new sheet**

Displays chart on its own
sheet, called a chart
sheet

**As object in**

Displays chart on the same
worksheet as the data

**12** Click **Finish** to
complete the chart.

**Do I have to create a new chart each time I change data in my worksheet?**

No. When you edit the data you used to create the chart, Excel will automatically update the chart to display the changes.

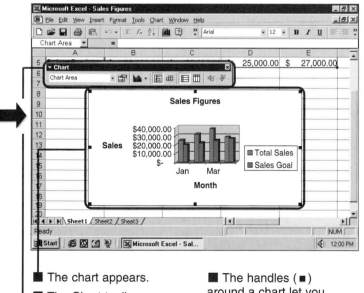

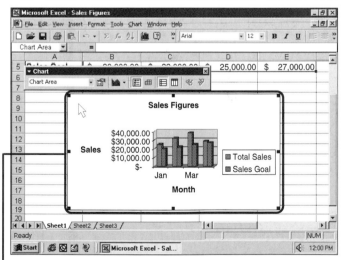

■ The chart appears.

■ The Chart toolbar also appears, displaying buttons that allow you to change the chart.

■ The handles (■) around a chart let you change the size of the chart. To hide the handles, click outside the chart.

*Note: To move or size a chart, see page 168.*

**DELETE A CHART**

**1** Click a blank area in the chart. Handles (■) appear around the chart.

**2** Press the Delete key.

*Note: To delete a chart displayed on a chart sheet, you must delete the sheet. To delete a worksheet, see page 105.*

# MOVE OR SIZE A CHART

After you create a chart, you can change the location and size of the chart.

- Move -

- Size -

## MOVE A CHART

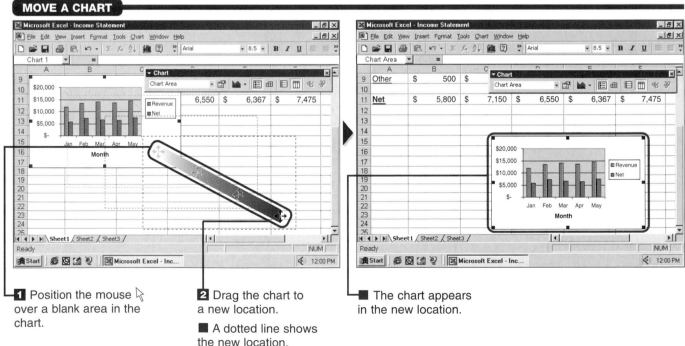

**1** Position the mouse ⬚ over a blank area in the chart.

**2** Drag the chart to a new location.

■ A dotted line shows the new location.

■ The chart appears in the new location.

**?** **What handle (■) should I use to size a chart?**

■ Changes the height of a chart

■ Changes the width of a chart

■ Changes the height and width of a chart at the same time

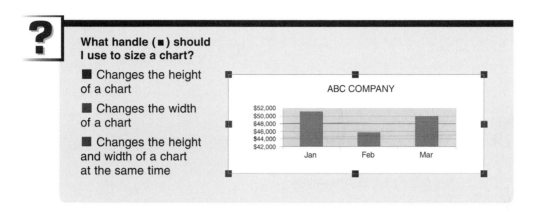

## SIZE A CHART

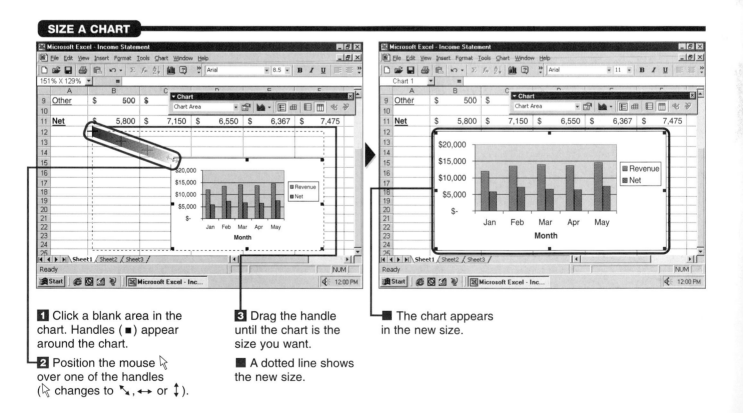

**1** Click a blank area in the chart. Handles (■) appear around the chart.

**2** Position the mouse ⌖ over one of the handles (⌖ changes to ↖, ↔ or ↕).

**3** Drag the handle until the chart is the size you want.

■ A dotted line shows the new size.

■ The chart appears in the new size.

169

# ADD DATA TO A CHART

After you create a chart, you can add new data to the chart.

Adding data to a chart is useful when you will need to update the chart over time. For example, you can add the latest sales figures to your chart each month.

## ADD DATA TO A CHART

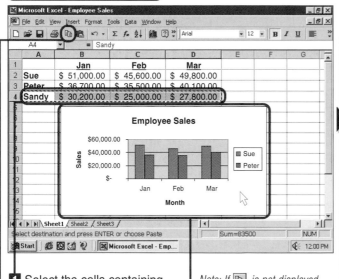

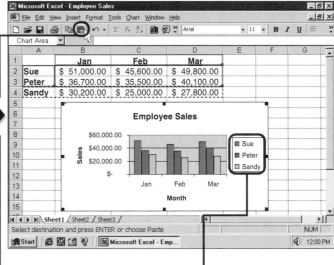

**1** Select the cells containing the data you want to add to the chart, including the row or column labels. To select cells, see page 98.

**2** Click 📋 to copy the data.

*Note: If 📋 is not displayed, click ⁇ on the Standard toolbar to display all the buttons.*

**3** Click the chart you want to add the data to.

**4** Click 📋 to add the data to the chart.

*Note: If 📋 is not displayed, click ⁇ on the Standard toolbar to display all the buttons.*

■ The data appears in the chart.

■ When you add data to a chart, Excel automatically updates the chart legend.

# PRINT A CHART

You can print
your chart with
the worksheet
data or on its
own page.

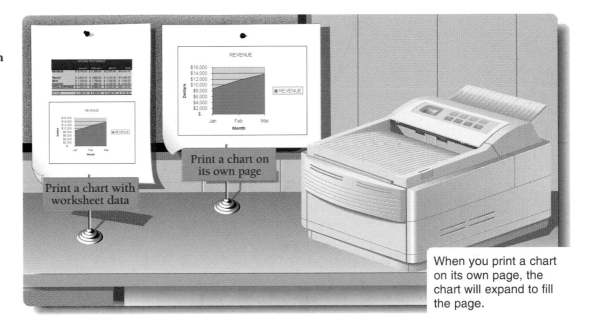

Print a chart on
its own page

Print a chart with
worksheet data

When you print a chart
on its own page, the
chart will expand to fill
the page.

## PRINT A CHART

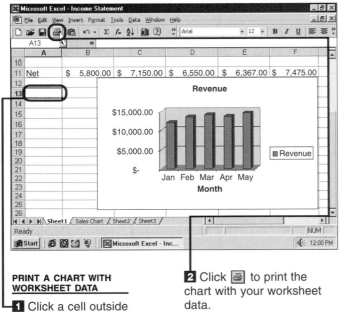

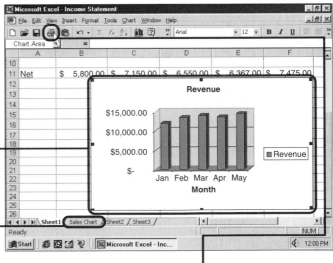

**PRINT A CHART WITH
WORKSHEET DATA**

■1 Click a cell outside
the chart.

■2 Click 🖨 to print the
chart with your worksheet
data.

*Note: If 🖨 is not displayed,
click ⏭ on the Standard toolbar
to display all the buttons.*

**PRINT A CHART ON ITS
OWN PAGE**

■1 To print a chart displayed
on a worksheet, click a
blank area in the chart.

■ To print a chart displayed
on a chart sheet, click the
tab for the chart sheet.

■2 Click 🖨 to print the
chart on its own page.

*Note: If 🖨 is not displayed,
click ⏭ on the Standard toolbar
to display all the buttons.*

# Using PowerPoint

# INTRODUCTION TO POWERPOINT

PowerPoint helps you plan, organize, design and deliver professional presentations.

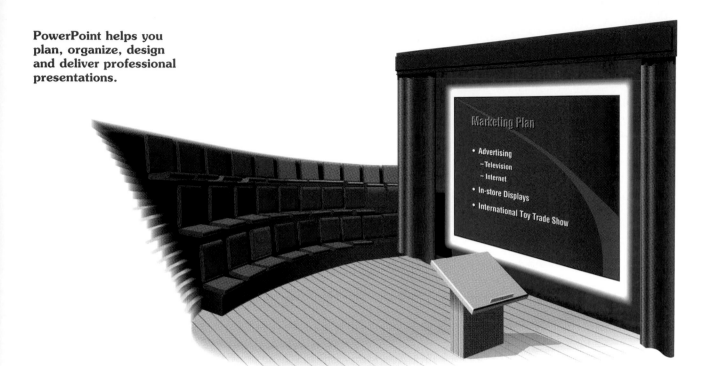

## Creating and Editing Presentations

You can use PowerPoint's AutoContent Wizard to quickly create a presentation. You can then add, delete or move text in the presentation and check the presentation for spelling errors. You can also add new slides to insert additional information.

## Enhancing Presentations

You can emphasize the text on a slide using a bold, italic, underline or shadow style. You can also change the font, size and color of text. You can enhance your slides by adding objects such as clip art images, AutoShapes, text effects and charts.

## Fine-Tuning Presentations

If you plan to deliver a presentation on a computer screen, you can add special effects called transitions to help you move from one slide to the next. You can also reorganize the slides in your presentation and delete slides you no longer need.

**PARTS OF A PRESENTATION**

### Slides

Slides display the information in a presentation. You can use a computer screen to present your slides to an audience. This is ideal for delivering a presentation to a small audience and allows you to add multimedia, such as animations, to your slides.

You can also use 35mm slides or overhead transparencies to present your slides. Many office supply stores sell overhead transparencies that you can print your slides on. You could also have a service bureau output your slides as overhead transparencies or 35mm slides for you.

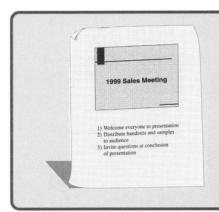

### Speaker Notes

Speaker notes are pages that contain copies of your slides with all the ideas you want to discuss during your presentation. Speaker notes can also include statistics or additional information that will help you answer questions from the audience.

### Handouts

You can print and distribute handouts to the audience to help them follow your presentation. Handouts display copies of the slides in your presentation and can provide space where the audience can write notes. Handouts are ideal for audience members who cannot clearly view the screen.

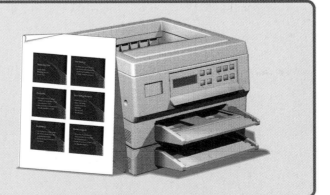

# START POWERPOINT

You can start PowerPoint
to create a professional
presentation.

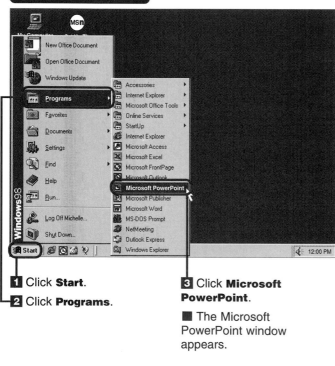

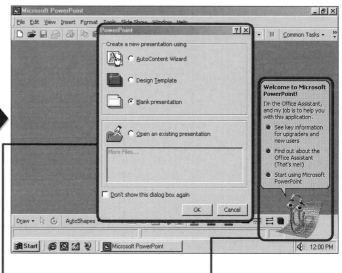

**1** Click **Start**.

**2** Click **Programs**.

**3** Click **Microsoft
PowerPoint**.

■ The Microsoft
PowerPoint window
appears.

■ The PowerPoint dialog
box appears each time
you start PowerPoint,
allowing you to create
or open a presentation.

*Note: To create a presentation,
see page 178. To open a
presentation, see page 188.*

■ The Office Assistant
welcome appears the
first time you start
PowerPoint.

*Note: For information on the
Office Assistant, see page 14.*

# THE POWERPOINT SCREEN

**The PowerPoint screen displays several items to help you perform tasks efficiently.**

### Menu Bar
Provides access to lists of commands available in PowerPoint.

### Formatting Toolbar
Contains buttons to help you select formatting commands, such as Bold and Underline.

### Standard Toolbar
Contains buttons to help you select common commands, such as Save and Open.

### Slide Pane
Displays the current slide.

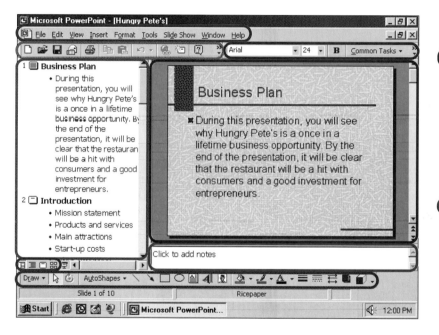

### Outline Pane
Displays all the text in your presentation.

### Notes Pane
Displays the speaker notes for the current slide.

### View Buttons
Allow you to quickly change the way your presentation is displayed on the screen.

### Drawing Toolbar
Contains buttons to help you work with objects in your presentation.

# CREATE A PRESENTATION

You can use the AutoContent Wizard to create a presentation. The wizard asks you a series of questions and then sets up a presentation based on your answers.

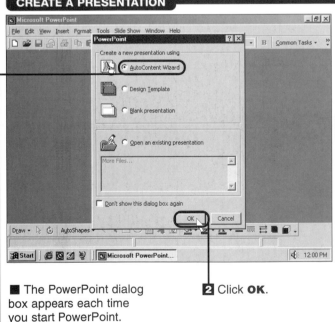

■ The PowerPoint dialog box appears each time you start PowerPoint.

**1** Click this option to create a new presentation using the AutoContent Wizard (○ changes to ⊙).

**2** Click **OK**.

■ The AutoContent Wizard appears.

■ This area describes the wizard.

Note: The Office Assistant may also appear. Click **No** to remove the Office Assistant from your screen. For more information on the Office Assistant, see page 14.

**3** Click **Next** to start creating your presentation.

178

**?** **Why does a dialog box appear when I select a presentation in the AutoContent Wizard?**

A dialog box appears if the presentation you selected is not installed on your computer. Insert the CD-ROM disc you used to install Office 2000 into your CD-ROM drive and then click **Yes** to install the presentation.

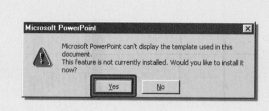

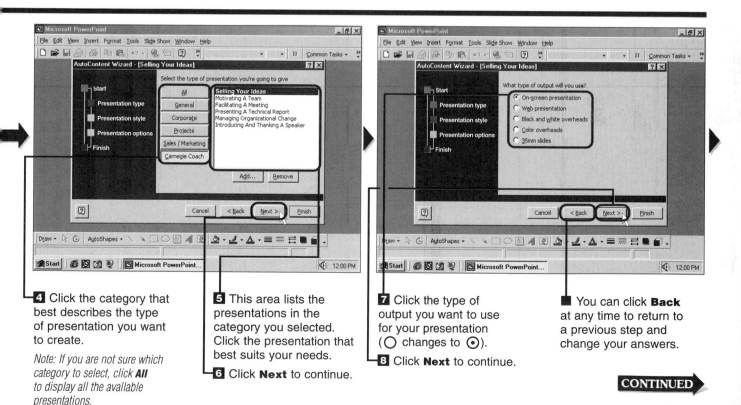

**4** Click the category that best describes the type of presentation you want to create.

*Note: If you are not sure which category to select, click **All** to display all the available presentations.*

**5** This area lists the presentations in the category you selected. Click the presentation that best suits your needs.

**6** Click **Next** to continue.

**7** Click the type of output you want to use for your presentation (○ changes to ⊙).

**8** Click **Next** to continue.

■ You can click **Back** at any time to return to a previous step and change your answers.

CONTINUED

# CREATE A PRESENTATION

The AutoContent Wizard allows you to specify a title for the first slide in your presentation. You can also specify information you want to appear on each slide.

Presentation title
Date last updated
Footer
Slide number

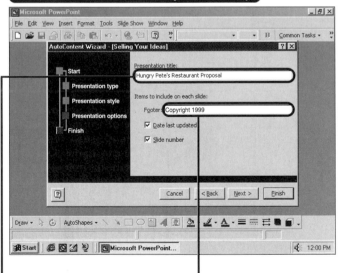

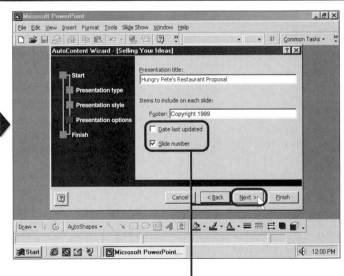

**9** Click this area and type the title you want to appear on the first slide in your presentation.

**10** To add footer text to each slide in your presentation, click this area and then type the text.

■ PowerPoint will add the current date and slide number to each slide in your presentation.

**11** If you do not want to add the current date or slide number, click the option you do not want to add (☑ changes to ☐).

**12** Click **Next** to continue.

**?**

**Why is there a yellow light bulb ( 💡 ) on a slide in my presentation?**

A yellow light bulb indicates the Office Assistant has a suggestion for improving the slide. Click the light bulb to display the suggestion. For more information on the Office Assistant, see page 14.

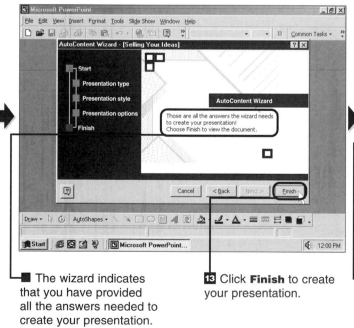

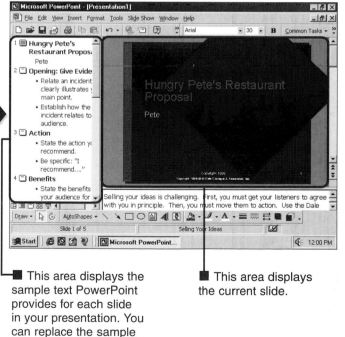

■ The wizard indicates that you have provided all the answers needed to create your presentation.

**13** Click **Finish** to create your presentation.

■ This area displays the sample text PowerPoint provides for each slide in your presentation. You can replace the sample text with your own text. To do so, see page 194.

■ This area displays the current slide.

# CHANGE THE VIEW

**PowerPoint offers several ways that you can view a presentation on your screen.**

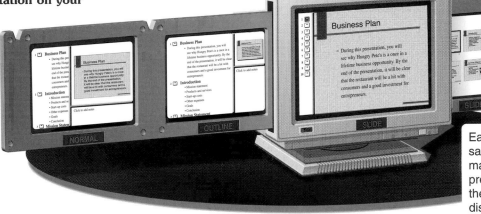

Each view displays the same presentation. If you make changes to your presentation in one view, the other views will also display the changes.

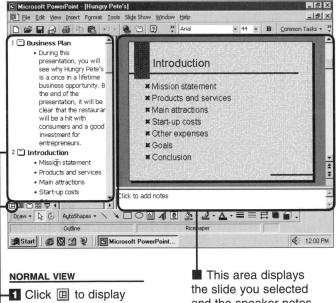

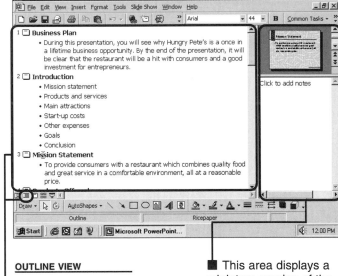

## NORMAL VIEW

**1** Click 📖 to display your presentation in the Normal view.

**2** This area displays all the text in your presentation. Click the text on a slide of interest.

■ This area displays the slide you selected and the speaker notes for the slide.

## OUTLINE VIEW

**1** Click 📄 to display your presentation in the Outline view.

**2** This area displays all the text in your presentation. Click the text on a slide of interest.

■ This area displays a miniature version of the slide you selected and the speaker notes for the slide.

182

**?**

**When would I use each view?**

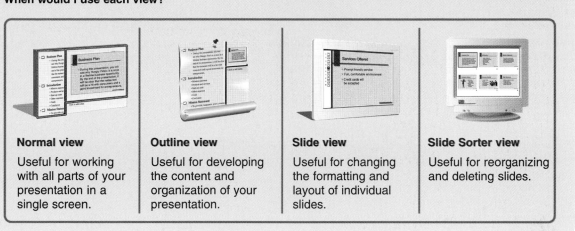

**Normal view**

Useful for working with all parts of your presentation in a single screen.

**Outline view**

Useful for developing the content and organization of your presentation.

**Slide view**

Useful for changing the formatting and layout of individual slides.

**Slide Sorter view**

Useful for reorganizing and deleting slides.

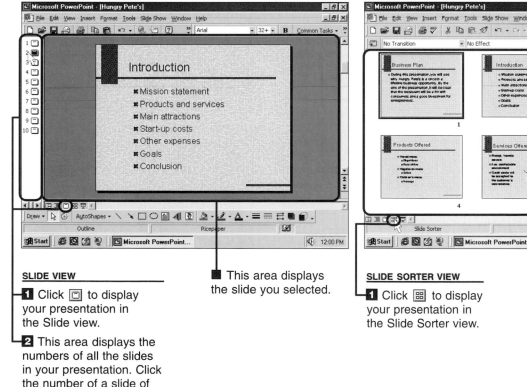

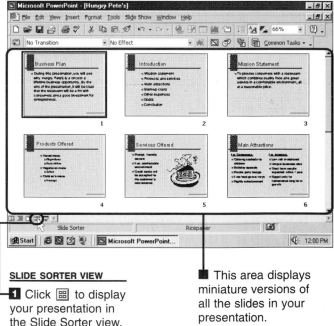

**SLIDE VIEW**

**1** Click 🔲 to display your presentation in the Slide view.

**2** This area displays the numbers of all the slides in your presentation. Click the number of a slide of interest.

■ This area displays the slide you selected.

**SLIDE SORTER VIEW**

**1** Click 🔠 to display your presentation in the Slide Sorter view.

■ This area displays miniature versions of all the slides in your presentation.

# BROWSE THROUGH A PRESENTATION

Your computer screen cannot display your entire presentation at once. You can browse through your presentation to view other areas of the presentation.

## BROWSE THROUGH A PRESENTATION

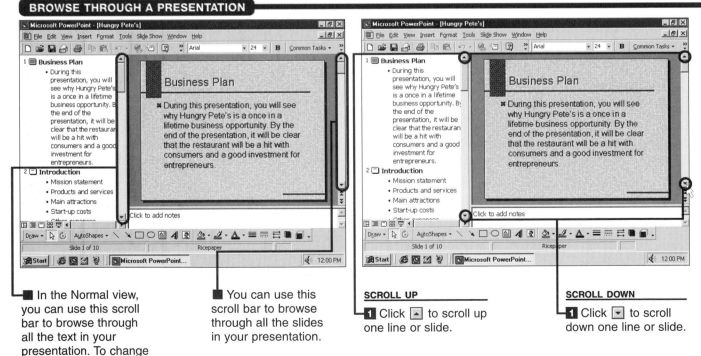

■ In the Normal view, you can use this scroll bar to browse through all the text in your presentation. To change the view, see page 182.

■ You can use this scroll bar to browse through all the slides in your presentation.

**SCROLL UP**

1 Click ▲ to scroll up one line or slide.

**SCROLL DOWN**

1 Click ▼ to scroll down one line or slide.

**How do I use a wheeled mouse to browse through my presentation?**

A wheeled mouse has a wheel between the left and right mouse buttons. Moving this wheel lets you quickly browse through your presentation. The Microsoft IntelliMouse is a popular example of a wheeled mouse.

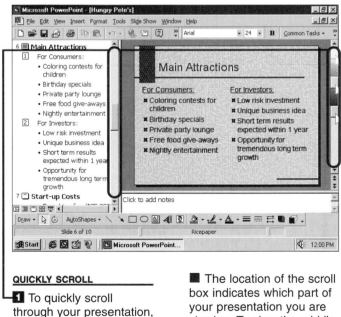

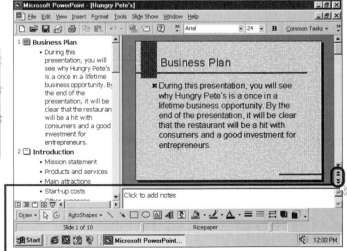

**QUICKLY SCROLL**

**1** To quickly scroll through your presentation, drag the scroll box along the scroll bar.

■ The location of the scroll box indicates which part of your presentation you are viewing. To view the middle of your presentation, drag the scroll box halfway down the scroll bar.

**DISPLAY PREVIOUS OR NEXT SLIDE**

**1** Click one of the following buttons.

⯅ Display previous slide

⯆ Display next slide

# SAVE A PRESENTATION

You can save your presentation to store it for future use. This allows you to later review and make changes to the presentation.

You should regularly save changes you make to a presentation to avoid losing your work.

## SAVE A PRESENTATION

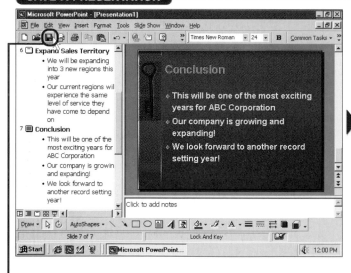

**1** Click 🖫 to save your presentation.

*Note: If 🖫 is not displayed, click ⏩ on the Standard toolbar to display all the buttons.*

■ The Save As dialog box appears.

*Note: If you previously saved your presentation, the Save As dialog box will not appear since you have already named the presentation.*

**2** Type a name for the presentation.

## ? What are the commonly used folders I can access?

**History**

Provides access to folders and presentations you recently used.

**My Documents**

Provides a convenient place to store a presentation.

**Desktop**

Lets you store a presentation on the Windows desktop.

**Favorites**

Provides a place to store a presentation you will frequently access.

**Web Folders**

Can help you store a presentation on the Web.

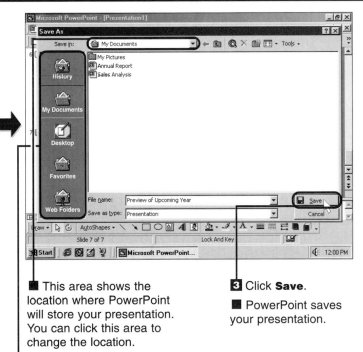

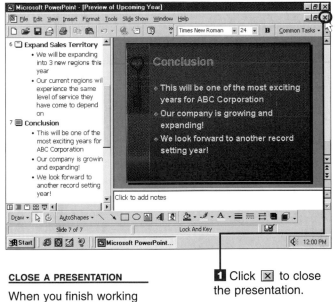

■ This area shows the location where PowerPoint will store your presentation. You can click this area to change the location.

■ This area allows you to access commonly used folders. To display the contents of a folder, click the folder.

**3** Click **Save**.

■ PowerPoint saves your presentation.

**CLOSE A PRESENTATION**

When you finish working with a presentation, you can close the presentation to remove it from your screen.

**1** Click ⊠ to close the presentation.

187

# OPEN A PRESENTATION

You can open a saved presentation and display it on your screen. This lets you review and make changes to the presentation.

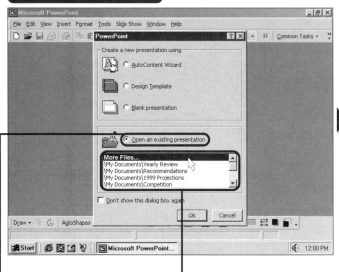

■ The PowerPoint dialog box appears each time you start PowerPoint.

**1** Click this option to open an existing presentation (○ changes to ⊙).

■ This area displays the names of the last presentations you worked with. To open one of these presentations, double-click the name of the presentation.

**2** If the presentation you want to open is not listed, double-click **More Files**.

■ The Open dialog box appears.

■ This area shows the location of the displayed presentations. You can click this area to change the location.

■ This area allows you to access commonly used folders. To display the contents of a folder, click the folder.

*Note: For information on the commonly used folders, see the top of page 187.*

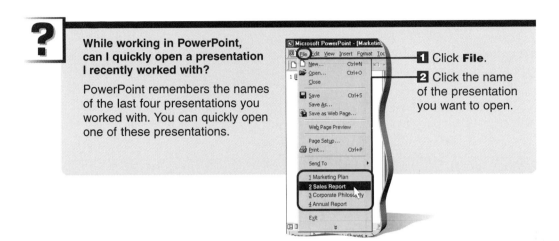

**?** While working in PowerPoint, can I quickly open a presentation I recently worked with?

PowerPoint remembers the names of the last four presentations you worked with. You can quickly open one of these presentations.

**1** Click **File**.

**2** Click the name of the presentation you want to open.

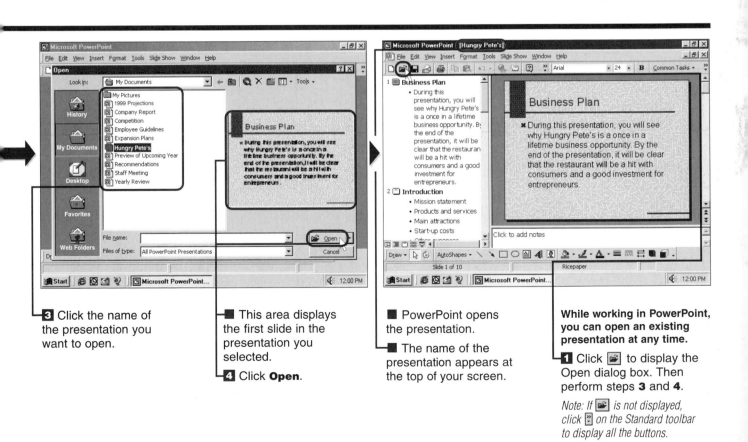

**3** Click the name of the presentation you want to open.

■ This area displays the first slide in the presentation you selected.

**4** Click **Open**.

■ PowerPoint opens the presentation.

■ The name of the presentation appears at the top of your screen.

**While working in PowerPoint, you can open an existing presentation at any time.**

**1** Click 📂 to display the Open dialog box. Then perform steps **3** and **4**.

*Note: If 📂 is not displayed, click 🔽 on the Standard toolbar to display all the buttons.*

# E-MAIL A PRESENTATION

You can e-mail
a presentation
to a friend,
family member
or colleague.

Before you can e-mail a
presentation, Microsoft
Outlook must be set up
on your computer.

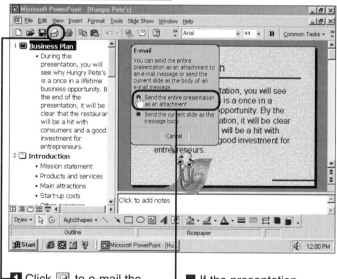

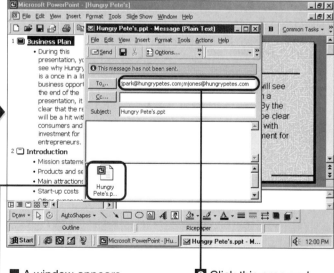

**1** Click 🔲 to e-mail the
current presentation.

*Note: If 🔲 is not displayed,
click 🔡 on the Standard toolbar
to display all the buttons.*

■ If the presentation
contains more than one
slide, a message appears,
asking if you want to send
the entire presentation or
just the current slide.

**2** Click this option to send
the entire presentation.

■ A window appears
for the e-mail message.

■ An icon for the
presentation appears
in the message.

**3** Click this area and
type the e-mail address
of each person you want
to receive the message.
Separate each address
with a semicolon (;).

190

**? How do I e-mail one slide in my presentation?**

To e-mail the slide currently displayed on your screen, perform steps **1** to **5** below, except select **Send the current slide as the message body** in step **2**. Then click **Send this Slide** to send the message. When you e-mail one slide, the slide appears in the body of the message.

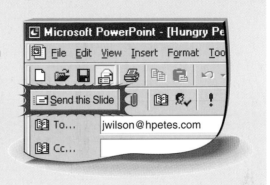

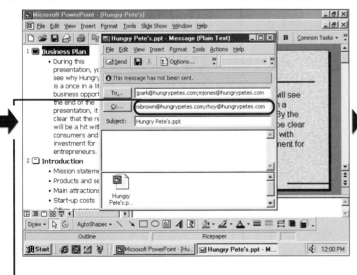

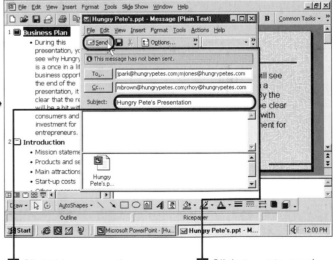

**4** To send a copy of the message, click this area and type the e-mail address of each person you want to receive a copy. Separate each address with a semicolon (;).

*Note: You may want to send a copy of the message to people who are not directly involved but would be interested in the message.*

**5** Click this area and type a subject for the message.

*Note: If a subject already exists, you can drag the mouse I over the existing subject and then type a new subject.*

**6** Click **Send** to send the message.

# SELECT TEXT

Before changing text in your presentation, you will often need to select the text you want to work with. Selected text appears highlighted on your screen.

Business Plan
• During this presentation, you will see why Hungry Pete's is a once in a lifetime business opportunity.

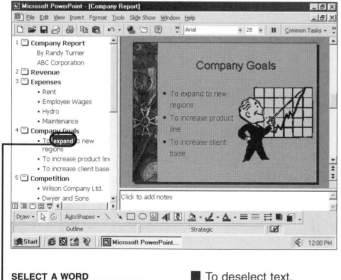

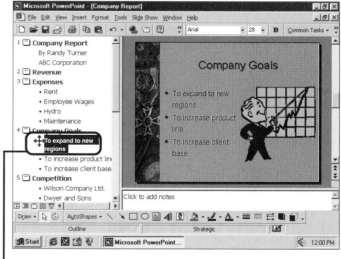

## SELECT A WORD

**1** Double-click the word you want to select.

■ To deselect text, click outside the selected area.

■ You can also select a word on a slide.

## SELECT A POINT

**1** Click the bullet ( • ) beside the point you want to select.

■ You can also select a point on a slide.

**How do I select all the text in my presentation?**

To quickly select all the text in your presentation, click the text in the Outline pane. Then press and hold down the `Ctrl` key as you press the `A` key.

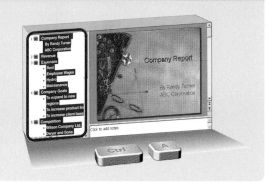

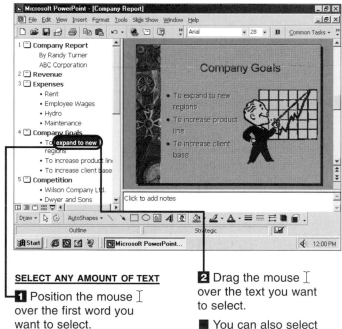

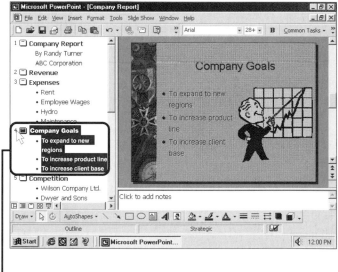

**SELECT ANY AMOUNT OF TEXT**

**1** Position the mouse I over the first word you want to select.

**2** Drag the mouse I over the text you want to select.

■ You can also select any amount of text on a slide.

**SELECT A SLIDE**

**1** Click the number of the slide you want to select.

# REPLACE SELECTED TEXT

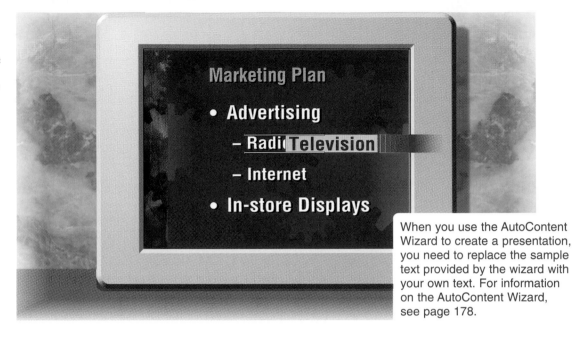

You can replace text you have selected in your presentation with new text.

When you use the AutoContent Wizard to create a presentation, you need to replace the sample text provided by the wizard with your own text. For information on the AutoContent Wizard, see page 178.

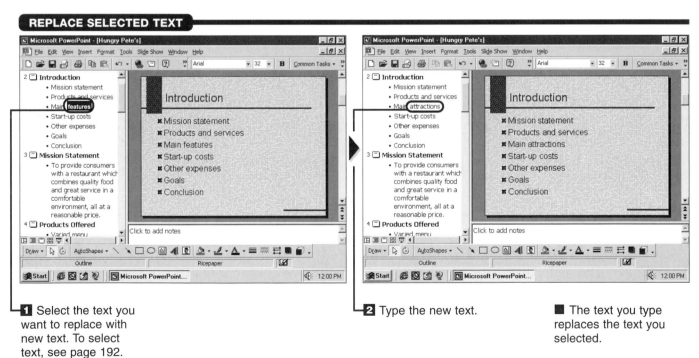

**1** Select the text you want to replace with new text. To select text, see page 192.

**2** Type the new text.

■ The text you type replaces the text you selected.

# UNDO CHANGES

PowerPoint remembers the last changes you made to your presentation. If you regret these changes, you can cancel them by using the Undo feature.

The Undo feature can cancel your last editing and formatting changes.

## UNDO CHANGES

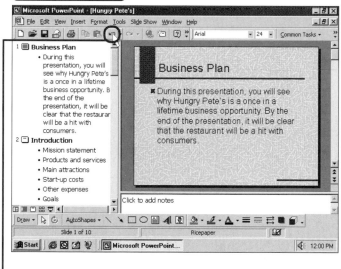

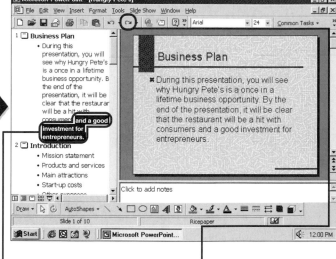

**1** Click ↶ to undo the last change you made to your presentation.

*Note: If ↶ is not displayed, click ⇒ on the Standard toolbar to display all the buttons.*

■ PowerPoint cancels the last change you made to your presentation.

■ You can repeat step **1** to cancel previous changes you made.

■ To reverse the results of using the Undo feature, click ↷ .

*Note: If ↷ is not displayed, click ⇒ on the Standard toolbar to display all the buttons.*

# INSERT TEXT

You can add new text
to your presentation to
update the presentation.

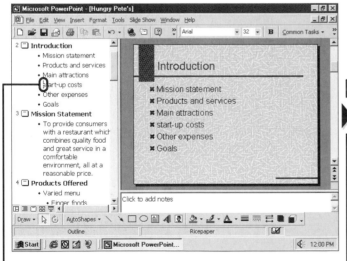

**1** Click where you want
to insert the new text.

■ The text you type
will appear where the
insertion point flashes
on your screen.

*Note: You can press the* ←,
↓, ↑ *or* → *key*
*to move the insertion point.*

**2** Type the text you
want to insert.

■ To insert a blank space,
press the **Spacebar**.

**?**

**Can I edit text directly on a slide?**

The Normal view displays all the text for your presentation in the Outline pane and also displays the current slide. You can edit text in the Outline pane or directly on the current slide. Editing the text in one area will change the text in the other area.

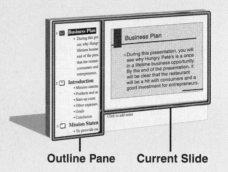

**Outline Pane        Current Slide**

## INSERT A NEW POINT

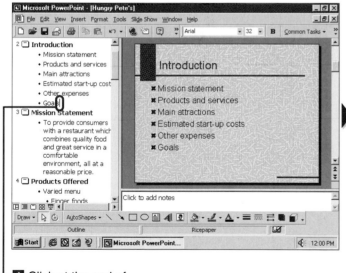

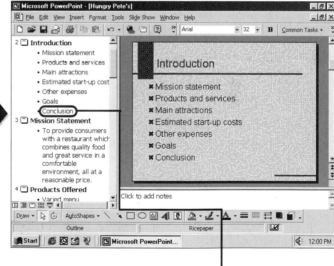

**1** Click at the end of the point directly above where you want to insert a new point.

**2** Press the `Enter` key to insert a blank line for the new point.

**3** Type the text for the new point.

# DELETE TEXT

You can remove text you no longer need from your presentation.

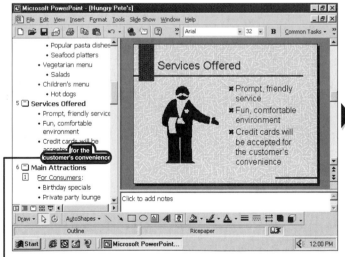

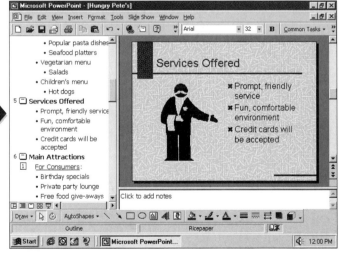

**1** Select the text you want to delete. To select text, see page 192.

**2** Press the Delete key to remove the text from your presentation.

■ The text disappears.

■ To delete a single character, click to the right of the character you want to delete and then press the Backspace key. PowerPoint will delete the character to the left of the flashing insertion point.

# MOVE TEXT

You can move text in your presentation to reorganize your ideas.

## MOVE TEXT

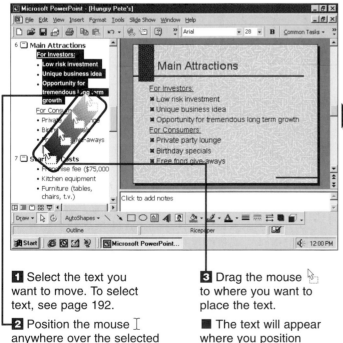

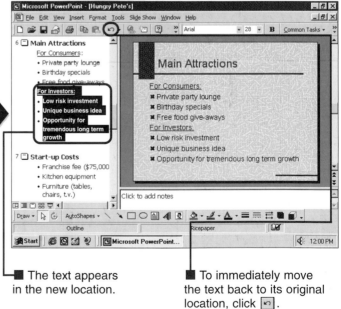

**1** Select the text you want to move. To select text, see page 192.

**2** Position the mouse I anywhere over the selected text ( I changes to ⤢).

**3** Drag the mouse ⤢ to where you want to place the text.

■ The text will appear where you position the solid line or dotted insertion point on your screen.

■ The text appears in the new location.

■ To immediately move the text back to its original location, click ⟲.

*Note: If ⟲ is not displayed, click ⟩⟩ on the Standard toolbar to display all the buttons.*

**199**

# CHANGE IMPORTANCE OF TEXT

You can increase or decrease the importance of text in your presentation.

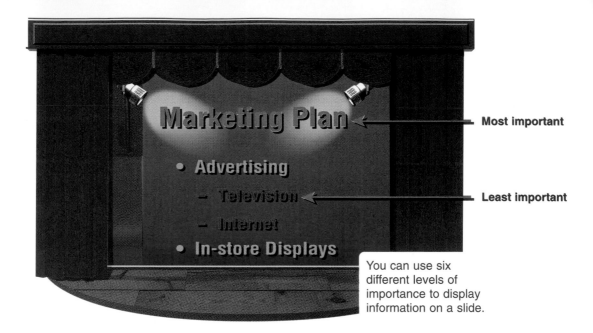

**Most important**

**Least important**

You can use six different levels of importance to display information on a slide.

## CHANGE IMPORTANCE OF TEXT

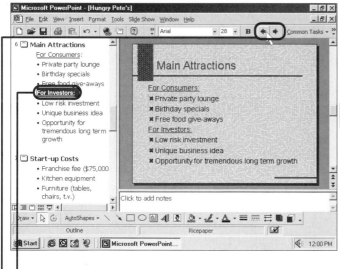

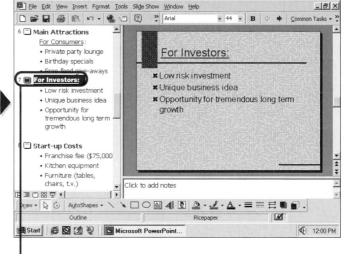

**1** Select the text you want to change. To select text, see page 192.

**2** Click one of the following buttons.

 Increase importance

Decrease importance

*Note: If the button you want is not displayed, click on the Formatting toolbar to display all the buttons.*

■ The text displays the new level of importance.

# HIDE SLIDE TEXT

You can display just the titles for each slide in your presentation and hide the remaining text. This lets you clearly view the overall structure of your presentation.

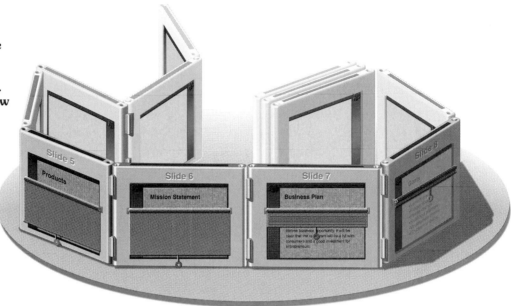

## HIDE SLIDE TEXT

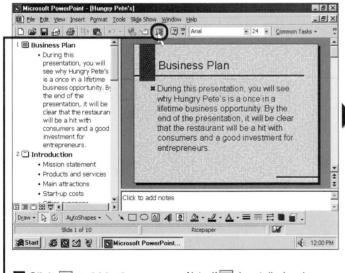

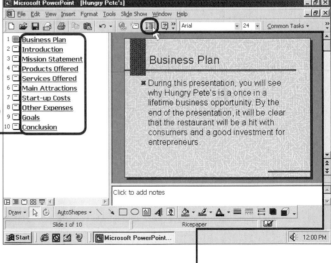

**1** Click 🔳 to hide the text on all the slides in your presentation.

*Note: If 🔳 is not displayed, click 📄 on the Standard toolbar to display all the buttons.*

■ A gray line appears below each slide title to indicate the text on the slide is hidden.

**2** Click 🔳 to once again display the text on all the slides.

# CHECK SPELLING

You can find and correct spelling errors in your presentation.

PowerPoint compares every word in your presentation to words in its dictionary. If a word in your presentation does not exist in PowerPoint's dictionary, PowerPoint considers the word misspelled.

## CHECK SPELLING

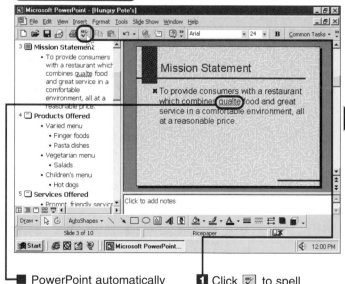

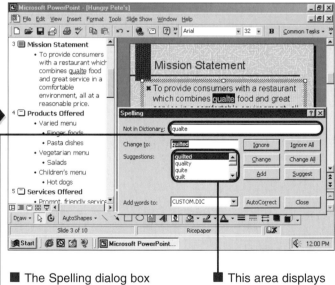

■ PowerPoint automatically underlines misspelled words in red. The underlines will not appear when you view the slide show or print your presentation.

**1** Click 🥄 to spell check your presentation.

*Note: If 🥄 is not displayed, click 🔽 on the Standard toolbar to display all the buttons.*

■ The Spelling dialog box appears if PowerPoint finds a misspelled word in your presentation.

■ This area displays the misspelled word.

■ This area displays suggestions for correcting the word.

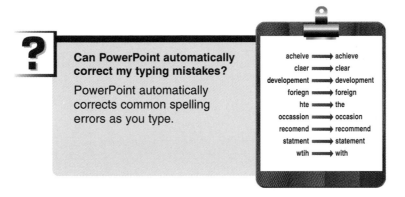

**Can PowerPoint automatically correct my typing mistakes?**

PowerPoint automatically corrects common spelling errors as you type.

| | | |
|---|---|---|
| acheive | ⟶ | achieve |
| claer | ⟶ | clear |
| developement | ⟶ | development |
| foriegn | ⟶ | foreign |
| hte | ⟶ | the |
| occassion | ⟶ | occasion |
| recomend | ⟶ | recommend |
| statment | ⟶ | statement |
| wtih | ⟶ | with |

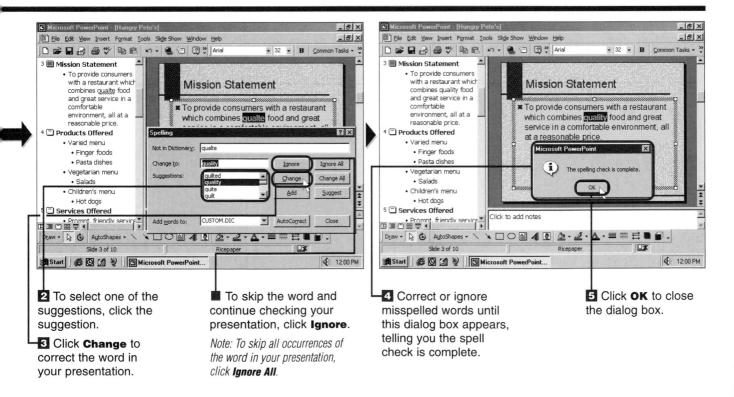

**2** To select one of the suggestions, click the suggestion.

**3** Click **Change** to correct the word in your presentation.

■ To skip the word and continue checking your presentation, click **Ignore**.

*Note: To skip all occurrences of the word in your presentation, click **Ignore All**.*

**4** Correct or ignore misspelled words until this dialog box appears, telling you the spell check is complete.

**5** Click **OK** to close the dialog box.

# ADD A NEW SLIDE

You can insert a new slide into your presentation to add a new topic you want to discuss.

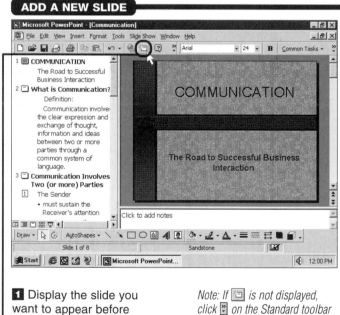

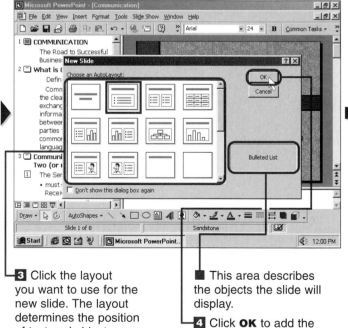

**1** Display the slide you want to appear before the new slide.

**2** Click 🖻 to add a new slide.

*Note: If 🖻 is not displayed, click 🔽 on the Standard toolbar to display all the buttons.*

■ The New Slide dialog box appears.

**3** Click the layout you want to use for the new slide. The layout determines the position of text and objects on the slide.

■ This area describes the objects the slide will display.

**4** Click **OK** to add the slide to your presentation.

**?**

## How much text should I display on a slide?

You should be careful not to include too much text on a slide in your presentation. Too much text on a slide can make the slide difficult to read and minimize the impact of important ideas. If a slide contains too much text, you should add a new slide to accommodate some of the text.

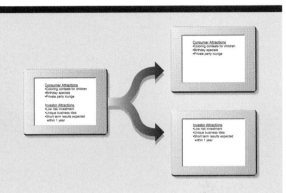

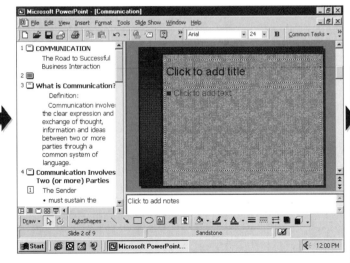

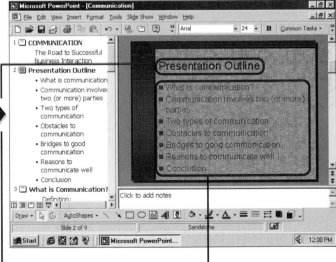

■ The new slide appears, displaying the layout you selected.

*Note: You can later change the layout. To change the slide layout, see page 206.*

**5** If the slide layout provides an area for a title, click the area and then type the title.

**6** If the slide layout provides an area for a list of points, click the area and then type a point. Press the **Enter** key each time you want to start a new point.

# CHANGE THE SLIDE LAYOUT

You can change the layout of a slide in your presentation to accommodate text and objects you want to add.

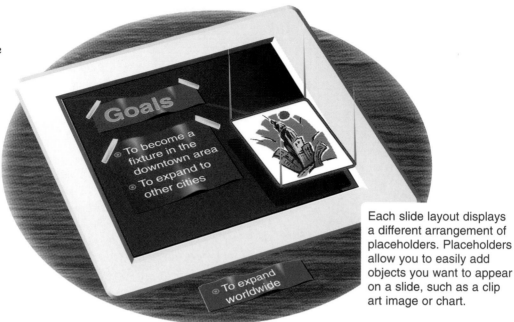

Each slide layout displays a different arrangement of placeholders. Placeholders allow you to easily add objects you want to appear on a slide, such as a clip art image or chart.

## CHANGE THE SLIDE LAYOUT

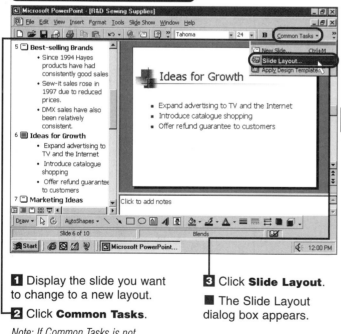

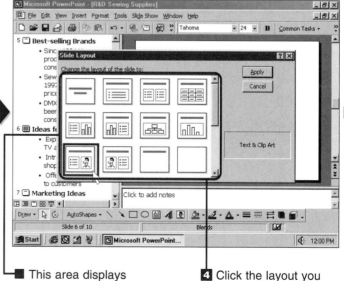

**1** Display the slide you want to change to a new layout.

**2** Click **Common Tasks**.

*Note: If Common Tasks is not displayed, click on the Formatting toolbar to display all the buttons.*

**3** Click **Slide Layout**.

■ The Slide Layout dialog box appears.

■ This area displays the available layouts. You can use the scroll bar to browse through the layouts.

**4** Click the layout you want to apply to the slide.

**Can I change the slide layout at any time?**

You should not change the slide layout after you have added an object to a slide. An object you have added will remain on the slide even after PowerPoint adds the placeholders for the new slide layout. This can cause the slide to become cluttered with overlapping objects and placeholders.

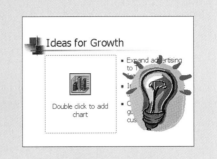

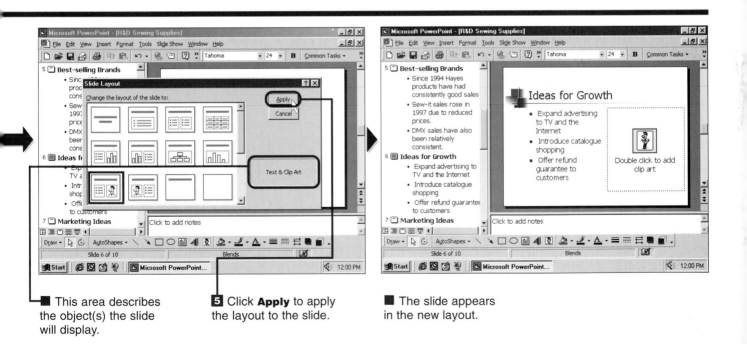

■ This area describes the object(s) the slide will display.

**5** Click **Apply** to apply the layout to the slide.

■ The slide appears in the new layout.

# ADD AN AUTOSHAPE

You can add
simple shapes,
called AutoShapes,
to the slides in
your presentation.

You can add AutoShapes
such as rectangles,
arrows, stars and banners.

## ADD AN AUTOSHAPE

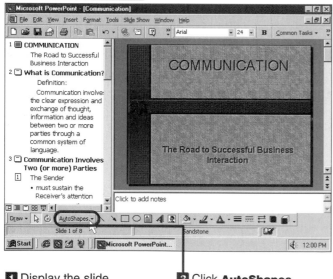

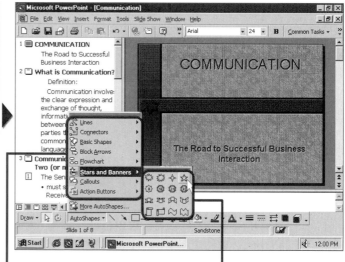

**1** Display the slide
you want to add an
AutoShape to.

**2** Click **AutoShapes**.

**3** Click the category for
the type of AutoShape
you want to add.

*Note: If the category you want
does not appear on the menu,
position the mouse ⓝ over the
bottom of the menu to display
all the menu commands.*

**4** Click the AutoShape
you want to add.

**?**

**Can I add text to an AutoShape?**

You can add text to most AutoShapes. This is particularly useful for AutoShapes such as banners. To add text to an AutoShape, click the AutoShape and then type the text you want the AutoShape to display.

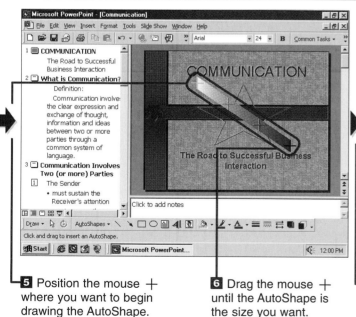

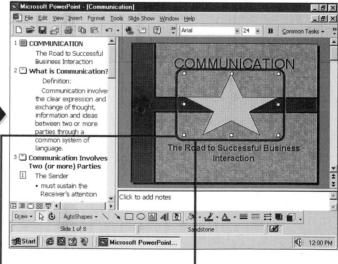

**5** Position the mouse + where you want to begin drawing the AutoShape.

**6** Drag the mouse + until the AutoShape is the size you want.

■ The AutoShape appears on the slide. The handles (□) around the AutoShape let you change the size of the AutoShape. To move or size an AutoShape, see page 218.

**7** To hide the handles, click outside the AutoShape.

**DELETE AN AUTOSHAPE**

**1** Click the AutoShape you want to delete. Then press the Delete key.

# ADD A TEXT EFFECT

You can add a text effect to a slide in your presentation. Text effects can enhance the appearance of a title or draw attention to an important point.

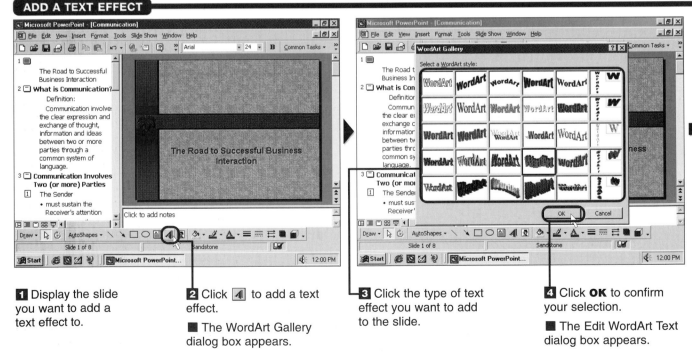

**1** Display the slide you want to add a text effect to.

**2** Click 📐 to add a text effect.

■ The WordArt Gallery dialog box appears.

**3** Click the type of text effect you want to add to the slide.

**4** Click **OK** to confirm your selection.

■ The Edit WordArt Text dialog box appears.

**?**

**How do I edit a text effect?**

Double-click the text effect to display the Edit WordArt Text dialog box. Then edit the text in the dialog box. When you finish editing the text effect, click **OK** to display the changes on the slide.

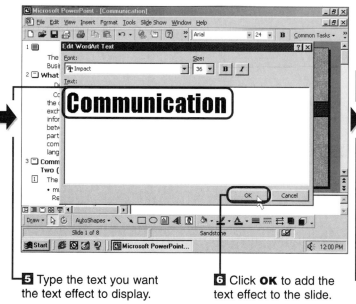

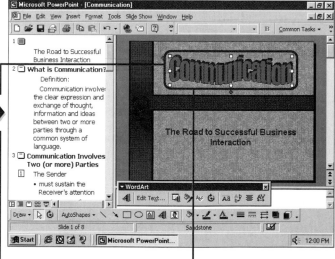

**5** Type the text you want the text effect to display.

**6** Click **OK** to add the text effect to the slide.

■ The text effect appears on the slide. The handles (□) around the text effect let you change the size of the text effect. To move or size a text effect, see page 218.

**7** To hide the handles, click outside the text effect.

**DELETE A TEXT EFFECT**

**1** Click the text effect you want to delete. Then press the Delete key.

# ADD CLIP ART

You can add a clip art image to a slide to make your presentation more interesting and entertaining.

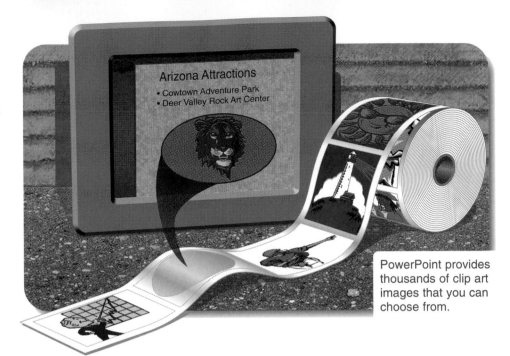

PowerPoint provides thousands of clip art images that you can choose from.

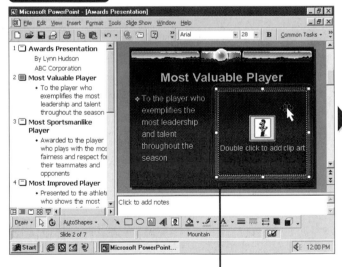

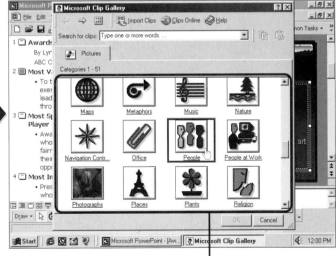

**1** Display the slide you want to add a clip art image to.

**2** Change the layout of the slide to one that includes space for a clip art image. To change the slide layout, see page 206.

**3** Double-click this area to add a clip art image to the slide.

■ The Microsoft Clip Gallery dialog box appears.

**4** Click the category of clip art images you want to display.

## Where can I find more clip art images?

If you are connected to the Internet, you can visit Microsoft's Clip Gallery Live Web site to find additional clip art images. In the Microsoft Clip Gallery dialog box, click **Clips Online**. In the dialog box that appears, click **OK** to connect to the Web site.

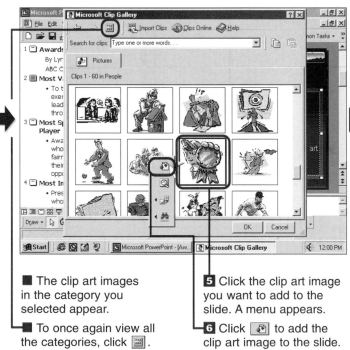

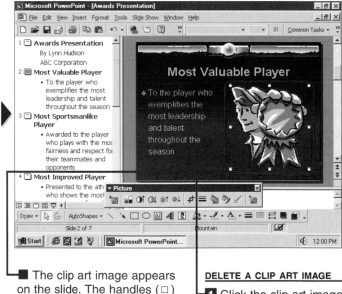

■ The clip art images in the category you selected appear.

■ To once again view all the categories, click ⊞.

**5** Click the clip art image you want to add to the slide. A menu appears.

**6** Click ⬛ to add the clip art image to the slide.

■ The clip art image appears on the slide. The handles (□) around the image let you change the size of the image. To move or size a clip art image, see page 218.

**7** To hide the handles, click outside the clip art image.

### DELETE A CLIP ART IMAGE

**1** Click the clip art image you want to delete. Then press the Delete key.

# ADD A CHART

You can add a
chart to a slide to
show trends and
compare data.

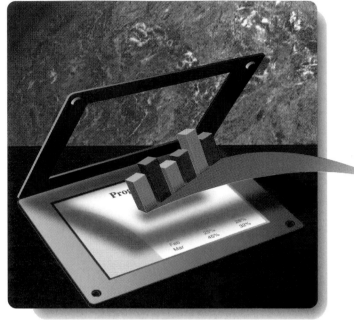

A chart is more
appealing and often
easier to understand
than a list of numbers.

## ADD A CHART

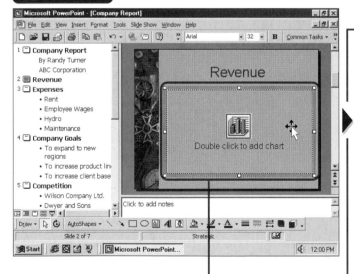

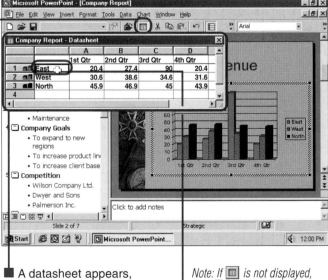

**1** Display the slide you
want to add a chart to.

**2** Change the layout
of the slide to one that
includes a placeholder
for a chart. To change the
slide layout, see page 206.

**3** Double-click this
area to add a chart
to the slide.

■ A datasheet appears,
displaying sample data
to show you where to
enter information.

■ If the datasheet does
not appear, click ▦ to
display the datasheet.

*Note: If ▦ is not displayed,
click » on the Standard toolbar
to display all the buttons.*

**4** To replace the data
in a cell, click the cell.
A thick border appears
around the cell.

**?**

**How do I change the data displayed in my chart?**

Double-click the chart to activate the chart and display the datasheet. You can then perform steps **4** to **7** below to change the data displayed in the chart.

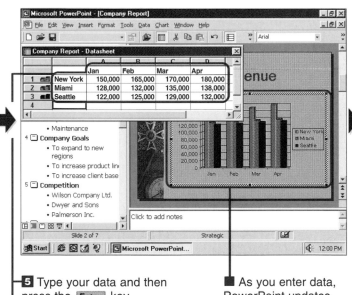

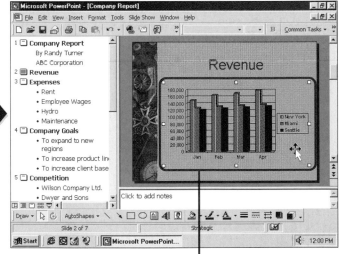

**5** Type your data and then press the Enter key.

*Note: To remove data from a cell and leave the cell empty, click the cell and then press the Delete key.*

**6** Repeat steps **4** and **5** until you finish entering all your data.

■ As you enter data, PowerPoint updates the chart on the slide.

**7** When you finish entering data for the chart, click a blank area on your screen.

■ The datasheet disappears and you can clearly view the chart on the slide.

*Note: To move or size a chart, see page 218.*

**DELETE A CHART**

**1** Click the chart you want to delete. Then press the Delete key.

# MAKE CHANGES TO A CHART

You can change
the chart type
to better suit
your data.

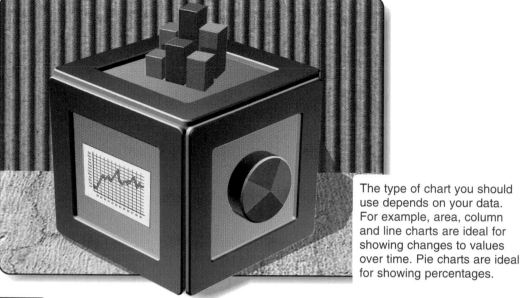

The type of chart you should
use depends on your data.
For example, area, column
and line charts are ideal for
showing changes to values
over time. Pie charts are ideal
for showing percentages.

## CHANGE THE CHART TYPE

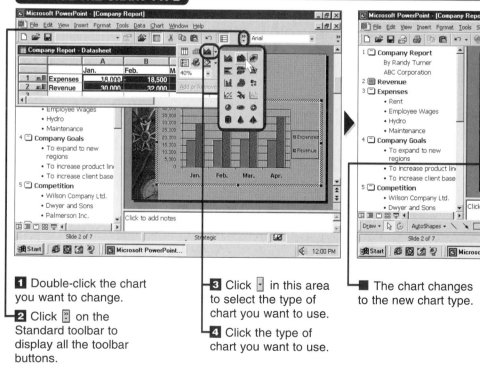

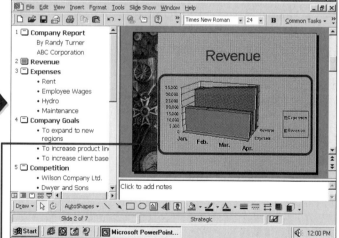

**1** Double-click the chart
you want to change.

**2** Click 🞂 on the
Standard toolbar to
display all the toolbar
buttons.

**3** Click ⏷ in this area
to select the type of
chart you want to use.

**4** Click the type of
chart you want to use.

■ The chart changes
to the new chart type.

**5** Click a blank area
on your screen to hide
the datasheet and
return to the slide.

You can change
the format of
numbers in a chart
without retyping
the numbers.

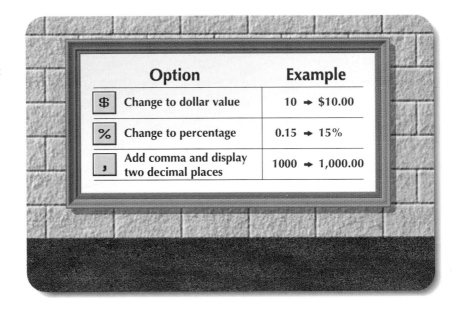

| | Option | Example |
|---|---|---|
| $ | Change to dollar value | 10 → $10.00 |
| % | Change to percentage | 0.15 → 15% |
| , | Add comma and display two decimal places | 1000 → 1,000.00 |

## CHANGE NUMBER FORMAT

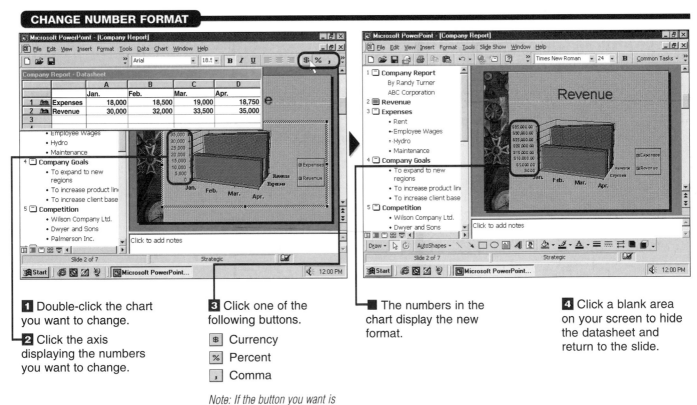

**1** Double-click the chart
you want to change.

**2** Click the axis
displaying the numbers
you want to change.

**3** Click one of the
following buttons.

$ Currency

% Percent

, Comma

*Note: If the button you want is
not displayed, click ⏷ on the
Formatting toolbar to display
all the buttons.*

■ The numbers in the
chart display the new
format.

**4** Click a blank area
on your screen to hide
the datasheet and
return to the slide.

# MOVE OR SIZE AN OBJECT

You can change the location or size of an object on a slide.

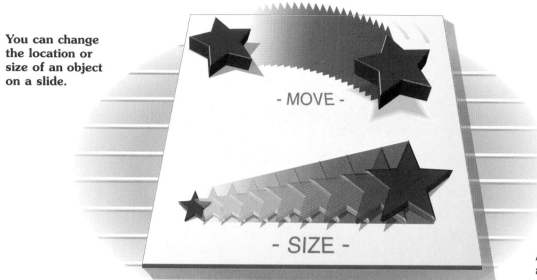

An object can include an AutoShape, chart, clip art image, text box or text effect.

## MOVE AN OBJECT

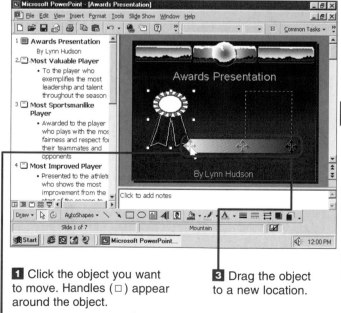

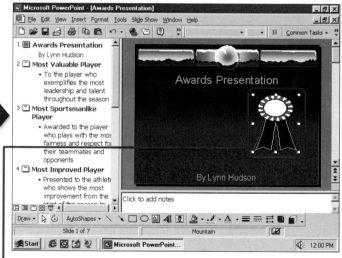

**1** Click the object you want to move. Handles (□) appear around the object.

**2** Position the mouse ⌖ over an edge of the object (⌖ changes to ✥).

**3** Drag the object to a new location.

■ The object appears in the new location.

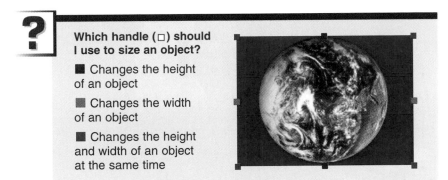

**Which handle (□) should I use to size an object?**

■ Changes the height of an object

■ Changes the width of an object

■ Changes the height and width of an object at the same time

## SIZE AN OBJECT

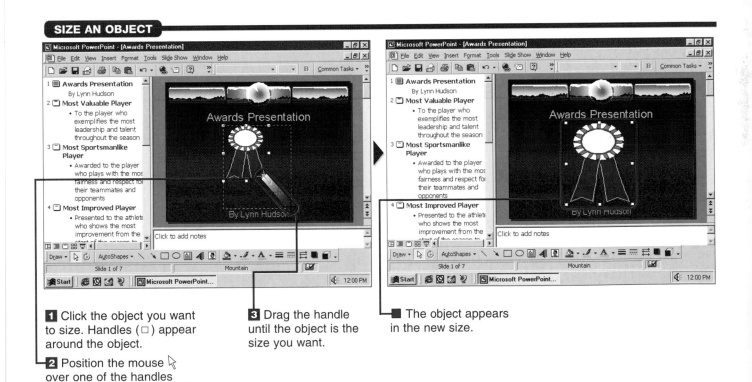

**1** Click the object you want to size. Handles (□) appear around the object.

**2** Position the mouse ⌖ over one of the handles (⌖ changes to ↖, ↔ or ↕).

**3** Drag the handle until the object is the size you want.

■ The object appears in the new size.

# CHANGE STYLE OF TEXT

You can use the Bold, Italic, Underline and Shadow features to change the style of text on a slide.

## CHANGE STYLE OF TEXT

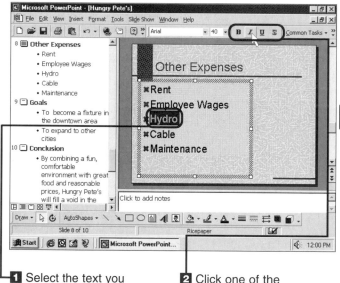

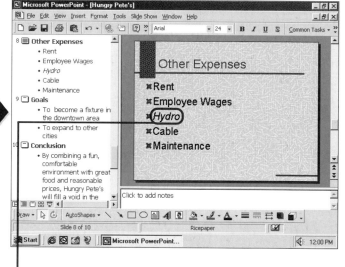

**1** Select the text you want to change. To select text, see page 192.

**2** Click one of the following buttons.

**B** Bold

**I** Italic

**U** Underline

**S** Shadow

*Note: If the button you want is not displayed, click ➤ on the Formatting toolbar to display all the buttons.*

■ The text you selected appears in the new style.

■ To deselect text, click outside the selected area.

■ To remove a style, repeat steps **1** and **2**.

# CHANGE ALIGNMENT OF TEXT

You can enhance the appearance of a slide by aligning text in different ways.

## CHANGE ALIGNMENT OF TEXT

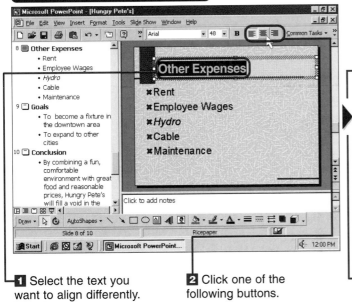

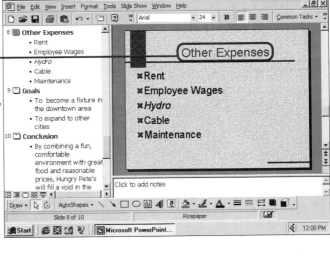

**1** Select the text you want to align differently. To select text, see page 192.

**2** Click one of the following buttons.

▤ Left align

▤ Center

▤ Right align

*Note: If the button you want is not displayed, click ▨ on the Formatting toolbar to display all the buttons.*

■ The text displays the new alignment.

■ To deselect text, click outside the selected area.

# CHANGE COLOR OF TEXT

You can change the color of text on a slide to enhance the appearance of the slide and draw attention to important information.

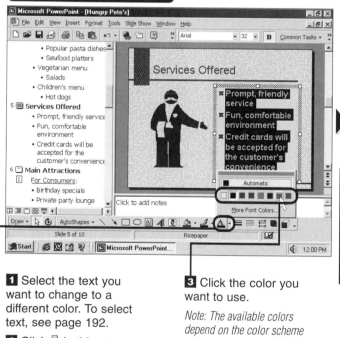

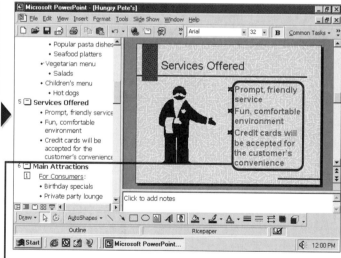

**1** Select the text you want to change to a different color. To select text, see page 192.

**2** Click ⏷ in this area to select a color.

**3** Click the color you want to use.

*Note: The available colors depend on the color scheme of the slide. For information on color schemes, see page 228.*

■ The text appears in the color you selected.

■ To deselect text, click outside the selected area.

■ To once again display the text in the default color, repeat steps **1** to **3**, except select **Automatic** in step **3**.

# CHANGE OBJECT COLOR

You can change the
color of an object
on a slide to enhance
the appearance of
the slide.

## CHANGE OBJECT COLOR

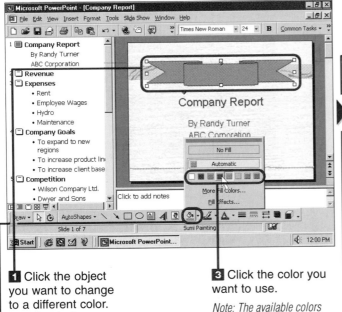

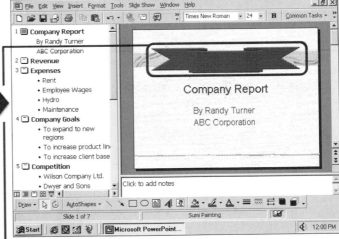

**1** Click the object
you want to change
to a different color.
Handles (□) appear
around the object.

**2** Click ⬝ in this area
to select a color.

**3** Click the color you
want to use.

*Note: The available colors
depend on the color scheme
of the slide. For information
on color schemes, see
page 228.*

■ The object appears
in the color you selected.

■ To deselect the object,
click outside the object.

# CHANGE DESIGN TEMPLATE

PowerPoint offers many design templates that you can choose from to give the slides in your presentation a new appearance.

CHANGE DESIGN TEMPLATE

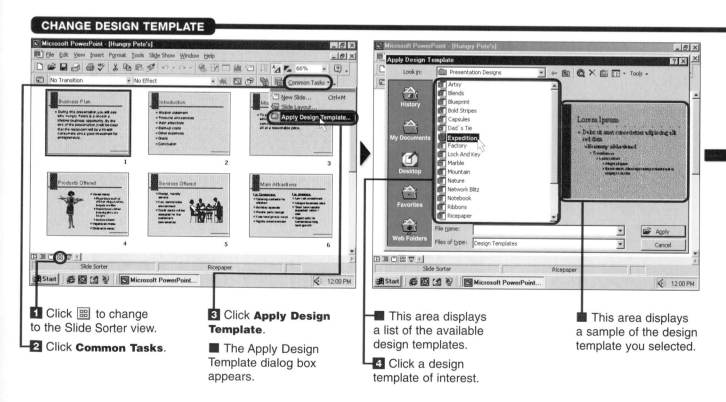

**1** Click 🔡 to change to the Slide Sorter view.

**2** Click **Common Tasks**.

**3** Click **Apply Design Template**.

■ The Apply Design Template dialog box appears.

■ This area displays a list of the available design templates.

**4** Click a design template of interest.

■ This area displays a sample of the design template you selected.

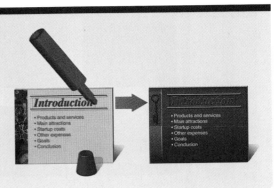

**When I changed the design template for my presentation, why did some parts of my slides not change?**

The new design template may not affect parts of a slide you have previously changed. For example, if you changed the color of text before changing the design template, the new design template will not affect the text you changed.

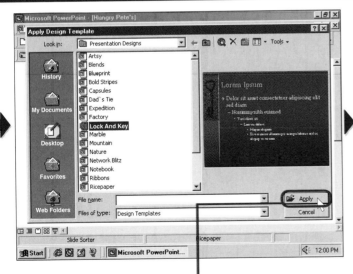

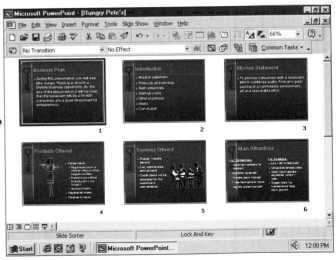

**5** Repeat step **4** until the design template you want to use appears.

**6** Click **Apply** to apply the design template to all the slides in your presentation.

■ The slides in your presentation display the new design template.

# ANIMATE SLIDES

You can add movement and sound effects to the objects on your slides. This can help keep your audience's attention throughout a presentation.

You can animate objects such as a title, list of points, AutoShape, text effect or clip art image.

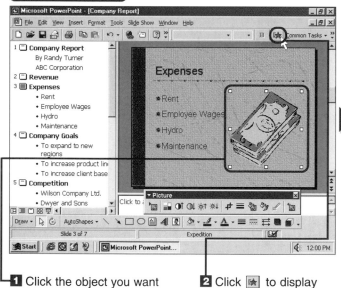

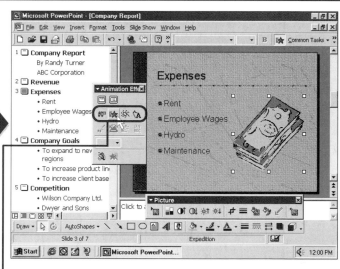

**1** Click the object you want to animate. Handles (□) appear around the object.

**2** Click ⭐ to display the Animation Effects toolbar.

*Note: If ⭐ is not displayed, click ⯯ on the Formatting toolbar to display all the buttons.*

■ The Animation Effects toolbar appears.

**3** Click the animation effect you want to use.

*Note: The available animation effects depend on the type of object you selected in step 1.*

**How do I display the animated objects in my slide show?**

When viewing your slide show, you must click the slide to display each animated object on the slide. For example, if you animated a list of points, you must click the slide each time you want a point to appear.

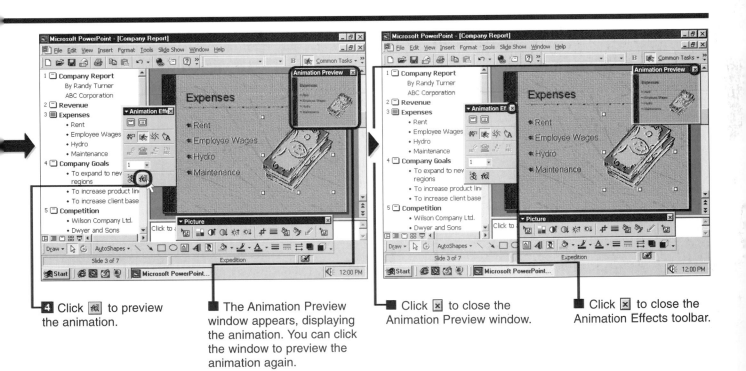

■4 Click 📷 to preview the animation.

■ The Animation Preview window appears, displaying the animation. You can click the window to preview the animation again.

■ Click ⌧ to close the Animation Preview window.

■ Click ⌧ to close the Animation Effects toolbar.

# REORDER SLIDES

You can change the order of the slides in your presentation.

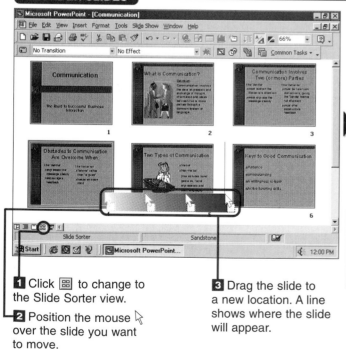

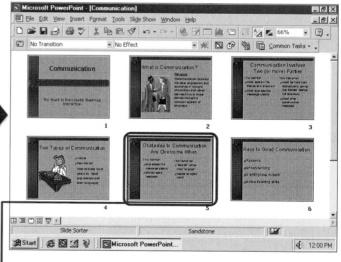

**1** Click ⊞ to change to the Slide Sorter view.

**2** Position the mouse ⇖ over the slide you want to move.

**3** Drag the slide to a new location. A line shows where the slide will appear.

■ The slide appears in the new location.

232

# DELETE A SLIDE

You can remove
a slide you no
longer need from
your presentation.

## DELETE A SLIDE

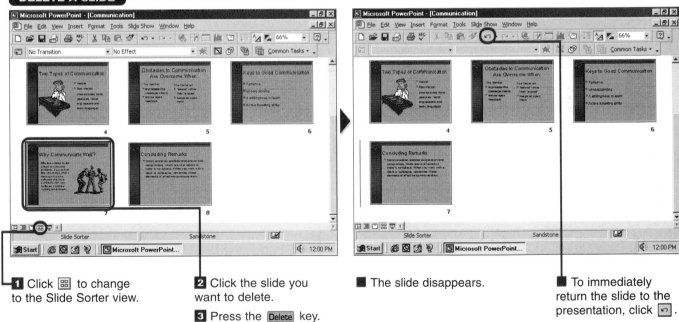

**1** Click ⊞ to change
to the Slide Sorter view.

**2** Click the slide you
want to delete.

**3** Press the Delete key.

■ The slide disappears.

■ To immediately
return the slide to the
presentation, click ↶ .

# ADD SLIDE TRANSITIONS

You can use effects called transitions to help you move from one slide to the next.

When you use the AutoContent Wizard to create a presentation, PowerPoint may automatically add slide transitions to the presentation for you. You can change these transitions at any time.

## ADD SLIDE TRANSITIONS

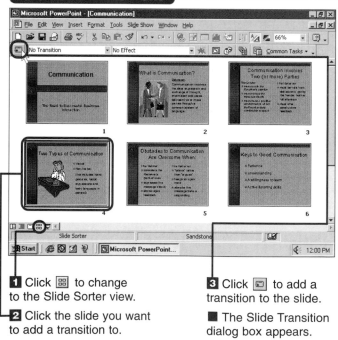

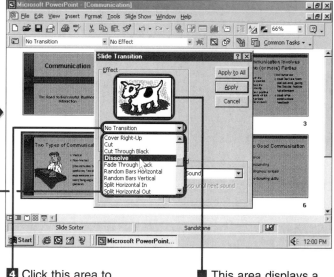

**1** Click ⊞ to change to the Slide Sorter view.

**2** Click the slide you want to add a transition to.

**3** Click 🖭 to add a transition to the slide.

■ The Slide Transition dialog box appears.

**4** Click this area to display a list of the available transitions.

**5** Click the transition you want to use.

■ This area displays a preview of the transition you selected. To see the preview again, click this area.

234

**?** **Can I add a different transition to each slide in my presentation?**

Although PowerPoint allows you to add a different transition to each slide in your presentation, using too many different transitions may distract the audience. The audience may focus on how each slide is introduced, rather than the information you are presenting.

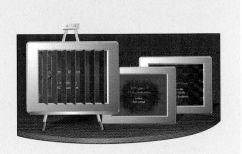

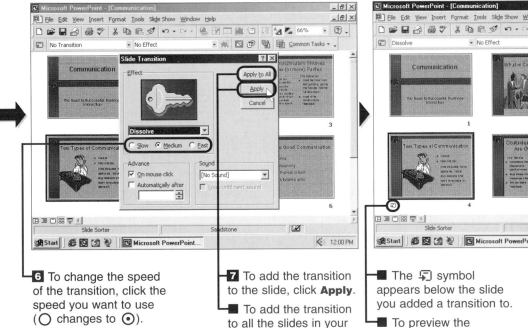

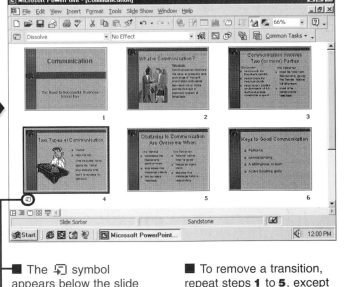

**6** To change the speed of the transition, click the speed you want to use (○ changes to ⊙).

**7** To add the transition to the slide, click **Apply**.

■ To add the transition to all the slides in your presentation, click **Apply to All**.

■ The 🔁 symbol appears below the slide you added a transition to.

■ To preview the transition for the slide, click 🔁 below the slide.

■ To remove a transition, repeat steps **1** to **5**, except select **No Transition** in step **5**. Then perform step **7**.

# VIEW A SLIDE SHOW

You can view a slide show of your presentation on a computer screen.

Business Proposal

By Marge Hill
Hill Ceramic Studios

Before presenting a slide show to an audience, you can view the slide show to rehearse your presentation.

## VIEW A SLIDE SHOW

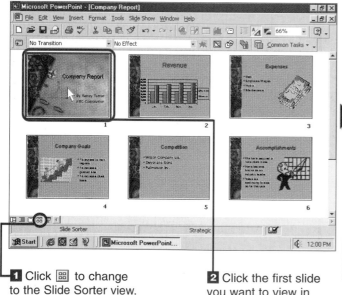

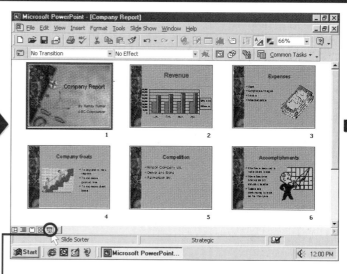

**1** Click ▦ to change to the Slide Sorter view.

**2** Click the first slide you want to view in the slide show.

**3** Click ▭ to start the slide show.

236

**?** **How can I use my keyboard to move through a slide show?**

| Task | Press this key |
|------|----------------|
| Display the next slide | Spacebar |
| Display the previous slide | Backspace |
| Display any slide | Type the number of the slide and then press Enter |
| End the slide show | Esc |
| Pause the slide show and turn the screen black | B (Press B again to return to the slide show.) |
| Pause the slide show and turn the screen white | W (Press W again to return to the slide show.) |

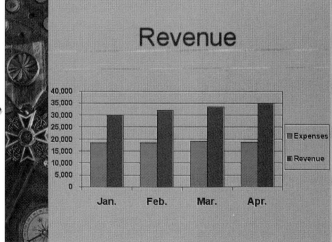

■ The first slide fills your screen.

*Note: You can press the* `Esc` *key to end the slide show at any time.*

**4** To display the next slide, click the current slide.

■ To return to the previous slide, press the `+Backspace` key.

■ The next slide appears.

■ Repeat step **4** until you finish viewing all the slides in the slide show.

# CREATE SPEAKER NOTES

You can create speaker notes that contain copies of your slides with all the ideas you want to discuss. You can use these notes as a guide when delivering your presentation.

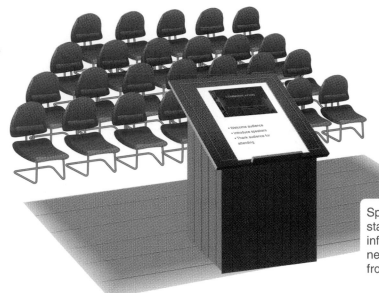

Speaker notes can include statistics or additional information that you may need to answer questions from the audience.

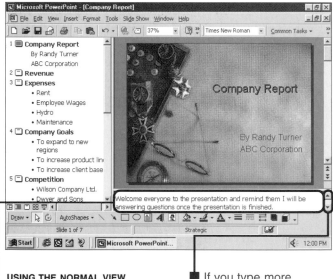

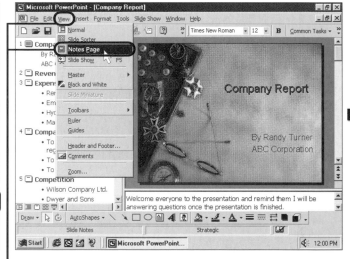

## USING THE NORMAL VIEW

**1** Display the slide you want to create speaker notes for.

**2** Click this area and then type the ideas you want to discuss when you display the slide during the presentation.

■ If you type more than one line of text, you can use the scroll bar to browse through the text.

## USING THE NOTES PAGE VIEW

**1** Click **View**.

**2** Click **Notes Page** to display the presentation in the Notes Page view.

*Note: If Notes Page does not appear on the menu, position the mouse ⟍ over the bottom of the menu to display all the menu commands.*

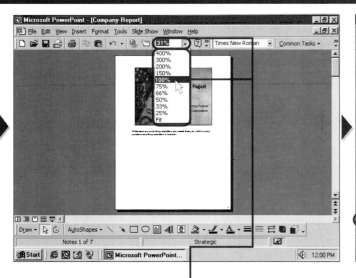

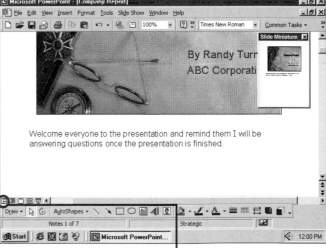

■ The notes page for the current slide appears.

*Note: You can use the scroll bar to view the notes pages for other slides.*

**3** To magnify the notes page so you can clearly view the notes, click ▬ in this area.

*Note: If the Zoom area is not displayed, click ▓ on the Standard toolbar to display all the buttons.*

**4** Click the magnification setting you want to use.

■ The notes page appears in the new magnification setting.

■ You can edit the text on the notes page as you would edit any text in your presentation.

*Note: To once again display the entire notes page, repeat steps 3 and 4, except select Fit in step 4.*

■ When you finish reviewing the notes pages, click 🔲 to return to the Normal view.

# PRINT A PRESENTATION

You can produce
a paper copy of a
presentation for
your own use or
to hand out to
the audience.

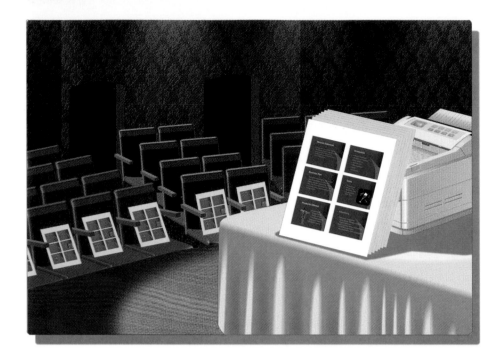

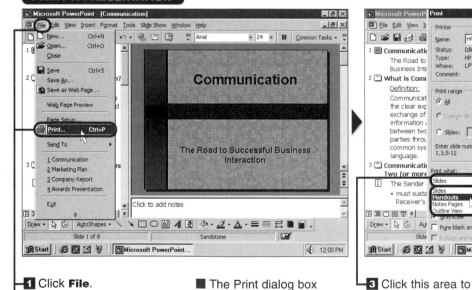

**1** Click **File**.

**2** Click **Print**.

■ The Print dialog box
appears.

**3** Click this area to
select the part of your
presentation you want
to print.

**4** Click the part of your
presentation you want
to print.

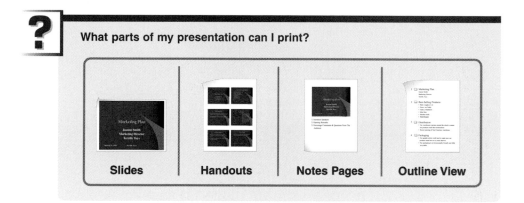

**What parts of my presentation can I print?**

**Slides**  |  **Handouts**  |  **Notes Pages**  |  **Outline View**

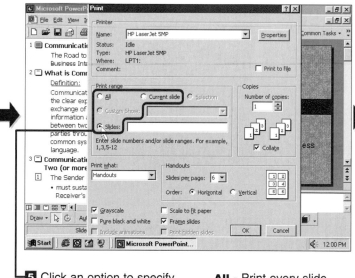

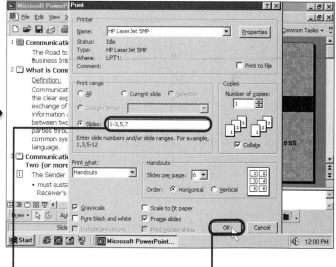

**5** Click an option to specify which slides you want to print (○ changes to ⊙).

**All** - Print every slide in your presentation

**Current slide** - Print the selected slide or the slide displayed on your screen

**Slides** - Print the slides you specify

**6** If you selected **Slides** in step **5**, type the numbers of the slides you want to print in this area (example: 1,3,4 or 2-4).

**7** Click **OK** to print your presentation.

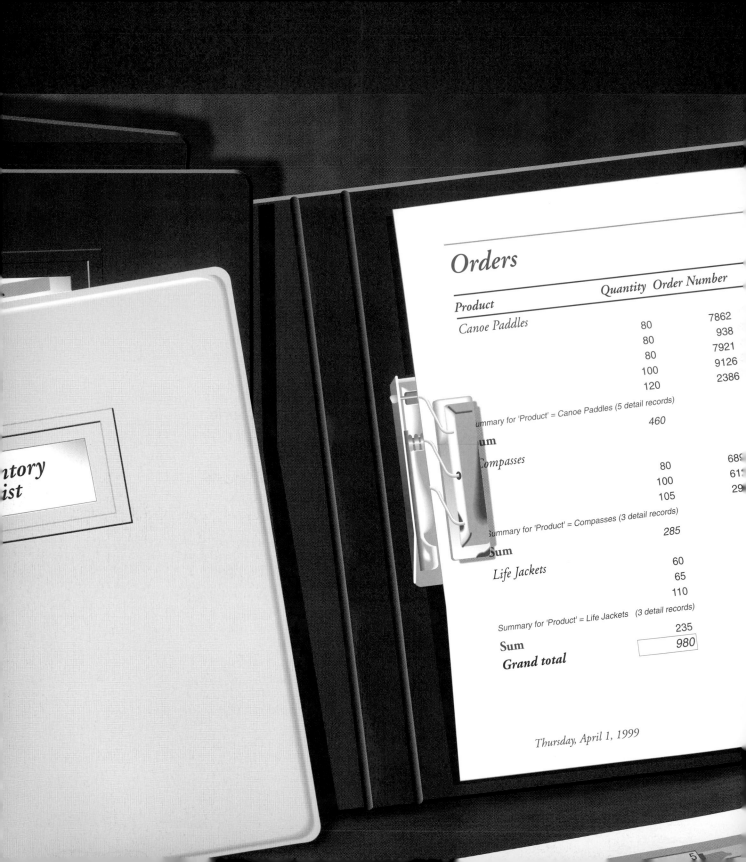

# Orders

| Product | Quantity | Order Number |
|---|---|---|
| Canoe Paddles | 80 | 7862 |
| | 80 | 938 |
| | 80 | 7921 |
| | 100 | 9126 |
| | 120 | 2386 |

Summary for 'Product' = Canoe Paddles (5 detail records)

**Sum** 460

| Compasses | 80 | 689 |
|---|---|---|
| | 100 | 61 |
| | 105 | 29 |

Summary for 'Product' = Compasses (3 detail records)

**Sum** 285

| Life Jackets | 60 | |
|---|---|---|
| | 65 | |
| | 110 | |

Summary for 'Product' = Life Jackets  (3 detail records)

**Sum** 235

**Grand total** 980

*Thursday, April 1, 1999*

# Using Access

Date

14/99
3/2/99
3/11/99
3/12/99
3/12/99

3/12/99
3/18/99
2/20/99

2/26/99
2/27/99
3/13/99

Page 1 of 1

Ready

Home Phone      (213) 749-6092
Work Phone      (213) 741-2291
Extension       3729
                (213) 740-9900

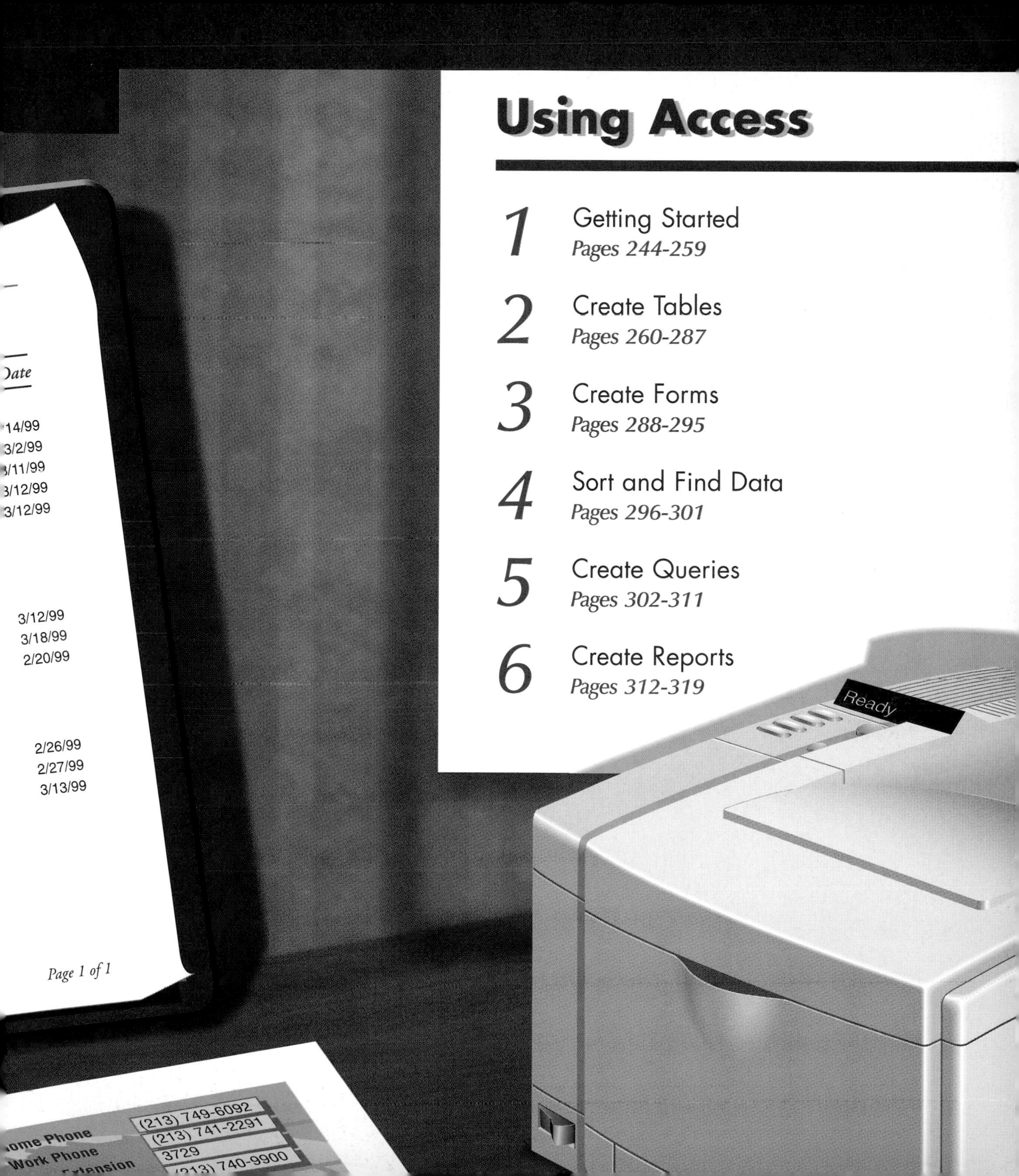

# INTRODUCTION TO ACCESS

Microsoft Access is a database program that allows you to store and manage large collections of information. Access provides you with all the tools you need to create an efficient and effective database.

A database contains a collection of information related to a particular topic. Databases are commonly used to store information such as a phone directory, inventory or expense information. A database consists of objects such as tables, forms, queries and reports.

## Tables

A table is a collection of information about a specific topic, such as a mailing list. You can have one or more tables in a database. A table consists of fields and records.

| Address ID | First Name | Last Name | Address | City | State/Province | Postal Code |
|---|---|---|---|---|---|---|
| 1 | Jim | Schmith | 258 Linton Ave. | New York | NY | 10010 |
| 2 | Brenda | Petterson | 50 Tree Lane | Boston | MA | 02117 |
| 3 | Todd | Talbot | 68 Cracker Ave. | San Francisco | CA | 94110 |
| 4 | Chuck | Dean | 47 Crosby Ave. | Las Vegas | NV | 89116 |
| 5 | Melanie | Robinson | 26 Arnold Cres. | Jacksonville | FL | 32256 |
| 6 | Susan | Hughes | 401 Idon Dr. | Nashville | TN | 37243 |
| 7 | Allen | Toppins | 10 Heldon St. | Atlanta | GA | 30375 |
| 8 | Greg | Kilkenny | 36 Buzzard St. | Boston | MA | 02118 |
| 9 | Jason | Marcuson | 15 Bizzo Pl. | New York | NY | 10020 |
| 10 | Jim | Martin | 890 Apple St. | San Diego | CA | 92121 |

## Field

A field is a specific category of information in a table, such as the first names of all your clients.

## Record

A record is a collection of information about one person, place or thing in a table, such as the name and address of one client.

## Forms

Forms provide a quick way to view, enter and change information in a database by presenting information in an easy-to-use format.

Forms display boxes that clearly show you where to enter information and usually display one record at a time.

## Queries

Queries allow you to find information of interest in a database. You specify criteria in a query to tell Access what information you want to find.

 Which clients live in California?

| Address ID | First Name | Last Name |
|---|---|---|
| 10 | Jim | Martin |
| 11 | Kathleen | Matthews |
| 3 | Todd | Talbot |
| 13 | John | Thyfault |
| 14 | Michael | Wolfe |

For example, you can create a query to find all clients who live in California.

## Reports

Reports are professional-looking documents that summarize data from the database. You can perform calculations, such as averages or totals, in a report to summarize information.

*Orders*

| Product | Quantity | Order Number | Date |
|---|---|---|---|
| Canoe Paddles | | | |
| | 80 | 7862 | 3/14/99 |
| | 80 | 938 | 3/2/99 |
| | 80 | 7921 | 3/11/99 |
| | 100 | 9126 | 3/12/99 |
| | 120 | 2386 | 3/12/99 |
| Summary for 'Product' = Canoe Paddles (5 detail records) | | | |
| **Sum** | 460 | | |
| Compasses | | | |
| | 80 | 6892 | 3/12/99 |
| | 100 | 6124 | 3/18/99 |
| | 105 | 2935 | 2/20/99 |
| Summary for 'Product' = Compasses (3 detail records) | | | |
| **Sum** | 285 | | |
| Life Jackets | | | |
| | 60 | 795 | 2/26/99 |
| | 65 | 1911 | 2/27/99 |
| | 110 | 6882 | 3/13/99 |
| Summary for 'Product' = Life Jackets (3 detail records) | | | |
| **Sum** | 235 | | |
| **Grand total** | 980 | | |

*Thursday, April 1, 1999* *Page 1 of 1*

For example, you can create a report that displays the total sales for each product.

# PLAN A DATABASE

You should take the time to plan your database. A well-planned database ensures that you will be able to perform tasks efficiently and accurately.

When planning your database, you must decide what information you want the database to store and how you will use the information. If other people will be using your database, you should also determine their needs.

## Determine the Tables You Need

➤ Gather all the information you want to store in your database and then divide the information into separate tables. A table should contain information for only one subject.

➤ The same information should not appear in more than one table in your database. You can work more efficiently and reduce errors if you only need to update information in one location.

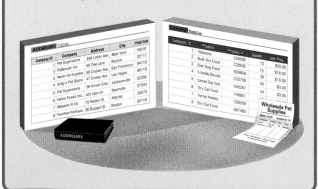

## Determine the Fields You Need

➤ Each field should relate directly to the subject of the table.

➤ Make sure you break information down into its smallest parts. For example, break down names into two fields called First Name and Last Name.

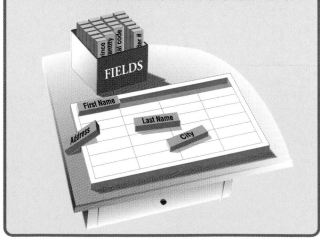

# START ACCESS

You can start
Access to create
a new database
or work with a
database you
previously created.

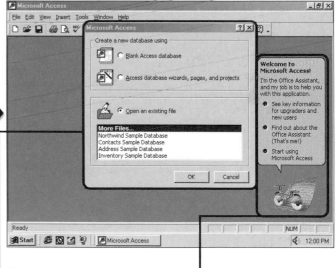

**1** Click **Start**.

**2** Click **Programs**.

**3** Click **Microsoft Access**.

■ The Microsoft Access window appears.

■ The Microsoft Access dialog box appears each time you start Access, allowing you to create or open a database.

*Note: To create a database, see page 248 or 254. To open a database, see page 258.*

■ The Office Assistant welcome appears the first time you start Access.

*Note: For information on the Office Assistant, see page 14.*

# CREATE A DATABASE USING A WIZARD

The Database Wizard lets you create a database quickly and efficiently. The wizard saves you time by providing ready-to-use objects, such as tables, forms, queries and reports.

You can use the Database Wizard to create several types of databases, such as the Contact Management, Expenses, Inventory Control and Order Entry databases.

## CREATE A DATABASE USING A WIZARD

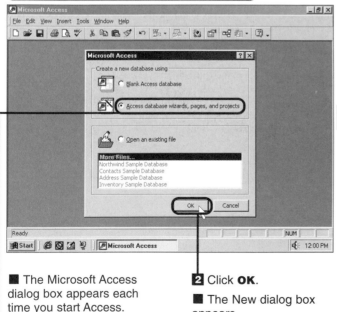

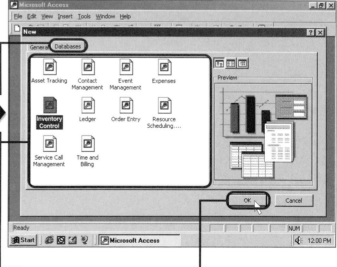

■ The Microsoft Access dialog box appears each time you start Access.

**1** Click this option to create a new database using the Database Wizard (○ changes to ⊙).

**2** Click **OK**.

■ The New dialog box appears.

**3** Click the **Databases** tab.

**4** Click the type of database you want to create.

**5** Click **OK**.

■ The File New Database dialog box appears.

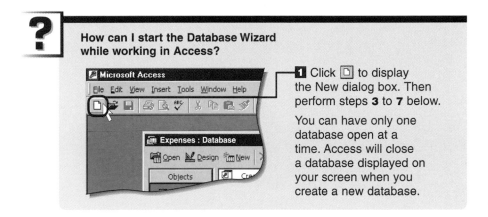

**How can I start the Database Wizard while working in Access?**

**1** Click ▢ to display the New dialog box. Then perform steps **3** to **7** below.

You can have only one database open at a time. Access will close a database displayed on your screen when you create a new database.

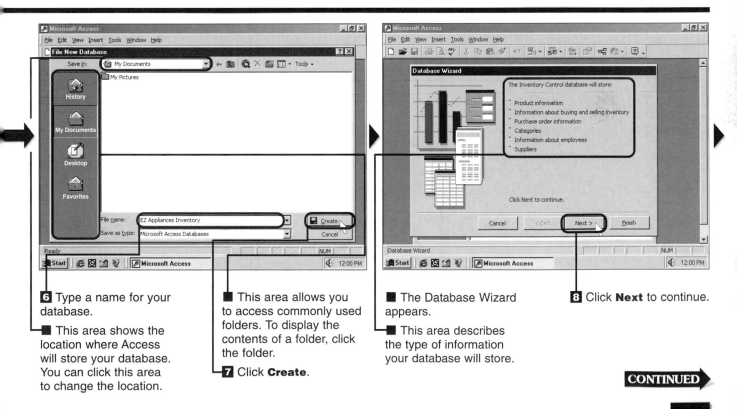

**6** Type a name for your database.

■ This area shows the location where Access will store your database. You can click this area to change the location.

■ This area allows you to access commonly used folders. To display the contents of a folder, click the folder.

**7** Click **Create**.

■ The Database Wizard appears.

■ This area describes the type of information your database will store.

**8** Click **Next** to continue.

CONTINUED

# CREATE A DATABASE USING A WIZARD

When using the Database Wizard to create a database, the wizard displays the fields that each table will include. You can choose to include other optional fields.

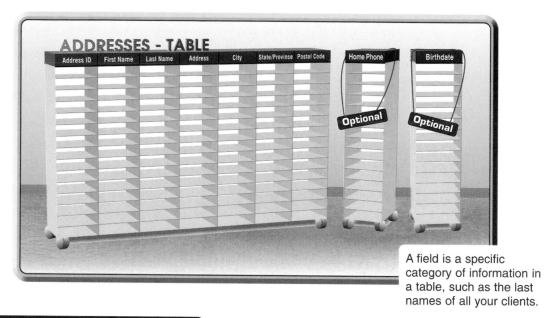

A field is a specific category of information in a table, such as the last names of all your clients.

## CREATE A DATABASE USING A WIZARD (CONTINUED)

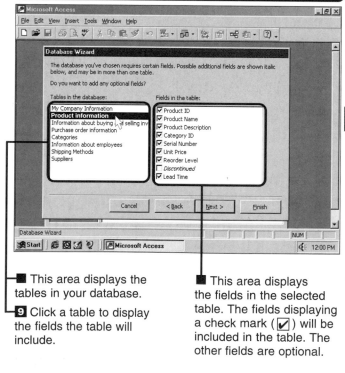

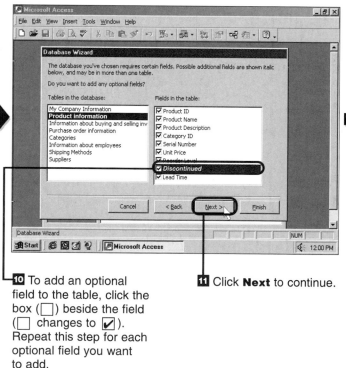

■ This area displays the tables in your database.

**9** Click a table to display the fields the table will include.

■ This area displays the fields in the selected table. The fields displaying a check mark (☑) will be included in the table. The other fields are optional.

**10** To add an optional field to the table, click the box (☐) beside the field (☐ changes to ☑). Repeat this step for each optional field you want to add.

**11** Click **Next** to continue.

250

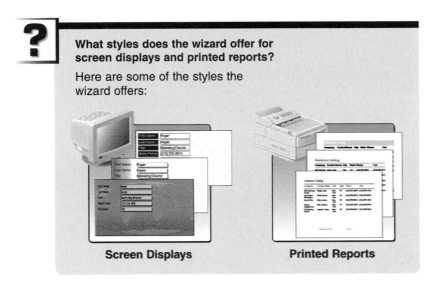

**?** **What styles does the wizard offer for screen displays and printed reports?**

Here are some of the styles the wizard offers:

**Screen Displays**          **Printed Reports**

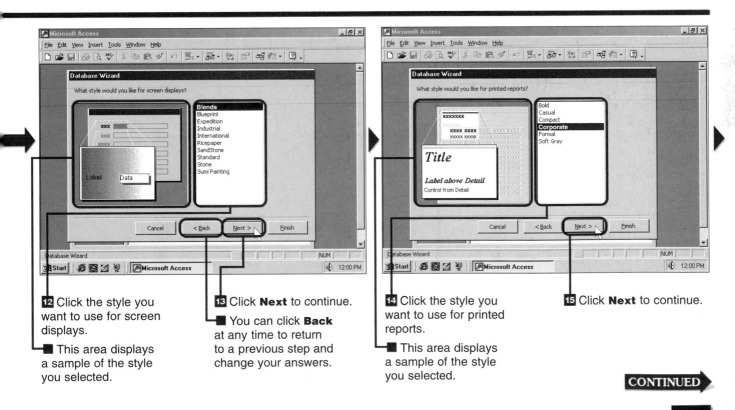

**12** Click the style you want to use for screen displays.

■ This area displays a sample of the style you selected.

**13** Click **Next** to continue.

■ You can click **Back** at any time to return to a previous step and change your answers.

**14** Click the style you want to use for printed reports.

■ This area displays a sample of the style you selected.

**15** Click **Next** to continue.

CONTINUED

# CREATE A DATABASE USING A WIZARD

When you finish creating a database, Access displays a switchboard to help you perform common tasks in the database.

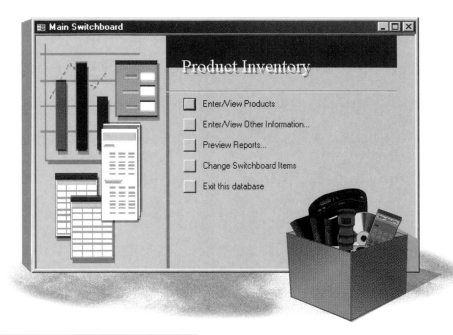

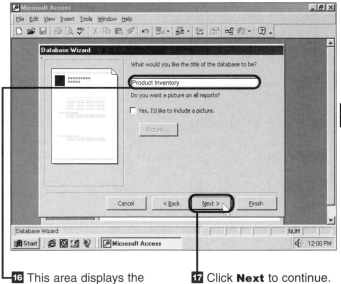

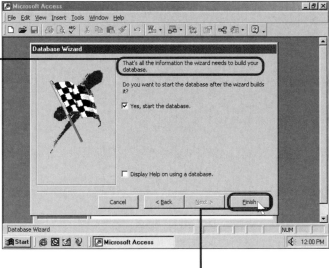

**16** This area displays the title of your database. To use a different title, type the title.

**17** Click **Next** to continue.

■ The wizard indicates that you have provided all the information needed to create your database.

**18** Click **Finish** to create your database.

**?**

**Why does this dialog box appear when I finish using the wizard?**

Access may need you to enter information, such as your company name and address, to finish setting up the database.

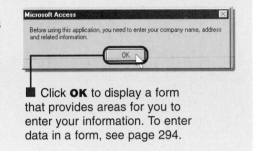

■ Click **OK** to display a form that provides areas for you to enter your information. To enter data in a form, see page 294.

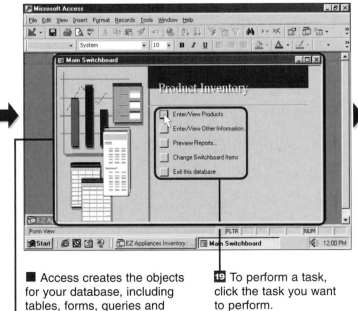

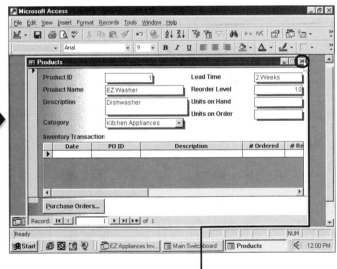

■ Access creates the objects for your database, including tables, forms, queries and reports.

■ The Main Switchboard window appears, which helps you perform common tasks.

**19** To perform a task, click the task you want to perform.

■ A database object that allows you to perform the task appears.

**20** When you finish using the object and want to return to the switchboard, click ✕ to close the object.

# CREATE A BLANK DATABASE

If you want to design your own database, you can create a blank database. Creating a blank database gives you the most flexibility and control.

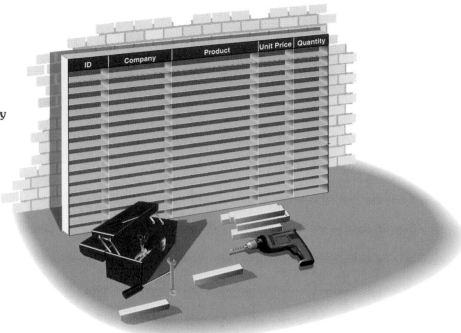

## CREATE A BLANK DATABASE

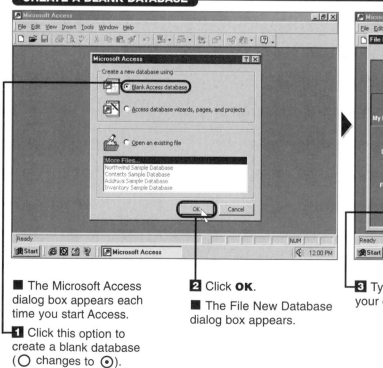

■ The Microsoft Access dialog box appears each time you start Access.

**1** Click this option to create a blank database (○ changes to ⊙).

**2** Click **OK**.

■ The File New Database dialog box appears.

**3** Type a name for your database.

■ This area shows the location where Access will store your database. You can click this area to change the location.

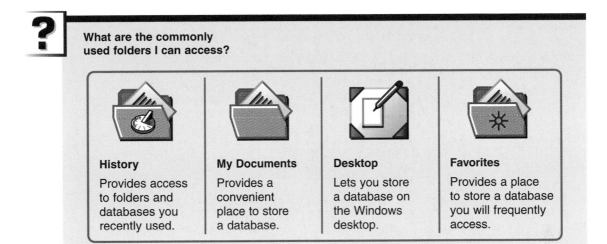

**What are the commonly used folders I can access?**

**History**
Provides access to folders and databases you recently used.

**My Documents**
Provides a convenient place to store a database.

**Desktop**
Lets you store a database on the Windows desktop.

**Favorites**
Provides a place to store a database you will frequently access.

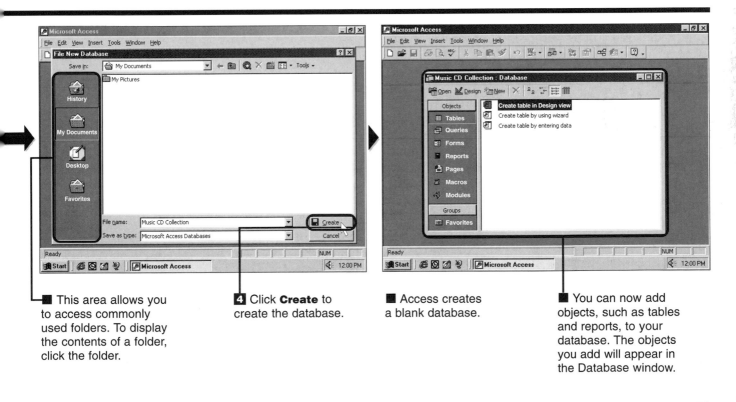

■ This area allows you to access commonly used folders. To display the contents of a folder, click the folder.

4 Click **Create** to create the database.

■ Access creates a blank database.

■ You can now add objects, such as tables and reports, to your database. The objects you add will appear in the Database window.

# OPEN A DATABASE OBJECT

You can use the
Database window
to open and work
with objects in your
database, including
tables, queries,
forms and reports.

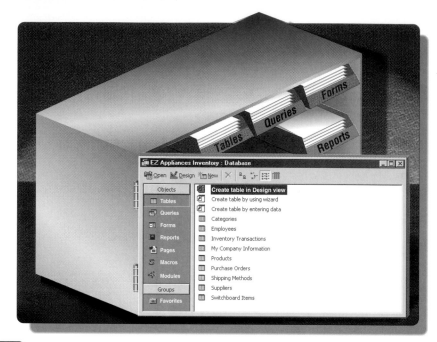

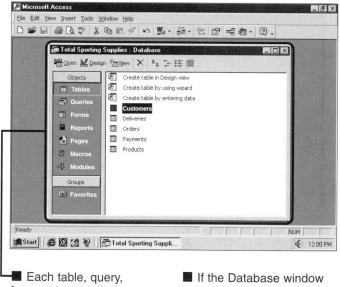

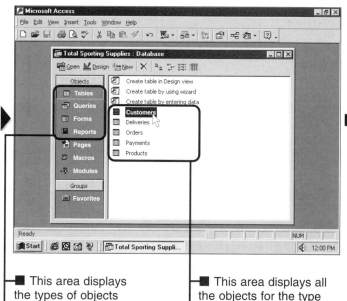

■ Each table, query,
form and report in the
database appears in
the Database window.

■ If the Database window
is hidden behind other
windows, press the F11
key to display the window.

■ This area displays
the types of objects
in the database.

**1** Click the type of
object you want to
work with.

■ This area displays all
the objects for the type
you selected.

**2** Double-click an object
to open the object.

**What types of objects can I open in the Database window?**

**Tables**

Contain information about a specific topic, such as a mailing list.

**Queries**

Allow you to find information of interest in your database.

**Forms**

Provide a quick way to view, enter and change data in your database.

**Reports**

Summarize and display data from your database in professional-looking documents.

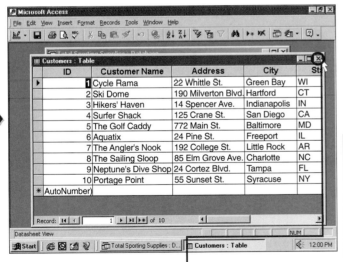

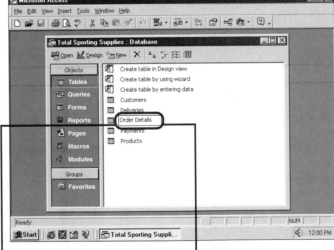

■ Access opens the object and displays its contents.

**3** When you finish working with the object, click ⊠ to close the object and return to the Database window.

**RENAME A DATABASE OBJECT**

**1** Click the name of the object you want to change.

**2** After a few seconds, click the name of the object again. A black border appears around the name of the object.

**3** Type a new name for the object and then press the Enter key.

# OPEN A DATABASE

You can open a database you previously created and display it on your screen. This lets you review and make changes to the database.

You can have only one database open at a time. Access will close a database displayed on your screen when you open another database.

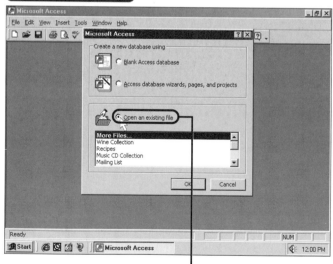

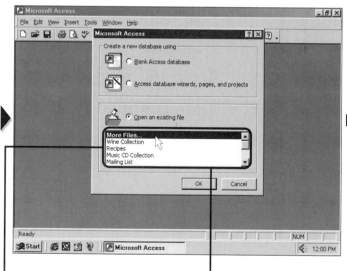

■ The Microsoft Access dialog box appears each time you start Access.

**1** Click this option to open an existing database (○ changes to ⊙).

■ This area displays the names of the last databases you worked with. To open one of these databases, double-click the name of the database.

*Note: The names of sample databases may also appear in the list.*

**2** If the database you want to open is not listed, double-click **More Files**.

■ The Open dialog box appears.

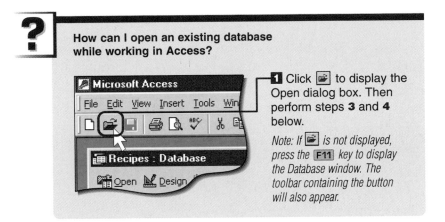

**?** **How can I open an existing database while working in Access?**

**1** Click 📂 to display the Open dialog box. Then perform steps **3** and **4** below.

*Note: If 📂 is not displayed, press the F11 key to display the Database window. The toolbar containing the button will also appear.*

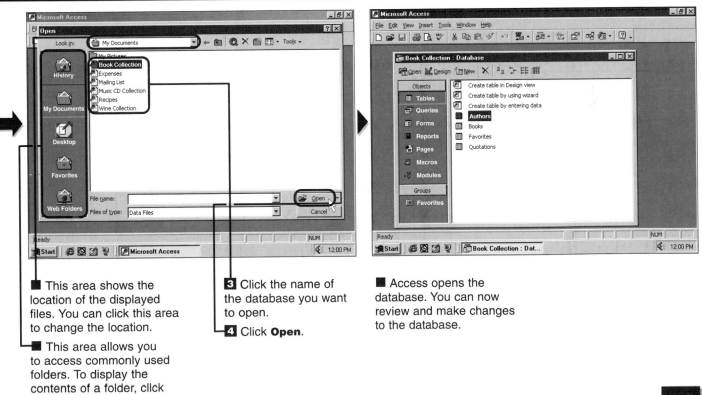

■ This area shows the location of the displayed files. You can click this area to change the location.

■ This area allows you to access commonly used folders. To display the contents of a folder, click the folder.

**3** Click the name of the database you want to open.

**4** Click **Open**.

■ Access opens the database. You can now review and make changes to the database.

# CREATE A TABLE

A table stores a collection of information about a specific topic, such as a list of client addresses. You can create a table to store new information in your database.

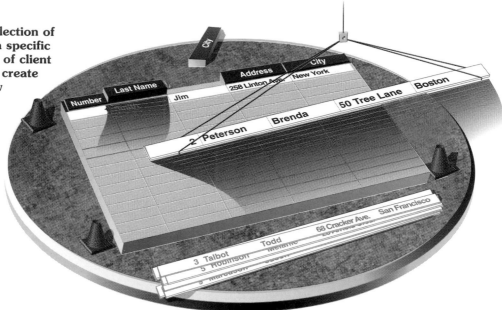

## CREATE A TABLE

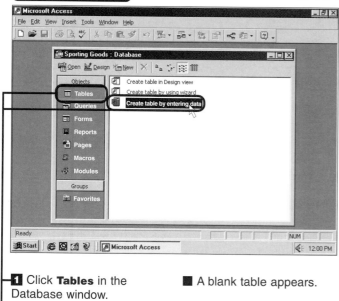

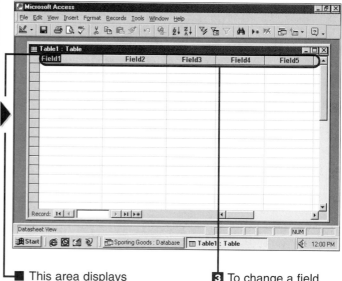

**1** Click **Tables** in the Database window.

**2** Double-click **Create table by entering data**.

■ A blank table appears.

■ This area displays the field names for each column in your table.

**3** To change a field name, double-click the field name to highlight the name.

## What are records and fields?

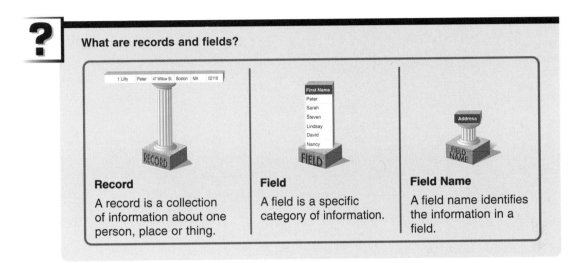

**Record**

A record is a collection of information about one person, place or thing.

**Field**

A field is a specific category of information.

**Field Name**

A field name identifies the information in a field.

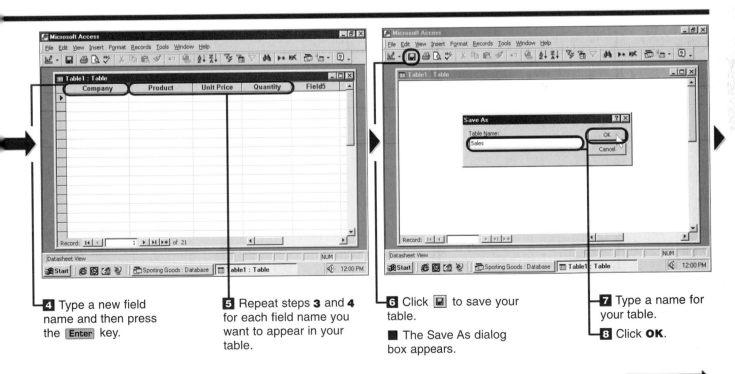

**4** Type a new field name and then press the **Enter** key.

**5** Repeat steps **3** and **4** for each field name you want to appear in your table.

**6** Click 🖫 to save your table.

■ The Save As dialog box appears.

**7** Type a name for your table.

**8** Click **OK**.

CONTINUED

# CREATE A TABLE

You can have Access set a primary key in your table for you. A primary key is one or more fields that uniquely identifies each record in a table, such as an ID number.

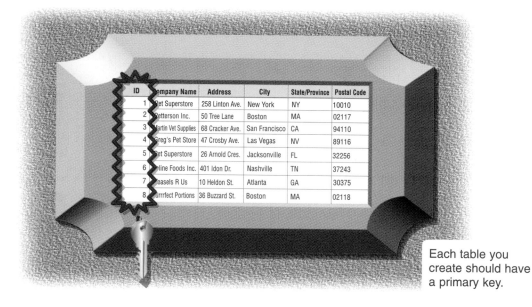

| ID | Company Name | Address | City | State/Province | Postal Code |
|----|--------------|---------|------|----------------|-------------|
| 1 | Pet Superstore | 258 Linton Ave. | New York | NY | 10010 |
| 2 | Petterson Inc. | 50 Tree Lane | Boston | MA | 02117 |
| 3 | Martin Vet Supplies | 68 Cracker Ave. | San Francisco | CA | 94110 |
| 4 | Greg's Pet Store | 47 Crosby Ave. | Las Vegas | NV | 89116 |
| 5 | Pet Superstore | 26 Arnold Cres. | Jacksonville | FL | 32256 |
| 6 | Feline Foods Inc. | 401 Idon Dr. | Nashville | TN | 37243 |
| 7 | Weasels R Us | 10 Heldon St. | Atlanta | GA | 30375 |
| 8 | Purrrfect Portions | 36 Buzzard St. | Boston | MA | 02118 |

Each table you create should have a primary key.

## CREATE A TABLE (CONTINUED)

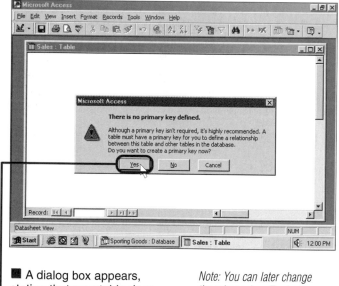

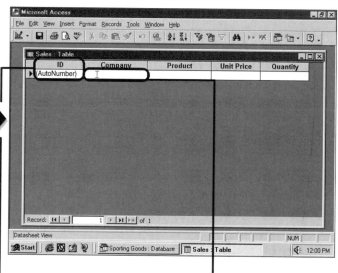

■ A dialog box appears, stating that your table does not have a primary key.

**9** To have Access create a primary key for you, click **Yes**.

*Note: You can later change the primary key. To change the primary key, see page 281.*

■ Access removes the rows and columns that do not contain data.

■ If you selected **Yes** in step **9**, Access adds an **ID** field to your table to serve as the primary key. The **ID** field will automatically number each record you add to your table.

**10** To enter the data for a record, click the first empty cell in the row.

262

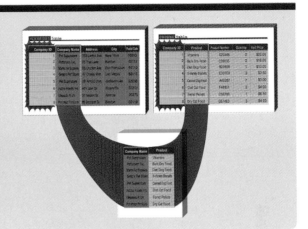

**Why do I need to set a primary key in a table?**

Access uses the primary key to match the records in one table with the records in another table. Setting up a primary key allows Access to bring together related information stored in the tables in your database. For information on relationships, see page 284.

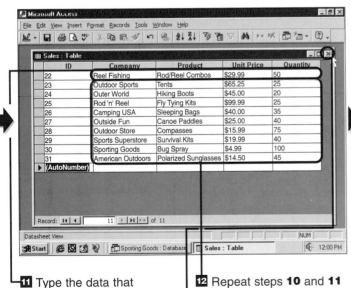

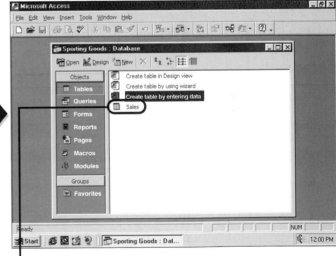

**11** Type the data that corresponds to the field and then press the [Enter] key to move to the next cell. Repeat this step until you finish entering all the data for the record.

**12** Repeat steps **10** and **11** for each record. Access automatically saves each record you enter.

**13** When you finish entering records, click ⊠ to close your table.

■ The name of your table appears in the Database window.

# RENAME A FIELD

You can give a field a different name to more accurately describe the contents of the field.

RECIPES Table

| Recipe ID | Recipe Name | Time | Meal | Servings |
|-----------|-------------|------|------|----------|
| 1 | Chicken Stir-fry | 25 minutes | Dinner | 4 |
| 2 | Omelet | 15 minutes | Breakfast | 1 |
| 3 | Veggie Pizza | 45 minutes | Lunch | 6 |
| | Lasagna | 45 minutes | Dinner | |
| | | 10 minutes | Breakf... | |

Preparation Time

## RENAME A FIELD

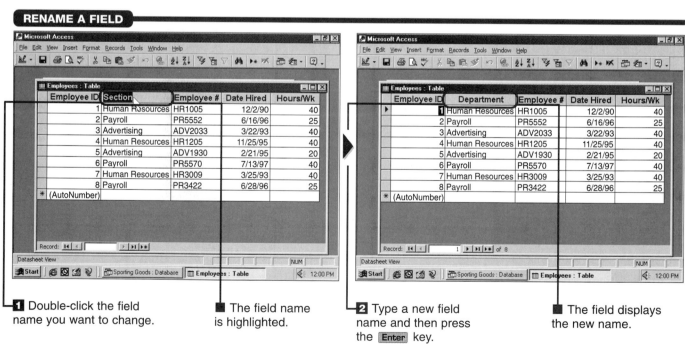

**1** Double-click the field name you want to change.

■ The field name is highlighted.

**2** Type a new field name and then press the **Enter** key.

■ The field displays the new name.

# REARRANGE FIELDS

You can change
the order of fields
to better organize
the information in
your table.

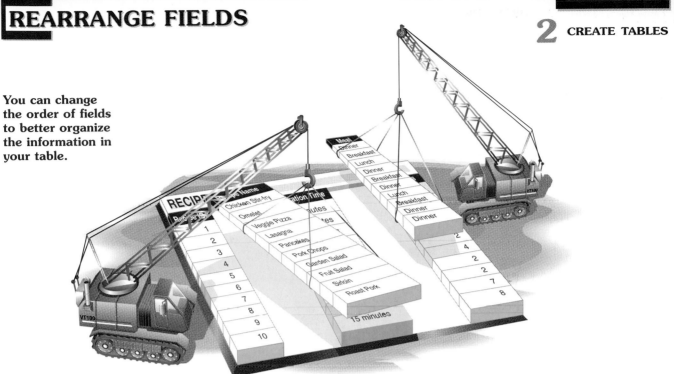

## REARRANGE FIELDS

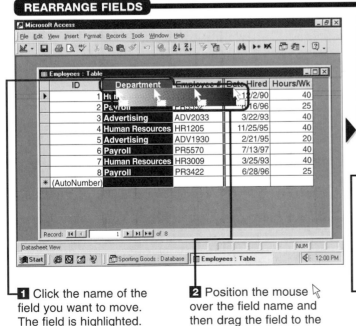

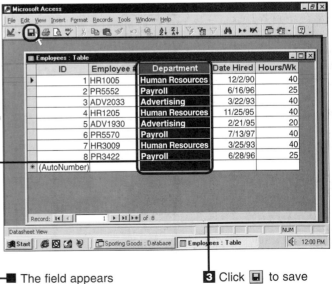

**1** Click the name of the field you want to move. The field is highlighted.

**2** Position the mouse ⓀⓀ over the field name and then drag the field to the new location.

■ A thick line shows where the field will appear.

■ The field appears in the new location.

**3** Click 🖫 to save the change you made to your table.

# ADD A FIELD

You can add a field
to a table when you
want to include an
additional category
of information.

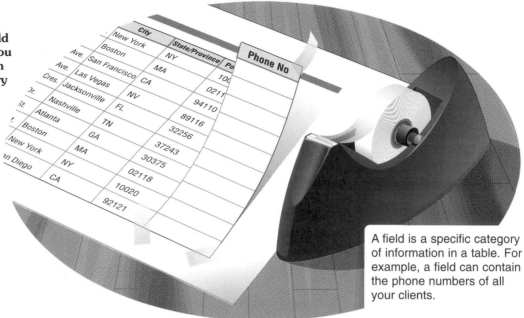

A field is a specific category
of information in a table. For
example, a field can contain
the phone numbers of all
your clients.

## ADD A FIELD

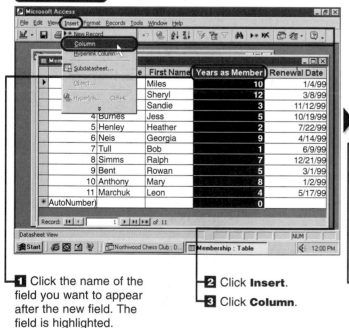

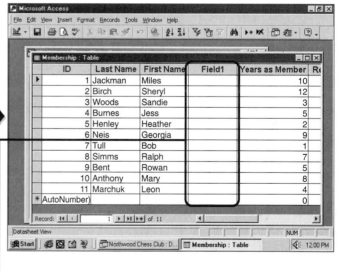

**1** Click the name of the
field you want to appear
after the new field. The
field is highlighted.

**2** Click **Insert**.

**3** Click **Column**.

■ The new field appears
in your table.

■ To give the field a
descriptive name, see
page 264.

# DELETE A FIELD

If you no longer need a field, you can permanently delete the field from your table.

Before you delete a field, make sure the field is not used in any other objects in your database, such as a form, query or report.

## DELETE A FIELD

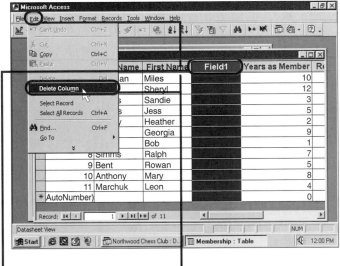

**1** Click the name of the field you want to delete. The field is highlighted.

**2** Click **Edit**.

**3** Click **Delete Column**.

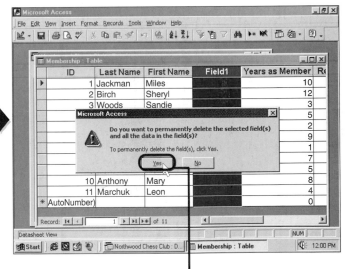

■ A dialog box appears, confirming the deletion.

**4** Click **Yes** to permanently delete the field.

■ The field disappears from your table.

# MOVE THROUGH DATA

You can easily move through the data in your table.

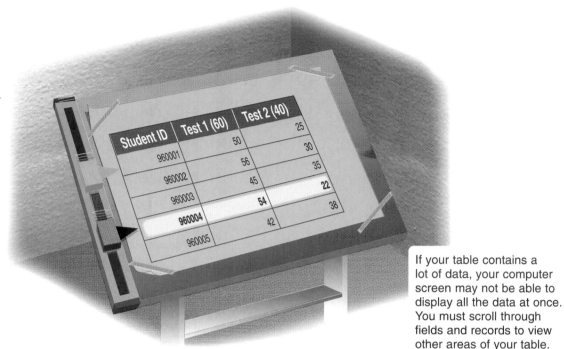

If your table contains a lot of data, your computer screen may not be able to display all the data at once. You must scroll through fields and records to view other areas of your table.

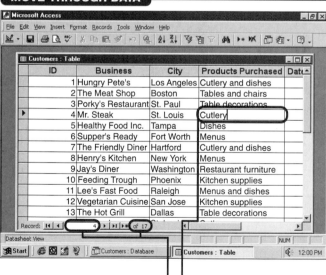

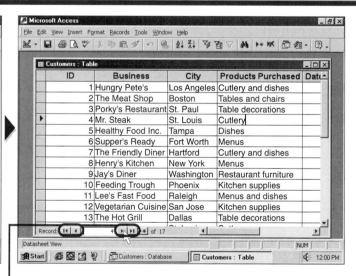

## MOVE THE INSERTION POINT

■ The flashing line on your screen, called the insertion point, indicates where the text you type will appear.

**1** To move the insertion point, click the cell you want to contain the insertion point.

■ This area displays the number of the record containing the insertion point and the total number of records in the table.

**2** To move the insertion point to another record, click one of the following buttons.

|◄ First Record

◄ Previous Record

► Next Record

►| Last Record

### How do I use my keyboard to move through data in a table?

| Press on Keyboard | Description |
|---|---|
| Page Up | Move up one screen of records |
| Page Down | Move down one screen of records |
| Tab | Move to the next field in the current record |
| ↑ | Move up one record in the same field |
| ↓ | Move down one record in the same field |

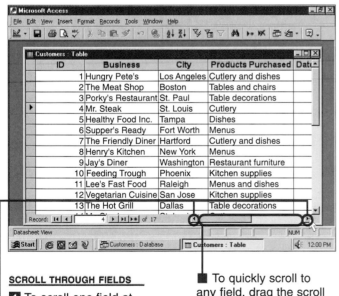

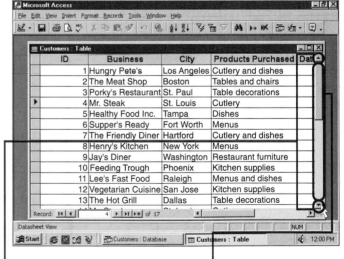

**SCROLL THROUGH FIELDS**

■1 To scroll one field at a time, click ◄ or ►.

*Note: You cannot scroll through fields if all the fields appear on your screen.*

■ To quickly scroll to any field, drag the scroll box along the scroll bar until the field you want to view appears.

**SCROLL THROUGH RECORDS**

■1 To scroll one record at a time, click ▲ or ▼.

*Note: You cannot scroll through records if all the records appear on your screen.*

■ To quickly scroll to any record, drag the scroll box along the scroll bar until a yellow box displays the number of the record you want to view.

# SELECT DATA

Before performing many tasks in a table, you must select the data you want to work with. Selected data appears highlighted on your screen.

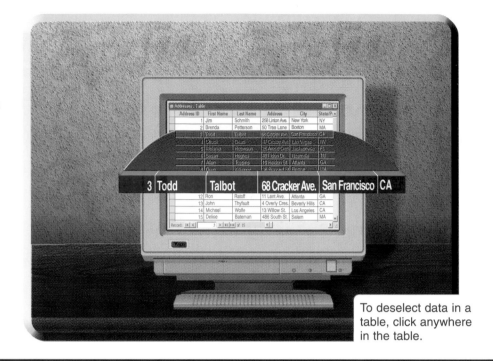

To deselect data in a table, click anywhere in the table.

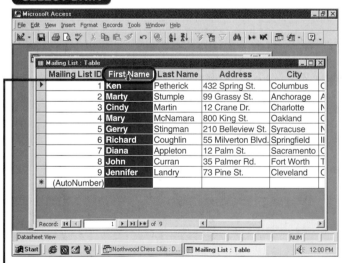

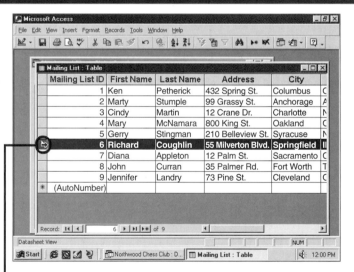

## SELECT A FIELD

**1** Position the mouse ⇧ over the name of the field you want to select (⇧ changes to ⬇) and then click to select the field.

■ To select multiple fields, position the mouse ⇧ over the name of the first field (⇧ changes to ⬇). Then drag the mouse ⬇ until you highlight all the fields you want to select.

## SELECT A RECORD

**1** Position the mouse ⇧ over the area to the left of the record you want to select (⇧ changes to ➡) and then click to select the record.

■ To select multiple records, position the mouse ⇧ over the area to the left of the first record (⇧ changes to ➡). Then drag the mouse ➡ until you highlight all the records you want to select.

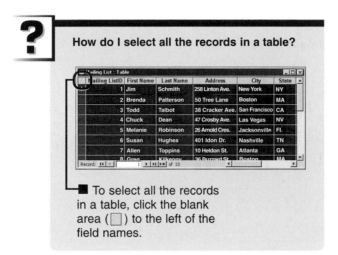

**How do I select all the records in a table?**

■ To select all the records in a table, click the blank area (☐) to the left of the field names.

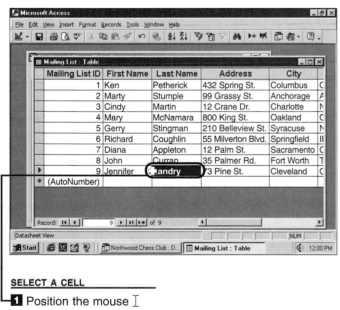

**SELECT A CELL**

**1** Position the mouse I over the left edge of the cell you want to select ( I changes to ⇩) and then click to select the cell.

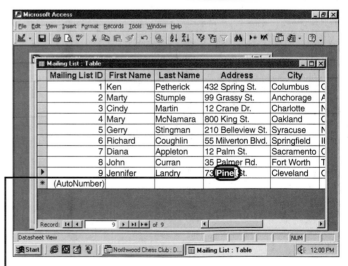

**SELECT DATA IN A CELL**

**1** Position the mouse I over the left edge of the data and then drag the mouse I until you highlight all the data you want to select.

■ To quickly select a word, double-click the word.

# EDIT DATA

After you enter data into your table, you can change the data to correct a mistake or update the data.

Access automatically saves the changes you make to your table.

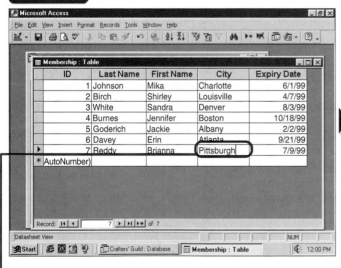

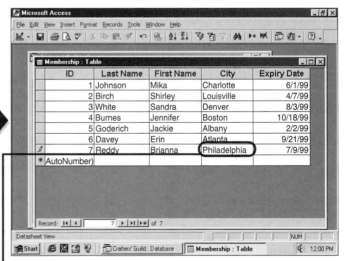

**1** Click the location in the cell where you want to change the data.

■ A flashing insertion point appears in the cell.

*Note: You can press the ← or → key to move the insertion point to where you want to change the data.*

**2** To remove the character to the left of the insertion point, press the ◆Backspace key.

**3** To insert data where the insertion point flashes on your screen, type the data.

**4** When you finish making changes to the data, press the Enter key.

**?**

**What are the symbols that appear to the left of the records?**

This is the current record.

You are editing this record.

You can enter data for a new record here.

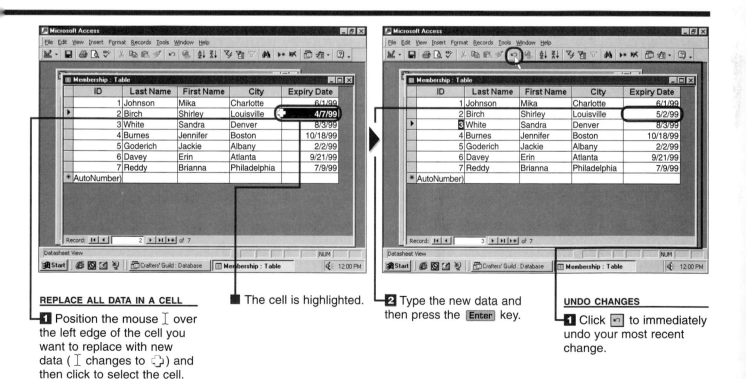

**REPLACE ALL DATA IN A CELL**

**1** Position the mouse I over the left edge of the cell you want to replace with new data ( I changes to ⇦) and then click to select the cell.

■ The cell is highlighted.

**2** Type the new data and then press the [Enter] key.

**UNDO CHANGES**

**1** Click 🔄 to immediately undo your most recent change.

# ZOOM INTO A CELL

You can zoom into
any cell in a table to
make the contents
of the cell easier to
review and edit.

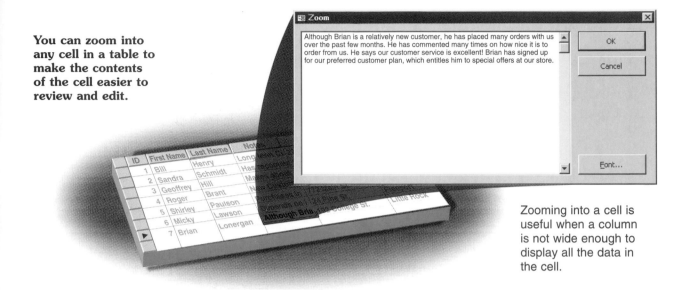

Zooming into a cell is
useful when a column
is not wide enough to
display all the data in
the cell.

## ZOOM INTO A CELL

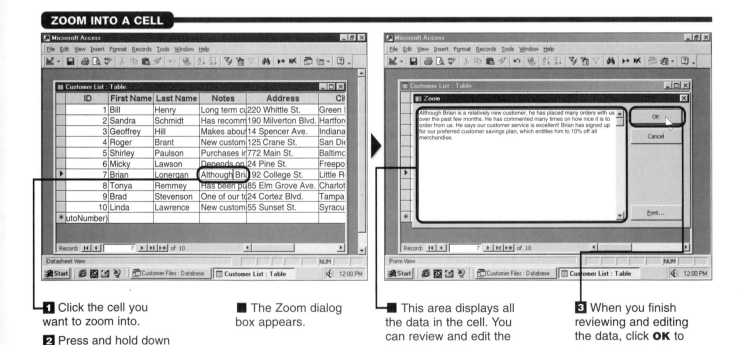

**1** Click the cell you
want to zoom into.

**2** Press and hold down
the **Shift** key as you
press the **F2** key.

■ The Zoom dialog
box appears.

■ This area displays all
the data in the cell. You
can review and edit the
data. To edit data, see
page 272.

**3** When you finish
reviewing and editing
the data, click **OK** to
close the dialog box.

■ The table will display
any changes you made
to the data.

# CHANGE COLUMN WIDTH

You can change the width of a column in your table. Increasing the width of a column lets you view data that is too long to display in the column.

| Address | First Na | Last Na | Address | City | State/Pr | Postal |
|---|---|---|---|---|---|---|
| 1 | Jim | Schmith | 258 Linton Ave. | New Yor | NY | 1001 |
| 2 | Brenda | Petterson | 50 Tree Lane | Boston | MA | 0211 |
| 3 | Todd | Talbot | 68 Cracker Ave. | San Fran | CA | 9411 |
| 4 | Chuck | Dean | 47 Crosby Ave. | Las Vega | NV | 8911 |
| 5 | Melanie | Robinson | 26 Arnold Cres. | Jackson | FL | 3225 |
| 6 | Susan | Hughes | 401 Idon Dr. | Nashville | TN | 3724 |
| 7 | Allen | Toppins | 10 Heldon St. | Atlanta | GA | 3037 |
| 8 | Greg | Kilkenny | 36 Buzzard St. | Boston | MA | 0211 |

Reducing the width of a column allows you to display more fields on your screen at once.

## CHANGE COLUMN WIDTH

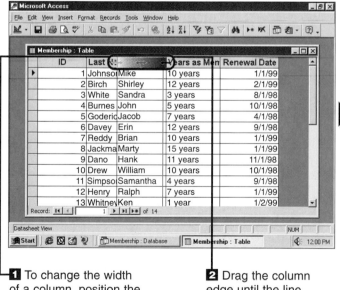

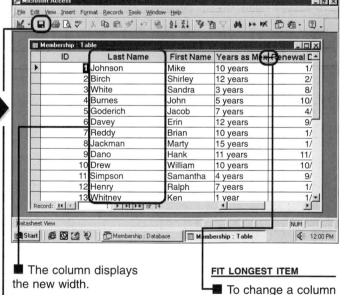

■1 To change the width of a column, position the mouse ⌖ over the right edge of the column heading (⌖ changes to ↔).

■2 Drag the column edge until the line displays the column width you want.

■ The column displays the new width.

■3 Click 🖫 to save the change.

**FIT LONGEST ITEM**

■ To change a column width to fit the longest item in the column, double-click the right edge of the column heading.

275

# ADD A RECORD

You can add a new record to insert additional information into your table. For example, you may want to add information about a new customer.

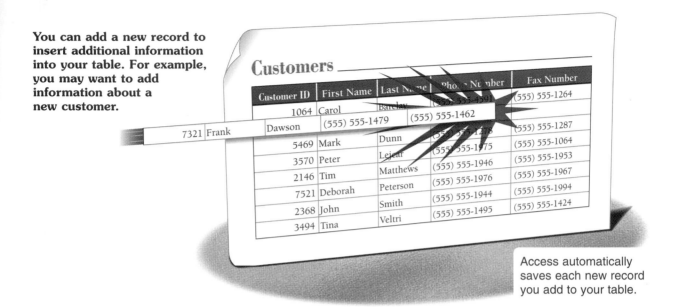

Access automatically saves each new record you add to your table.

## ADD A RECORD

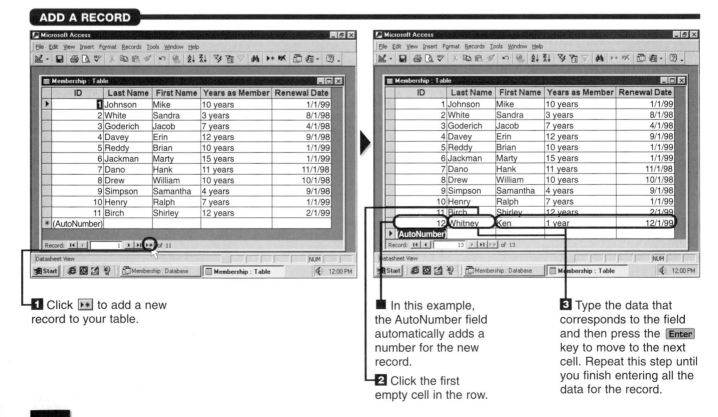

**1** Click ▶* to add a new record to your table.

■ In this example, the AutoNumber field automatically adds a number for the new record.

**2** Click the first empty cell in the row.

**3** Type the data that corresponds to the field and then press the Enter key to move to the next cell. Repeat this step until you finish entering all the data for the record.

# DELETE A RECORD

You can delete a record to permanently remove information you no longer need. Deleting records saves storage space on your computer and keeps your database from becoming cluttered with unnecessary information.

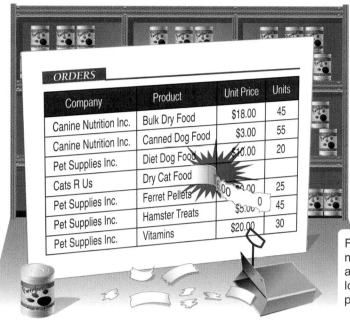

For example, you may want to remove a customer who no longer orders your products.

## DELETE A RECORD

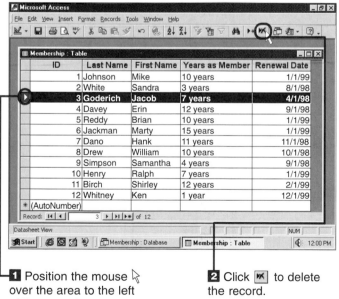

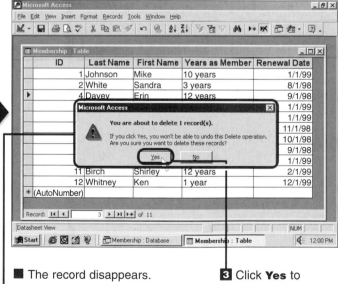

**1** Position the mouse ⌖ over the area to the left of the record you want to delete (⌖ changes to ➡) and then click to select the record.

**2** Click ⋈ to delete the record.

■ The record disappears.

■ A warning dialog box appears, confirming the deletion.

**3** Click **Yes** to permanently delete the record.

There are two ways you can view a table. Each view allows you to perform different tasks.

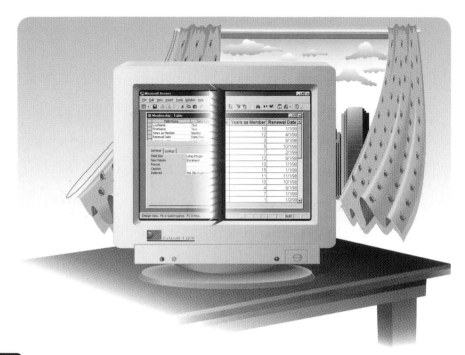

## CHANGE VIEW OF TABLE

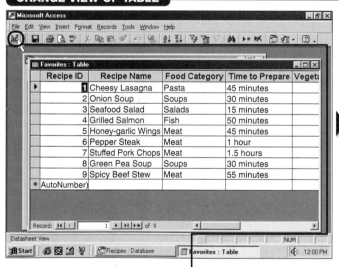

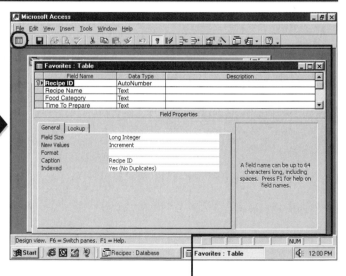

■ In this example, the table appears in the Datasheet view.

**1** Click  to display the table in the Design view.

■ The table appears in the Design view.

■ The View button changes to. You can click the View button to quickly switch between the Design () and Datasheet () views.

278

## THE TABLE VIEWS

### DATASHEET VIEW

The Datasheet view displays all the records in a table. You can enter, edit and review records in this view.

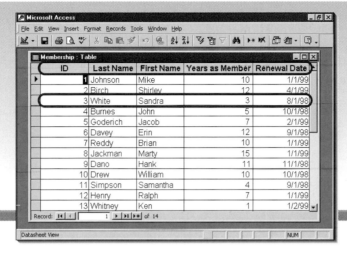

**Field Name**

A field name identifies the information within a field.

**Record**

A record is a collection of information about one person, place or thing.

### DESIGN VIEW

The Design view displays the structure of a table. You can change the settings in this view to specify the kind of information you can enter in a table.

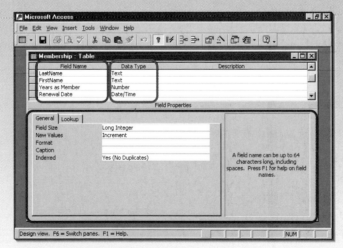

**Field Name**

A field name identifies the information within a field.

**Data Type**

The data type determines the type of information you can enter in a field, such as text, numbers or dates. Specifying a data type helps ensure that you enter the correct type of information in a field. For example, you cannot enter text in a field that has the Number data type.

**Field Properties**

The field properties are a set of characteristics that provide additional control over the information you can enter in a field. For example, you can specify the maximum number of characters a field will accept.

# DISPLAY A SUBDATASHEET

When viewing the records in a table, you can display a subdatasheet to view and edit related data from another table.

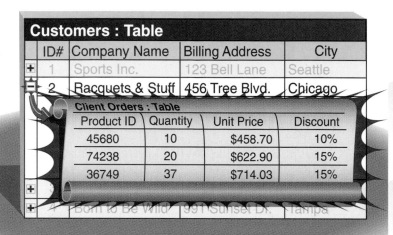

**Customers : Table**

| ID# | Company Name | Billing Address | City |
|-----|--------------|-----------------|------|
| 1 | Sports Inc. | 123 Bell Lane | Seattle |
| 2 | Racquets & Stuff | 456 Tree Blvd. | Chicago |

**Client Orders : Table**

| Product ID | Quantity | Unit Price | Discount |
|------------|----------|------------|----------|
| 45680 | 10 | $458.70 | 10% |
| 74238 | 20 | $622.90 | 15% |
| 36749 | 37 | $714.03 | 15% |

For example, in a table containing the addresses of all your clients, you can display a subdatasheet to review the orders for a particular client.

You can only display a subdatasheet when the table you are working with is related to another table. For information on relationships between tables, see page 284.

## DISPLAY A SUBDATASHEET

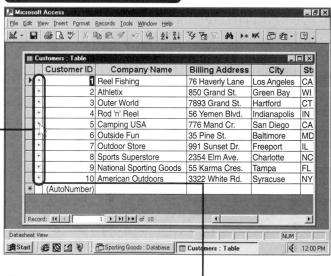

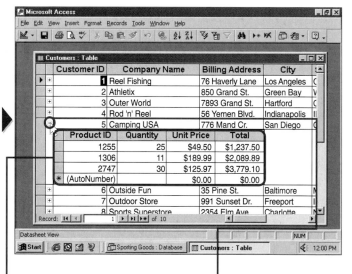

■ When records in a table relate to data in another table, a plus sign ( + ) appears beside each record.

**1** Click the plus sign ( + ) beside a record to display the related data from the other table ( + changes to − ).

■ The related data from the other table appears. You can review and edit the data. To edit data, see page 272.

**2** To once again hide the related data, click the minus sign ( − ) beside the record.

# SET THE PRIMARY KEY

A primary key is a field that contains a unique value for each record in a table, such as a social security number. Each table in a database should have a primary key.

| Social Security ID | Position | Salary | Hrs. Per Week |
|---|---|---|---|
| 111-11-1111 | Assistant | $25,000 | 40 |
| 222-22-2222 | Secretary | $30,000 | 40 |
| 333-33-3333 | Editor | $28,000 | 35 |
| 444-44-4444 | Sales Rep | $75,000 | 38 |
| 600-60-6000 | Designer | $39,000 | 38 |
| 777-77-7777 | Sales Rep | $42,000 | 40 |
| 888-88-8888 | Editor | $32,000 | 42 |
| 999-99-9999 | Writer | $50,000 | 44 |

You cannot enter the same value in a primary key more than once.

You should not change the primary key in a table that has a relationship with another table in the database. For information on relationships between tables, see page 284.

## SET THE PRIMARY KEY

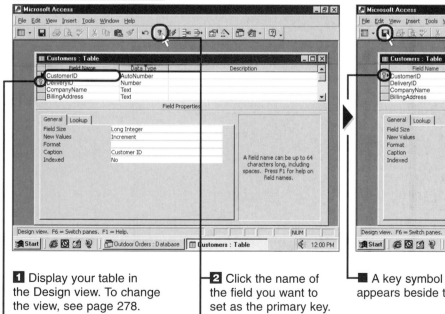

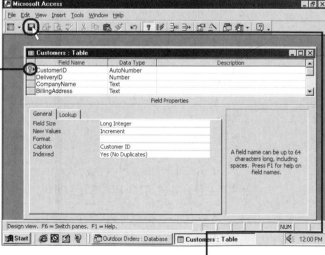

**1** Display your table in the Design view. To change the view, see page 278.

■ The field that is currently set as the primary key displays a key symbol (🔑).

*Note: You may have had Access set a primary key for you when you created the table.*

**2** Click the name of the field you want to set as the primary key.

**3** Click 🔑 to set the field as the primary key.

■ A key symbol (🔑) appears beside the field.

**4** Click 💾 to save the table.

# CHANGE A DATA TYPE

You can change the type of data you can enter in a field.

| Order ID | Company Name | Product | Quantity | Unit Price |
|---|---|---|---|---|
| AutoNumber | Text | | | Currency |
| 1 | Pet Superstore | | | $20.00 |
| 2 | Petterson Inc. | | | $18.00 |
| 3 | Martin Vet Supplies | | | $10.00 |
| 4 | Feline Foods Inc. | | | $3.50 |
| 5 | | 10 | | $3.00 |
| 6 | Weasels R Us | | | $4.00 |
| 7 8 | Purrrfect Portions | | | $6.50 |
| 10 9 | Doggone Yummy Inc. | | | $4.00 $1.25 $5.00 |

Changing the data type helps prevent errors when entering data. Access will not accept entries that do not match the data type you specify. For example, you cannot enter text in a field with the Number data type.

## CHANGE A DATA TYPE

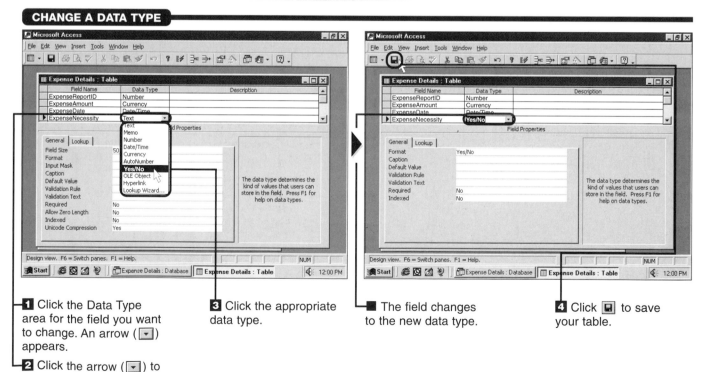

**1** Click the Data Type area for the field you want to change. An arrow ( ▼ ) appears.

**2** Click the arrow ( ▼ ) to display a list of data types.

**3** Click the appropriate data type.

■ The field changes to the new data type.

**4** Click 🖫 to save your table.

## DATA TYPES

### Text

Accepts entries up to 255 characters long that include any combination of text and numbers, such as an address. Make sure you use this data type for numbers you do not want to use in calculations, such as phone numbers or zip codes.

### Memo

Accepts entries up to 65,535 characters long that include any combination of text and numbers, such as notes, comments or lengthy descriptions.

### Number

Accepts numbers you want to use in calculations.

### Date/Time

Accepts only dates and times.

### Currency

Accepts only monetary values.

### AutoNumber

Automatically numbers each record for you.

### Yes/No

Accepts only one of two values–Yes/No, True/False or On/Off.

### OLE Object

Accepts OLE objects. An OLE object is an object created in another program, such as a document created in Word or a chart created in Excel. OLE objects can also include sounds and pictures.

### Hyperlink

Accepts hyperlinks you can select to jump to another document or a Web page.

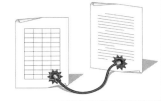

# ESTABLISH RELATIONSHIPS BETWEEN TABLES

You can create relationships between tables. Relationships allow you to bring together related information in your database.

If you used the Database Wizard to create your database, the wizard automatically created relationships between tables for you. For information on the Database Wizard, see page 248.

## ESTABLISH RELATIONSHIPS BETWEEN TABLES

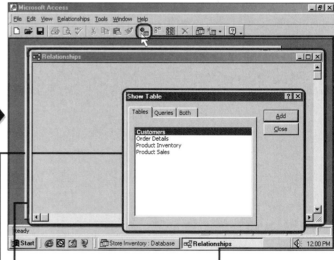

**1** Click ⊞ to display the Relationships window.

*Note: If ⊞ is not available, make sure the Database window is displayed and you do not have any other windows open on your screen. You can press the F11 key to display the Database window.*

■ The Relationships window appears. If any relationships exist between the tables in your database, a box for each table appears in the window.

■ The Show Table dialog box may also appear, listing all the tables in your database.

**2** If the Show Table dialog box does not appear, click ⊞ to display the dialog box.

**Why do I need to establish relationships between the tables in my database?**

Relationships between tables are essential for creating a form, report or query that uses information from more than one table in your database.

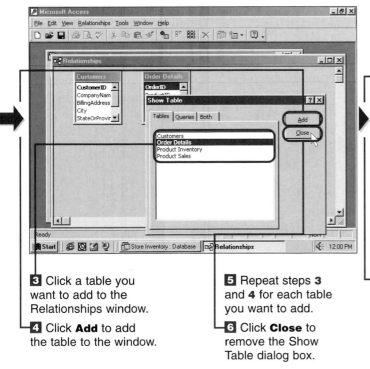

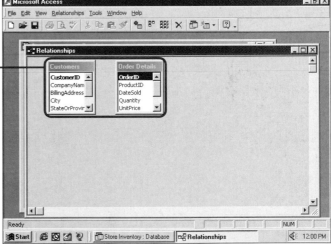

**3** Click a table you want to add to the Relationships window.

**4** Click **Add** to add the table to the window.

**5** Repeat steps **3** and **4** for each table you want to add.

**6** Click **Close** to remove the Show Table dialog box.

■ The Relationships window displays a box for each table. Each box displays the fields for a table.

■ The primary key in each table appears in **bold**. The primary key contains a unique value for each record in a table.

CONTINUED

# CREATE A FORM

When creating a form, you can choose from several layouts for the form. The layout of a form determines the arrangement of information on the form.

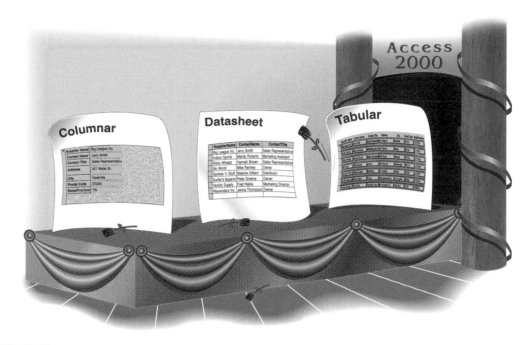

Columnar

Datasheet

Tabular

Access 2000

---

## CREATE A FORM (CONTINUED)

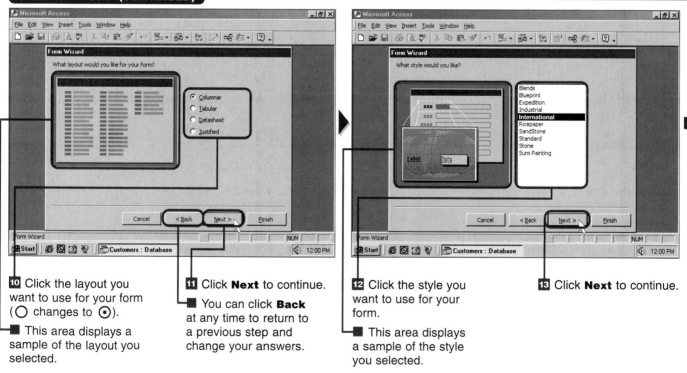

**10** Click the layout you want to use for your form (○ changes to ⊙).

■ This area displays a sample of the layout you selected.

**11** Click **Next** to continue.

■ You can click **Back** at any time to return to a previous step and change your answers.

**12** Click the style you want to use for your form.

■ This area displays a sample of the style you selected.

**13** Click **Next** to continue.

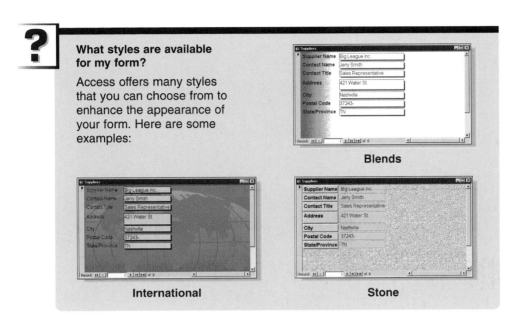

**What styles are available for my form?**

Access offers many styles that you can choose from to enhance the appearance of your form. Here are some examples:

**Blends**

**International**

**Stone**

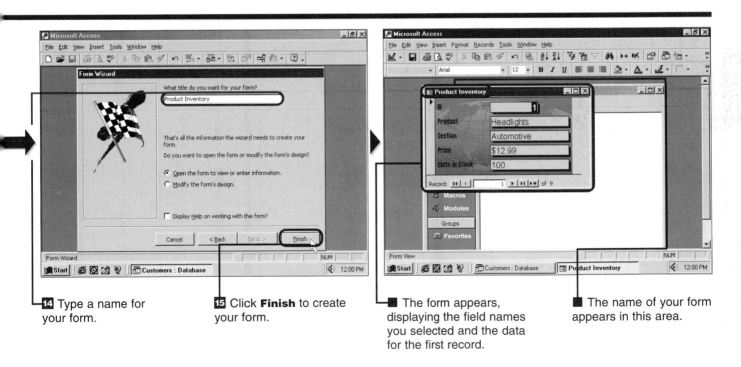

■14 Type a name for your form.

■15 Click **Finish** to create your form.

■ The form appears, displaying the field names you selected and the data for the first record.

■ The name of your form appears in this area.

# MOVE THROUGH RECORDS

You can move through
the records in a form
to review or edit
information.

## MOVE THROUGH RECORDS

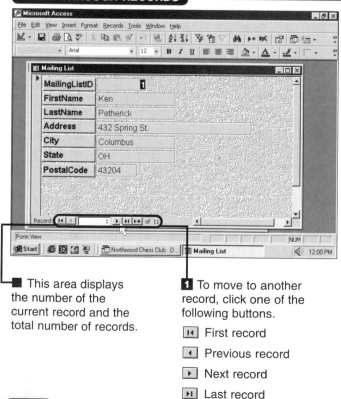

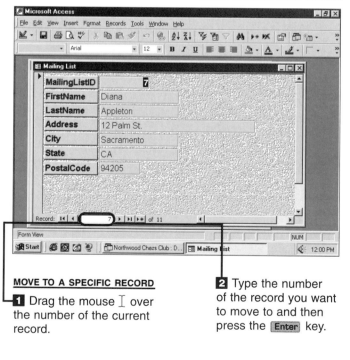

■ This area displays
the number of the
current record and the
total number of records.

**1** To move to another
record, click one of the
following buttons.

|◄| First record

◄| Previous record

|► Next record

►| Last record

**MOVE TO A SPECIFIC RECORD**

**1** Drag the mouse I over
the number of the current
record.

**2** Type the number
of the record you want
to move to and then
press the Enter key.

# EDIT DATA

You can change data
in a record to correct
a mistake or update
the data.

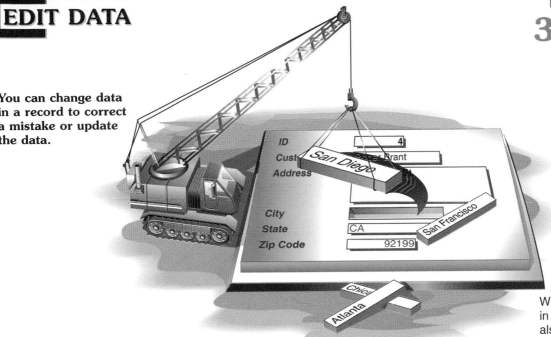

When you change data
in a form, Access will
also change the data
in the table you used
to create the form.

## EDIT DATA

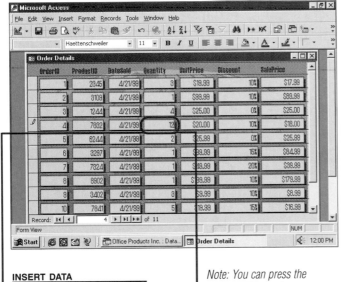

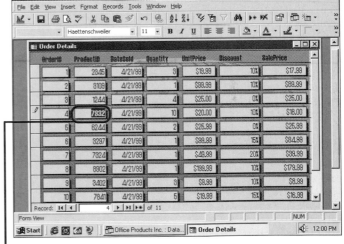

### INSERT DATA

**1** Click the location in
the cell where you want
to insert data.

■ A flashing insertion
point appears in the cell,
indicating where the data
you type will appear.

*Note: You can press the
← or → key to move
the insertion point.*

**2** Type the data you
want to insert.

### DELETE DATA

**1** To select the data you
want to delete, drag the
mouse I over the data.
Then press the Delete key.

■ To delete a single
character, click to the
right of the character you
want to delete and then
press the Backspace key.
Access will delete the
character to the left of the
flashing insertion point.

# ADD A RECORD

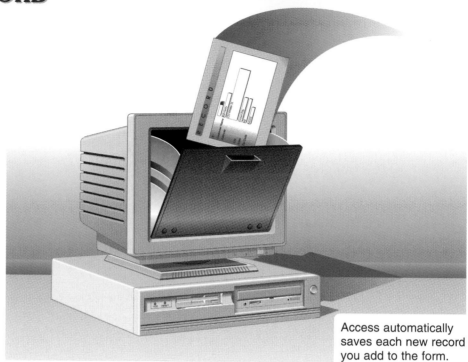

You can add a record to a form to insert new information into your database. For example, you may want to add information about a new client.

Access automatically saves each new record you add to the form.

## ADD A RECORD

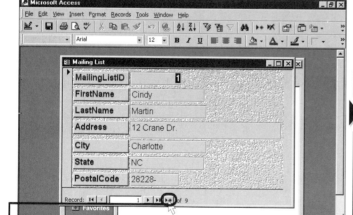

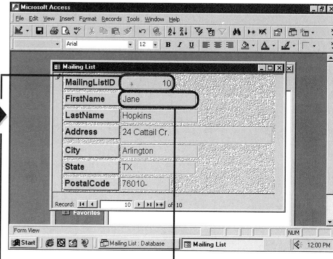

**1** Click ▶✱ to add a record.

■ A blank form appears.

■ In this example, the AutoNumber field automatically adds a number for the new record.

**2** Click the first empty field.

**3** Type the data that corresponds to the field and then press the `Tab` key to move to the next field. Repeat this step until you finish entering all the data for the record.

# DELETE A RECORD

You can delete a record to permanently remove information you no longer need. Deleting records saves storage space on your computer and keeps your database from becoming cluttered with unnecessary information.

For example, you may want to remove information about a product you no longer manufacture.

## DELETE A RECORD

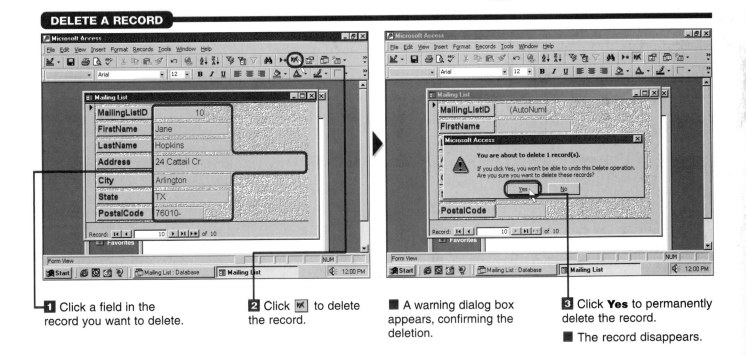

**1** Click a field in the record you want to delete.

**2** Click ⋈ to delete the record.

■ A warning dialog box appears, confirming the deletion.

**3** Click **Yes** to permanently delete the record.

■ The record disappears.

# SORT RECORDS

You can change the order of records in a table, query or form. This can help you find, organize and analyze data.

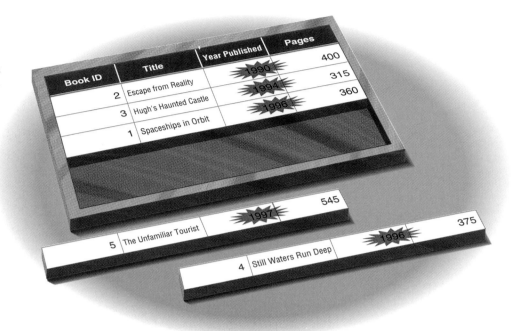

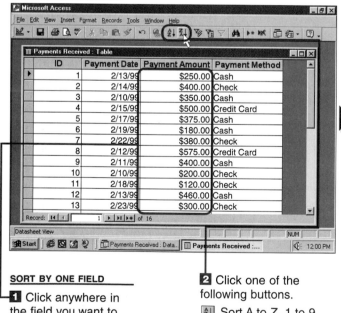

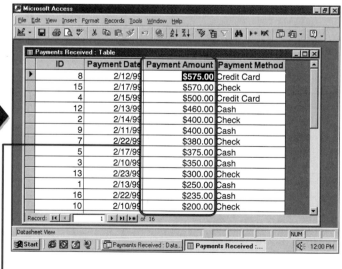

**SORT BY ONE FIELD**

**1** Click anywhere in the field you want to use to sort the records.

**2** Click one of the following buttons.

$\begin{array}{c}\text{A}\downarrow\\\text{Z}\end{array}$ Sort A to Z, 1 to 9

$\begin{array}{c}\text{Z}\downarrow\\\text{A}\end{array}$ Sort Z to A, 9 to 1

■ The records appear in the new order. In this example, the records are sorted by payment amount.

**?** **How do I remove a sort from my records?**

If you no longer want to display your records in the sort order you specified, you can return your records to the original order at any time.

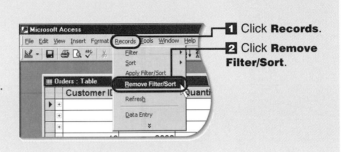

**1** Click **Records**.

**2** Click **Remove Filter/Sort**.

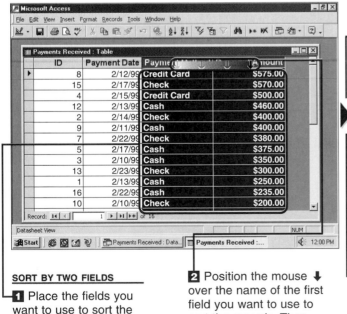

## SORT BY TWO FIELDS

**1** Place the fields you want to use to sort the records side-by-side and in the order you want to perform the sort. To rearrange fields, see page 265.

**2** Position the mouse ↓ over the name of the first field you want to use to sort the records. Then drag the mouse ↓ until you highlight the second field.

**3** Click one of the following buttons.

⬆ Sort A to Z, 1 to 9

⬇ Sort Z to A, 9 to 1

■ The records appear in the new order. In this example, the records are sorted by payment method. All records with the same payment method are also sorted by payment amount.

# FIND DATA

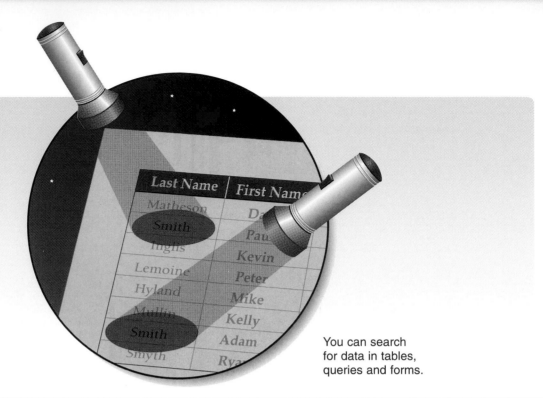

You can search
for records that
contain specific
data.

You can search
for data in tables,
queries and forms.

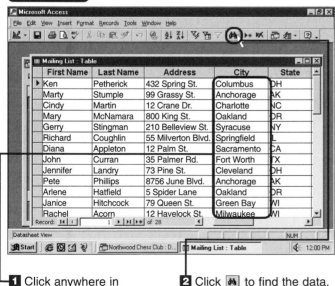

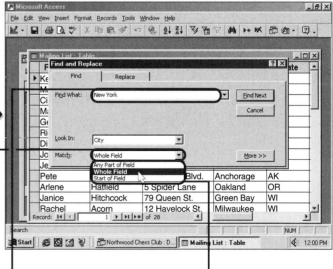

**1** Click anywhere in
the field containing the
data you want to find.

**2** Click 🔍 to find the data.

■ The Find and Replace
dialog box appears.

**3** Type the data you
want to find.

**4** To specify how you
want to search for the
data, click this area.

**5** Click the option you
want to use.

*Note: For information on the
available options, see the top
of page 299.*

298

**How can Access search for data in a field?**

**Any Part of Field**

Finds data anywhere in the field. For example, **smith** finds **Smith**, **Smithson** and **Macsmith**.

**Whole Field**

Finds data that is exactly the same. For example, **smith** finds **Smith**, but not **Smithson** or **Macsmith**.

**Start of Field**

Finds data only at the beginning of the field. For example, **smith** finds **Smith** and **Smithson**, but not **Macsmith**.

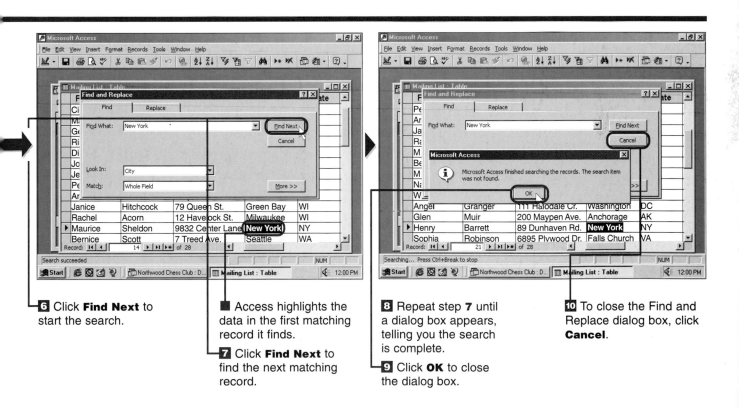

**6** Click **Find Next** to start the search.

■ Access highlights the data in the first matching record it finds.

**7** Click **Find Next** to find the next matching record.

**8** Repeat step **7** until a dialog box appears, telling you the search is complete.

**9** Click **OK** to close the dialog box.

**10** To close the Find and Replace dialog box, click **Cancel**.

# FILTER DATA BY SELECTION

You can filter data to display only records containing data of interest. This can help you review and analyze information in your database.

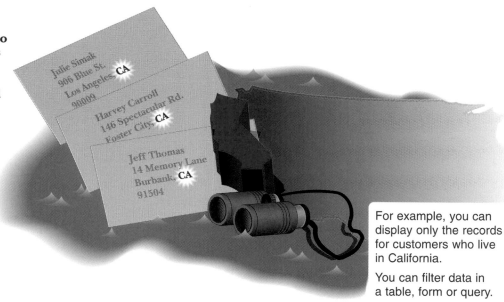

For example, you can display only the records for customers who live in California.

You can filter data in a table, form or query.

## FILTER DATA BY SELECTION

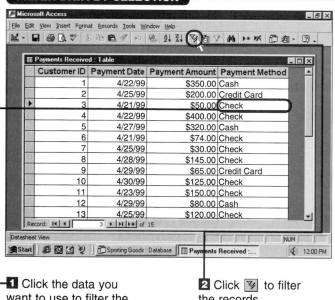

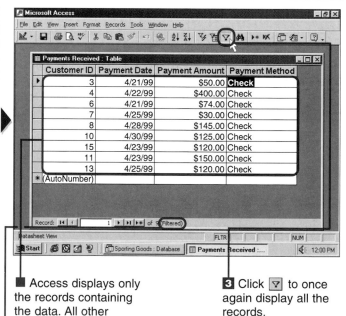

**1** Click the data you want to use to filter the records. Access will display only records that contain exactly the same data.

**2** Click ▽ to filter the records.

■ Access displays only the records containing the data. All other records are hidden.

■ The word **Filtered** appears in this area to indicate that you are looking at filtered records.

**3** Click ▽ to once again display all the records.

# FILTER DATA USING CRITERIA

You can filter data by entering criteria to display specific records in your database. Criteria are conditions that identify which records you want to display.

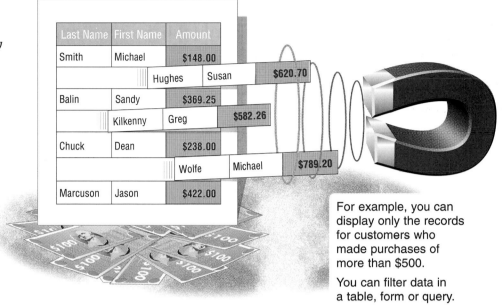

For example, you can display only the records for customers who made purchases of more than $500.

You can filter data in a table, form or query.

## FILTER DATA USING CRITERIA

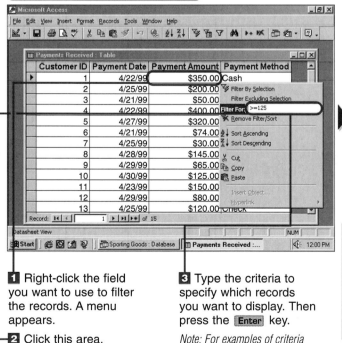

**1** Right-click the field you want to use to filter the records. A menu appears.

**2** Click this area.

**3** Type the criteria to specify which records you want to display. Then press the **Enter** key.

*Note: For examples of criteria you can use, see page 311.*

■ Access displays only the records that match the criteria you specified. All other records are hidden.

■ The word **Filtered** appears in this area to indicate that you are looking at filtered records.

**4** Click ▼ to once again display all the records.

# CREATE A QUERY

You can create
a query to find
information of
interest in your
database.

Which wines were
made before 1965?

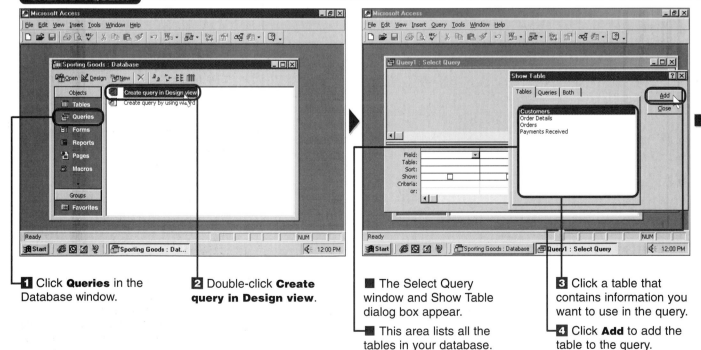

**1** Click **Queries** in the
Database window.

**2** Double-click **Create
query in Design view**.

■ The Select Query
window and Show Table
dialog box appear.

■ This area lists all the
tables in your database.

**3** Click a table that
contains information you
want to use in the query.

**4** Click **Add** to add the
table to the query.

**How do I add another table to a query?**

You can click 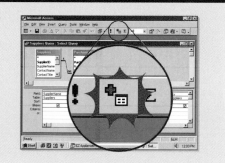 at any time to redisplay the Show Table dialog box and add another table to the query.

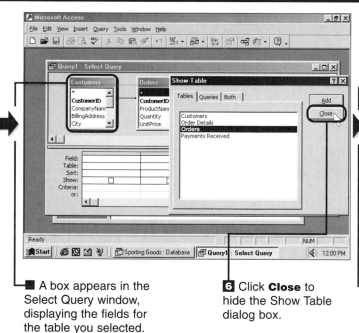

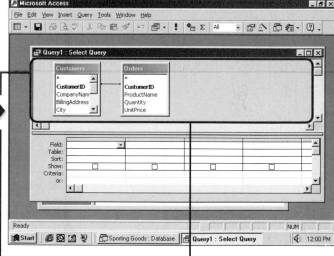

■ A box appears in the Select Query window, displaying the fields for the table you selected.

**5** Repeat steps **3** and **4** for each table you want to use in the query.

**6** Click **Close** to hide the Show Table dialog box.

■ Each box in this area displays the fields for one table.

*Note: If the tables are related, Access displays a line joining the related fields. For information on relationships, see page 284.*

■ If you accidentally added a table to the query, click the table and then press the Delete key. This removes the table from the query but not from the database.

**CONTINUED**

# CREATE A QUERY

You can select
which fields you
want to include
in your query.

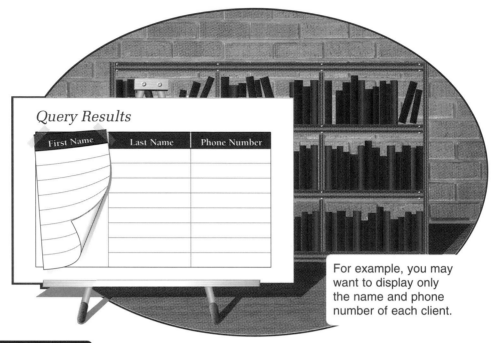

*Query Results*

| First Name | Last Name | Phone Number |
|---|---|---|
| | | |
| | | |
| | | |
| | | |
| | | |

For example, you may
want to display only
the name and phone
number of each client.

## CREATE A QUERY (CONTINUED)

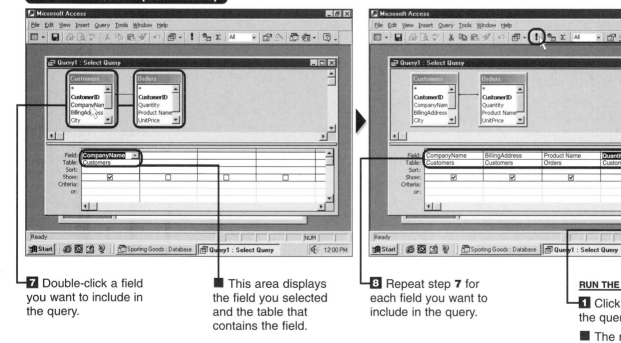

**7** Double-click a field
you want to include in
the query.

■ This area displays
the field you selected
and the table that
contains the field.

**8** Repeat step **7** for
each field you want to
include in the query.

**RUN THE QUERY**

**1** Click ▮ to run
the query.

■ The results of
the query appear.

**Does a query store data?**

No. A query gathers data from your database to answer a question you specify. When you save a query, Access stores only the question. This allows you to ask the same question again later to review the most up-to-date information. For example, you can run the same query each month to display the names of the top sales representatives for the month.

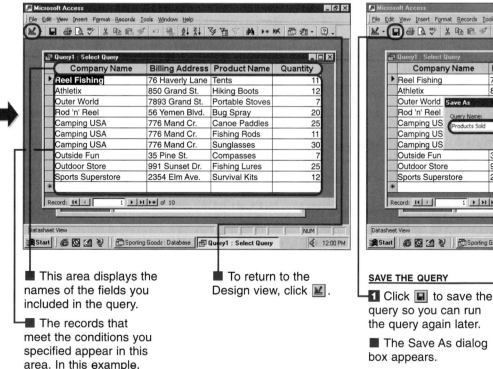

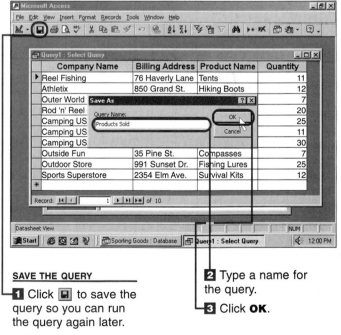

■ This area displays the names of the fields you included in the query.

■ The records that meet the conditions you specified appear in this area. In this example, all of the records are displayed.

■ To return to the Design view, click 🔟.

**SAVE THE QUERY**

**1** Click 🔲 to save the query so you can run the query again later.

■ The Save As dialog box appears.

**2** Type a name for the query.

**3** Click **OK**.

# CHANGE VIEW OF QUERY

You can change the way you view your query. Each view allows you to perform different tasks.

Datasheet View

Design View

Select View

**Datasheet view**

Allows you to view the results of your query.

**Design view**

Allows you to plan your query.

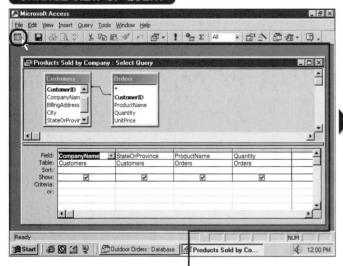

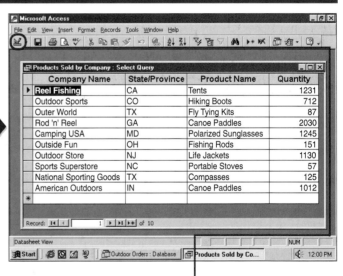

■ In this example, the query appears in the Design view.

**1** Click 🔲 to display the query in the Datasheet view.

■ The query appears in the Datasheet view.

■ The View button 🔲 changes to 📐. You can click the View button to quickly switch between the Design (📐) and Datasheet (🔲) views.

# SORT THE QUERY RESULTS

You can sort the results of a query to better organize the results. This can help you quickly find information of interest.

Sort "scores" in ascending order

There are two ways you can sort the results of a query.

**Ascending**
Sorts A to Z, 1 to 9

**Descending**
Sorts Z to A, 9 to 1

## SORT THE QUERY RESULTS

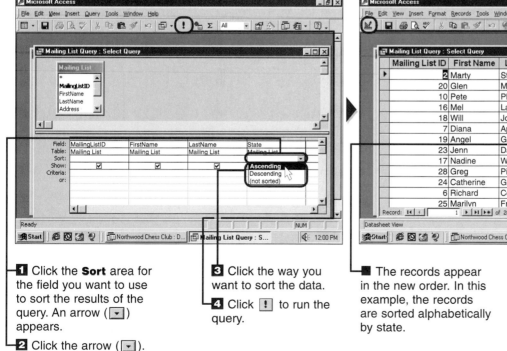

**1** Click the **Sort** area for the field you want to use to sort the results of the query. An arrow ( ▼ ) appears.

**2** Click the arrow ( ▼ ).

**3** Click the way you want to sort the data.

**4** Click ! to run the query.

■ The records appear in the new order. In this example, the records are sorted alphabetically by state.

■ To return to the Design view, click ☒.

# HIDE A FIELD

You can hide a field used in a query. Hiding a field is useful when you need a field to find information in your database, but do not want the field to appear in the results of the query.

Which clients live in Florida?

For example, you can hide the State field if you want to find clients in Florida, but do not want the State field to appear in the query results.

## HIDE A FIELD

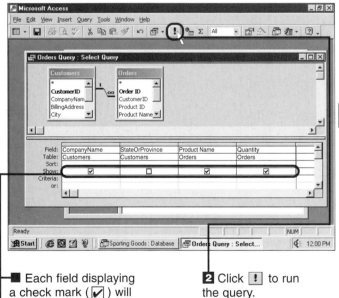

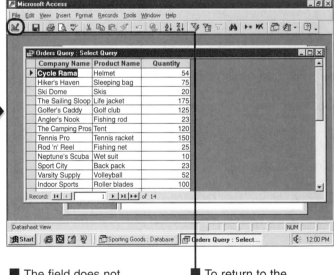

■ Each field displaying a check mark (☑) will appear in the results of the query.

**1** If you do not want a field to appear in the results of the query, click the **Show** box for the field (☑ changes to ☐).

**2** Click ! to run the query.

■ The field does not appear in the results of the query.

■ To return to the Design view, click ⬚.

# DELETE A FIELD

You can delete a
field you no longer
need in your query.

## DELETE A FIELD

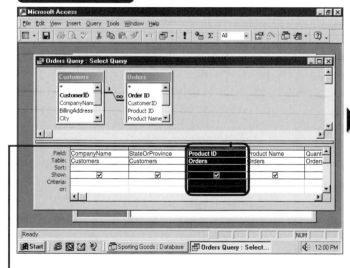

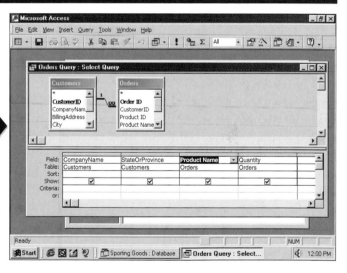

**1** Position the mouse ⃗
directly above the field
you want to delete
(⃗ changes to ↓) and
then click to select the
field.

**2** Press the Delete key.

■ The field disappears
from your query.

# SET CRITERIA

You can use criteria to find specific records in your database. Criteria are conditions that identify which records you want to find.

Which clients live in California?

State = CA

Which students scored greater than 80% on their final grade?

Final grade >80%

Which recipes take less than 15 minutes to prepare?

Preparation Time <15 min

## SET CRITERIA

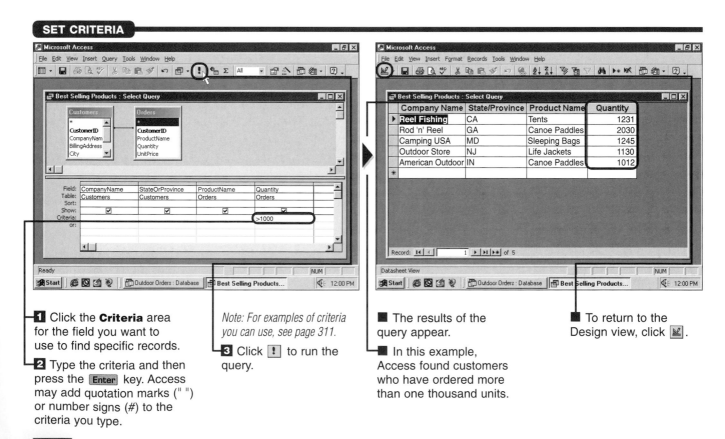

**1** Click the **Criteria** area for the field you want to use to find specific records.

**2** Type the criteria and then press the Enter key. Access may add quotation marks (" ") or number signs (#) to the criteria you type.

*Note: For examples of criteria you can use, see page 311.*

**3** Click ! to run the query.

■ The results of the query appear.

■ In this example, Access found customers who have ordered more than one thousand units.

■ To return to the Design view, click ✍.

# EXAMPLES OF CRITERIA

Here are examples of criteria
that you can use to find records
in your database. Criteria are
conditions that identify the
records you want to find.

## Exact matches

| | |
|---|---|
| =100 | Finds the number 100. |
| =California | Finds California. |

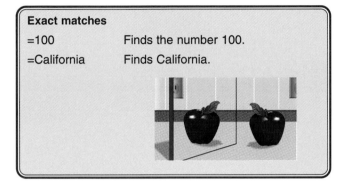

## Less than

| | |
|---|---|
| <100 | Finds numbers less than 100. |
| <1/5/99 | Finds dates before 5-Jan-99. |

## Less than or equal to

| | |
|---|---|
| <=100 | Finds numbers less than or equal to 100. |
| <=1/5/99 | Finds dates on and before 5-Jan-99. |

## Greater than

| | |
|---|---|
| >100 | Finds numbers greater than 100. |
| >1/5/99 | Finds dates after 5-Jan-99. |

## Greater than or equal to

| | |
|---|---|
| >=100 | Finds numbers greater than or equal to 100. |
| >=1/5/99 | Finds dates on and after 5-Jan-99. |

## Not equal to

| | |
|---|---|
| <>California | Finds text not equal to California. |
| <>1/5/99 | Finds dates not on 5-Jan-99. |

## Empty fields

| | |
|---|---|
| Is Null | Finds records that do not contain data in the field. |
| Is Not Null | Finds records that contain data in the field. |

**Last Name**

Carroll

Lessels

Duncan

Thomas

## Find list of items

| | |
|---|---|
| In (100,101) | Finds the numbers 100 and 101. |
| In (#1/5/99#,#1/6/99#) | Finds the dates 5-Jan-99 and 6-Jan-99. |

## Between...And...

| | |
|---|---|
| Between 100 And 200 | Finds numbers from 100 to 200. |
| Between 1/5/99 And 1/15/99 | Finds dates on and between 5-Jan-99 and 15-Jan-99. |

# CREATE A REPORT

You can use the Report Wizard to create a professionally designed report that summarizes data from your database.

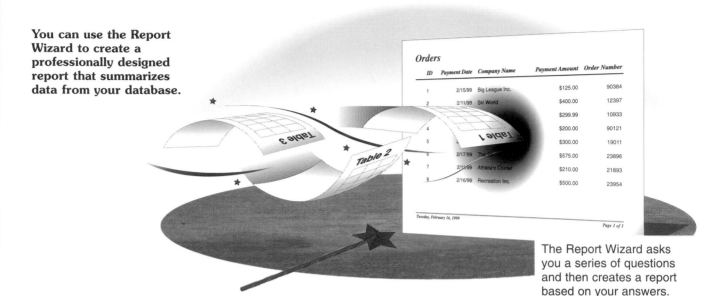

The Report Wizard asks you a series of questions and then creates a report based on your answers.

## CREATE A REPORT

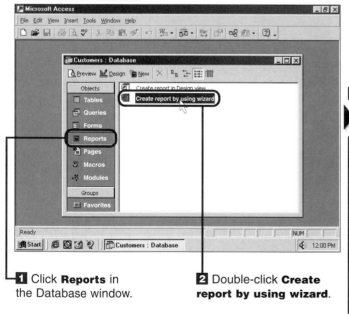

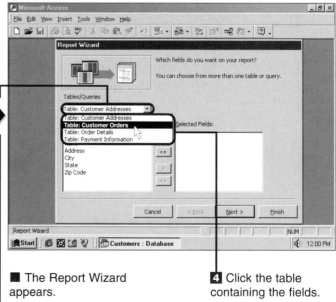

**1** Click **Reports** in the Database window.

**2** Double-click **Create report by using wizard**.

■ The Report Wizard appears.

**3** Click ▼ in this area to select the table containing the fields you want to include in your report.

**4** Click the table containing the fields.

**?** **Why would I group related data together in my report?**

Grouping related data can help you better organize and summarize the data that will appear in your report. For example, you can group data by the State field to place all the clients from the same state together.

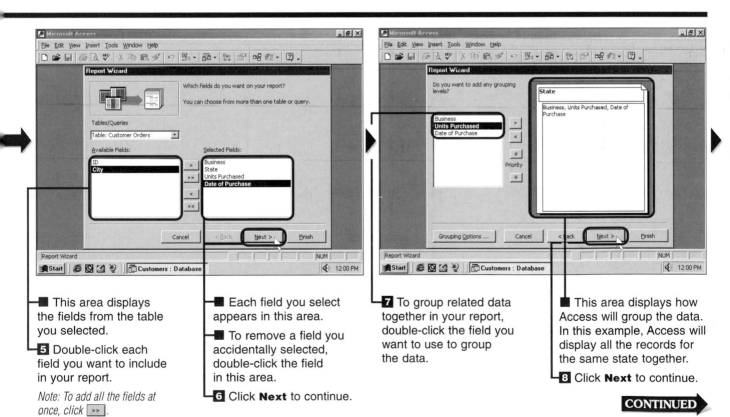

■ This area displays the fields from the table you selected.

**5** Double-click each field you want to include in your report.

*Note: To add all the fields at once, click* >> *.*

■ Each field you select appears in this area.

■ To remove a field you accidentally selected, double-click the field in this area.

**6** Click **Next** to continue.

**7** To group related data together in your report, double-click the field you want to use to group the data.

■ This area displays how Access will group the data. In this example, Access will display all the records for the same state together.

**8** Click **Next** to continue.

CONTINUED

# CREATE A REPORT

You can sort the records in your report to better organize the records.

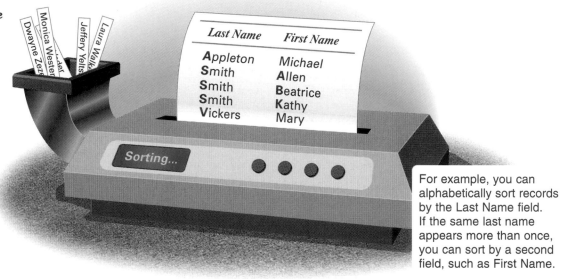

For example, you can alphabetically sort records by the Last Name field. If the same last name appears more than once, you can sort by a second field, such as First Name.

## CREATE A REPORT (CONTINUED)

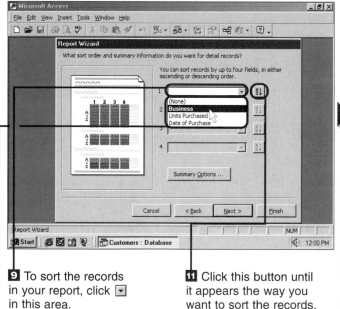

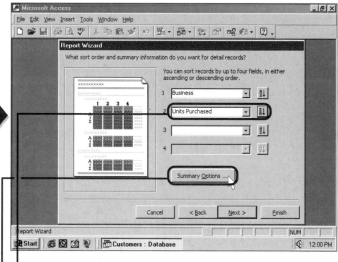

**9** To sort the records in your report, click ▾ in this area.

**10** Click the field you want to use to sort the records.

**11** Click this button until it appears the way you want to sort the records.

▲↓ Sort A to Z, 1 to 9

▲↓ Sort Z to A, 9 to 1

**12** To sort by a second field, repeat steps **9** to **11** in this area.

**13** To show calculations in your report, click **Summary Options**.

*Note: Summary Options may not be available for some reports. If Summary Options is not available, skip to step 18 to continue creating the report.*

■ The Summary Options dialog box appears.

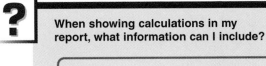

**When showing calculations in my report, what information can I include?**

**Detail and Summary**

Display all the records and the summary. For example, show all orders and the total orders for each month.

**Summary Only**

Display only the summary. For example, show only the total orders for each month.

**Calculate percent of total for sums**

Display the percentage of the total that each group represents. For example, show the percentage of the total orders that each month represents.

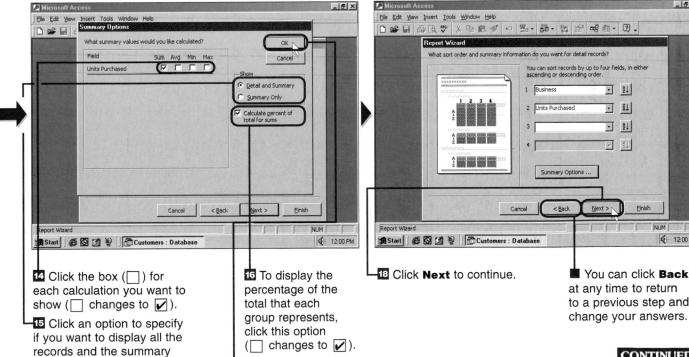

14 Click the box (□) for each calculation you want to show (□ changes to ✔).

15 Click an option to specify if you want to display all the records and the summary or just the summary (○ changes to ⊙).

16 To display the percentage of the total that each group represents, click this option (□ changes to ✔).

17 Click **OK**.

18 Click **Next** to continue.

■ You can click **Back** at any time to return to a previous step and change your answers.

CONTINUED ▶

# CREATE A REPORT

You can choose between several layouts for your report. The layout determines the arrangement of data in your report.

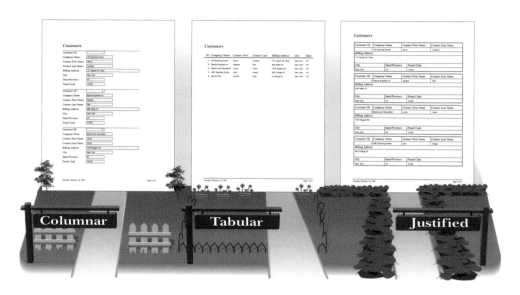

**Columnar**     **Tabular**     **Justified**

## CREATE A REPORT (CONTINUED)

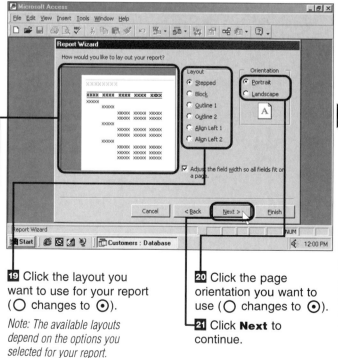

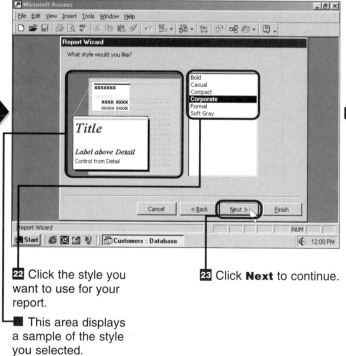

**19** Click the layout you want to use for your report (○ changes to ⊙).

*Note: The available layouts depend on the options you selected for your report.*

■ This area displays a sample of the layout you selected.

**20** Click the page orientation you want to use (○ changes to ⊙).

**21** Click **Next** to continue.

**22** Click the style you want to use for your report.

■ This area displays a sample of the style you selected.

**23** Click **Next** to continue.

**?**

**Do I need to create a new report each time I change the data in my database?**

No. Each time you open your report, Access will automatically gather the most current data from your database. This ensures that the report will always display the most up-to-date information.

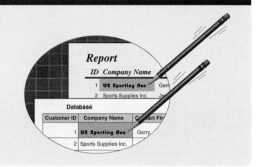

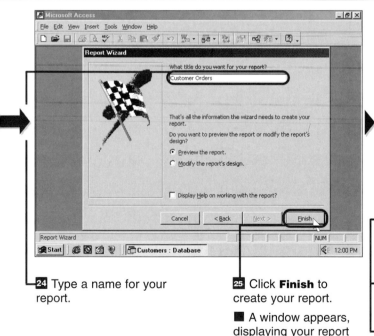

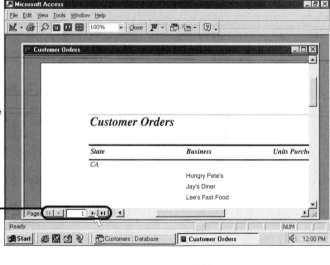

**24** Type a name for your report.

**25** Click **Finish** to create your report.

■ A window appears, displaying your report as it will look when printed.

■ This area shows the number of the page displayed on your screen.

**26** If your report contains more than one page, click one of these buttons to display another page.

|◀ First page

◀ Previous page

▶ Next page

▶| Last page

*Note: If a button is dimmed, the button is currently not available.*

# PRINT A REPORT

You can produce
a paper copy of the
report displayed on
your screen.

You can also use the
method described
below to print a table,
form or query in your
database.

## PRINT A REPORT

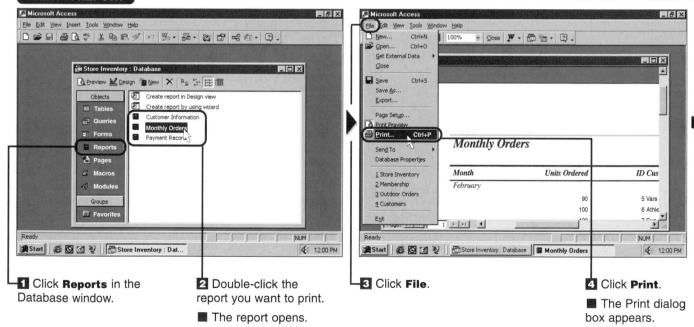

**1** Click **Reports** in the
Database window.

**2** Double-click the
report you want to print.

■ The report opens.

**3** Click **File**.

**4** Click **Print**.

■ The Print dialog
box appears.

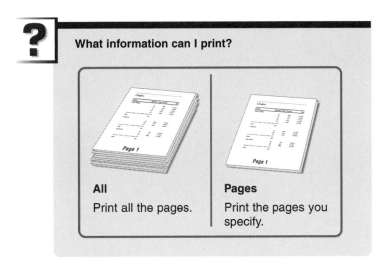

**What information can I print?**

**All**
Print all the pages.

**Pages**
Print the pages you specify.

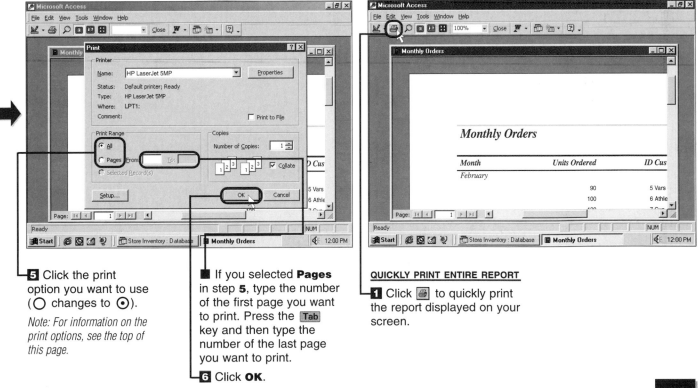

**5** Click the print option you want to use (○ changes to ⊙).

*Note: For information on the print options, see the top of this page.*

■ If you selected **Pages** in step **5**, type the number of the first page you want to print. Press the Tab key and then type the number of the last page you want to print.

**6** Click **OK**.

**QUICKLY PRINT ENTIRE REPORT**

**1** Click 🖨 to quickly print the report displayed on your screen.

# XYZ Corporation Weekly

## Record year for XYZ Corporation

The figures are in, and 1998 has been a record year for XYZ Corporation!

Company President, John Williams, credits his dedicated staff for the successful year.

"Everyone here worked really hard all year, and we have become an industry leader," said an elated Williams.

XYZ Corporation achieved their success by expanding their product line and concentrating on providing excellent customer service.

"We pride ourselves on customer service," said Williams. "We go the extra mile to ensure all our customers are very happy with the service we provide."

There will be a staff party to celebrate the achievement at the Breton Banquet Hall on Feb. 12.

Williams hopes all staff members and their families will be able to attend.

"This is our way of thanking a staff that made this achievement possible," said a proud Williams.

As for this year, there are reasons to believe XYZ Corporation will be even more successful!

The product line will continue to expand, and the company is growing rapidly.

*XYZ Corporation's logo, above, has become very well known as the company continues to expand.*

"We look forward to following up this record year with another excellent year," said Williams.

XYZ Corporation has become an industry leader, and the future looks bright for this company and its employees.

## XYZ Corporation Opens Doors to Public

XYZ Corporation has opened its doors to its future employees, by offering tours of the company to schools and interested members of the public.

Liz Brown, Public Relations Director, said tours will enable people to see how the company operates on a day-to-day basis and get a better understanding of how the company works.

"This is a great opportunity for young people and people in the community to see what we do here and how efficiently and safely we do it," said Brown. Tours will begin next month, and run continuously throughout the year.

So far, feedback from the community has been excellent, and several groups have already signed up for tours.

Photo

A weekly new
for the pho
enthusiast!

# Using Publisher

**Brown's**

**Brown's Construction**
124 King St. West • Los Angeles, CA • 90052

**Lloyd Brown**
*Owner*

Phone: 213 555 5205

# INTRODUCTION TO PUBLISHER

**Publisher is a desktop publishing program that helps you design professional publications.**

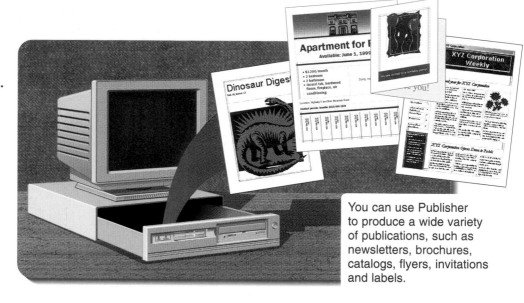

You can use Publisher to produce a wide variety of publications, such as newsletters, brochures, catalogs, flyers, invitations and labels.

### Creating Publications

Publisher provides wizards that can help you create publications. A wizard provides sample text and formatting for a publication so you can concentrate on the content.

When you want more control over the layout and design of a publication, you can create a blank publication. Publisher can help you make changes to a blank publication. For example, you can quickly change the overall design or color scheme.

### Adding Objects to Publications

You can enhance a publication by adding pictures stored on your computer or professionally designed clip art images. You can also add text effects to emphasize titles in your publication. After you add an object to your publication, you can move or size the object to suit your needs.

# START PUBLISHER

You can start Publisher to create a professional publication.

## START PUBLISHER

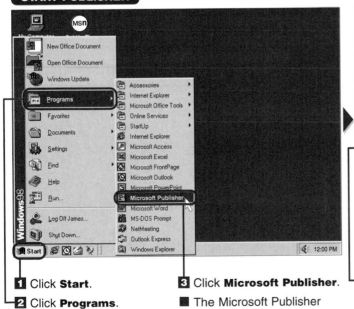

**1** Click **Start**.

**2** Click **Programs**.

**3** Click **Microsoft Publisher**.

■ The Microsoft Publisher window appears.

■ The Catalog dialog box appears each time you start Publisher, allowing you to create or open a publication.

*Note: To create a publication, see page 324 or 328. To open a publication, see page 332.*

# CREATE A PUBLICATION USING A WIZARD

You can use a wizard to create a publication. Publisher offers wizards to help you create many types of publications, such as newsletters, brochures and advertisements.

A wizard guides you step by step through the process of creating a publication. A wizard also provides the layout and formatting for a publication so you can concentrate on the content.

## CREATE A PUBLICATION USING A WIZARD

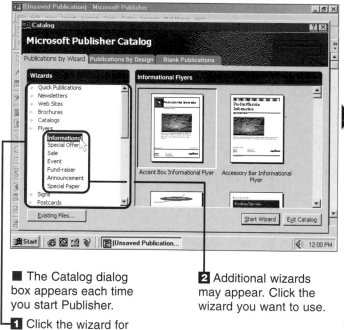

■ The Catalog dialog box appears each time you start Publisher.

**1** Click the wizard for the type of publication you want to create.

**2** Additional wizards may appear. Click the wizard you want to use.

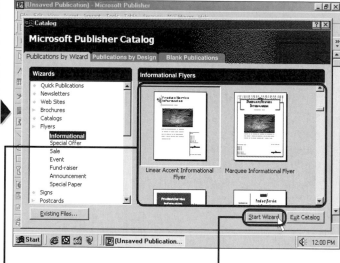

■ This area displays the available designs for the wizard you selected.

**3** Click the design you want to use.

**4** Click **Start Wizard**.

**?** **Why does a dialog box appear, asking for my personal information?**

Publisher asks you to provide your personal information the first time you use a wizard. Personal information includes items such as your name, address and telephone number. Many wizards use your personal information in the publications you create. Click **OK** to display the Personal Information dialog box and enter your personal information.

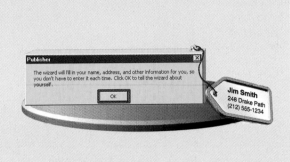

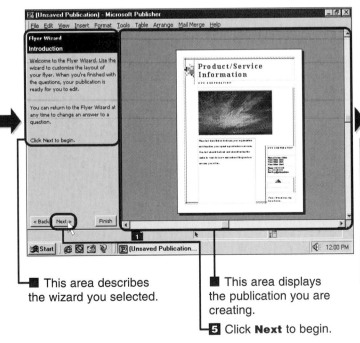

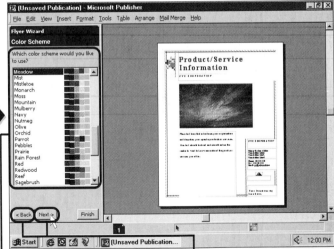

■ This area describes the wizard you selected.

■ This area displays the publication you are creating.

**5** Click **Next** to begin.

**6** Answer each question asked by the wizard. Each wizard will ask you a different set of questions.

■ The results of the choices you make instantly appear in the publication.

**7** When you finish answering a question, click **Next** to continue.

■ You can click **Back** at any time to return to a previous step and change your answers.

CONTINUED ▶

# CREATE A PUBLICATION USING A WIZARD

When you finish creating your publication, you can use the wizard to make quick changes to the publication.

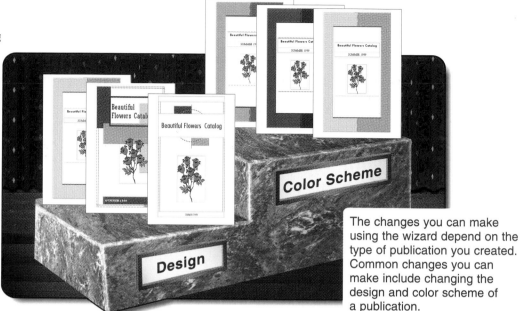

The changes you can make using the wizard depend on the type of publication you created. Common changes you can make include changing the design and color scheme of a publication.

## CREATE A PUBLICATION USING A WIZARD (CONTINUED)

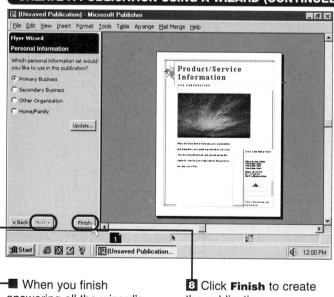

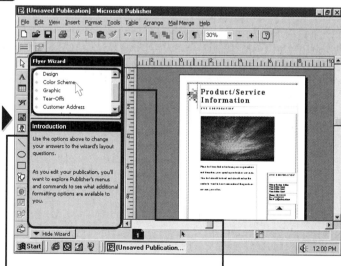

■ When you finish answering all the wizard's questions, the **Next** button becomes dimmed.

**8** Click **Finish** to create the publication.

■ Publisher creates the publication.

■ This area displays the wizard. You can use the wizard to make quick changes to the publication.

**9** This area displays each topic you covered in the wizard. To once again view the options for a topic, click the topic.

**?**

**Why does a yellow box appear on my screen when I am working with my publication?**

As you work with your publication, Publisher may display a yellow box containing a tip that can help you work more efficiently. You can click outside the yellow box to hide the tip.

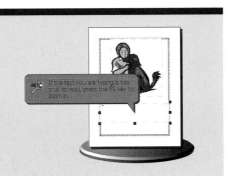

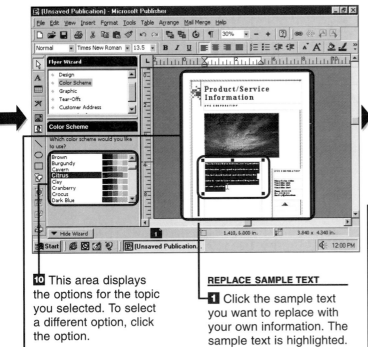

**10** This area displays the options for the topic you selected. To select a different option, click the option.

■ The publication displays the change.

**REPLACE SAMPLE TEXT**

**1** Click the sample text you want to replace with your own information. The sample text is highlighted.

**2** Press the `F9` key to increase the size of the publication so you can clearly view the text you type.

■ The sample text appears magnified.

**3** Type the text you want to appear in the publication.

**4** When you finish typing the text, press the `F9` key again so you can clearly view the publication.

# CREATE A BLANK PUBLICATION

If you want to design your own publication, you can create a blank publication. Creating a blank publication gives you the most flexibility and control.

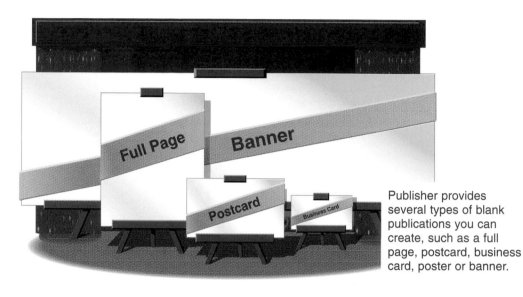

Publisher provides several types of blank publications you can create, such as a full page, postcard, business card, poster or banner.

## CREATE A BLANK PUBLICATION

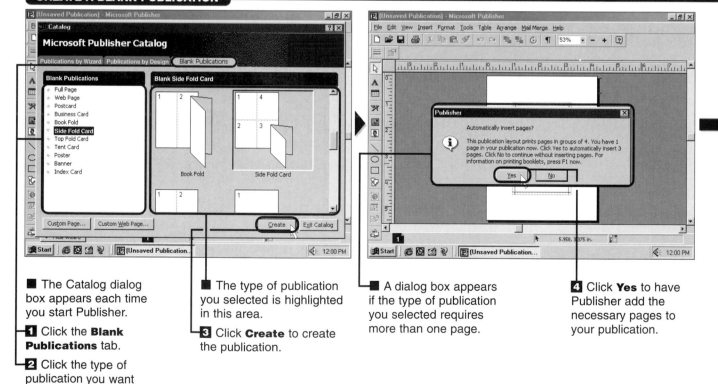

■ The Catalog dialog box appears each time you start Publisher.

**1** Click the **Blank Publications** tab.

**2** Click the type of publication you want to create.

■ The type of publication you selected is highlighted in this area.

**3** Click **Create** to create the publication.

■ A dialog box appears if the type of publication you selected requires more than one page.

**4** Click **Yes** to have Publisher add the necessary pages to your publication.

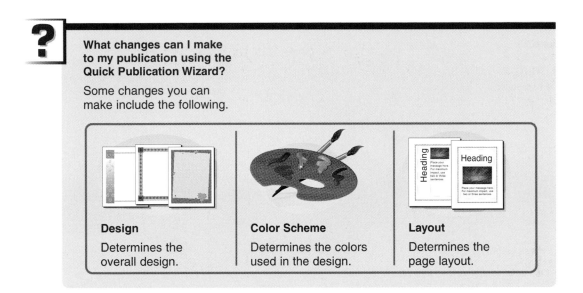

**?**

**What changes can I make to my publication using the Quick Publication Wizard?**

Some changes you can make include the following.

**Design**
Determines the overall design.

**Color Scheme**
Determines the colors used in the design.

**Layout**
Determines the page layout.

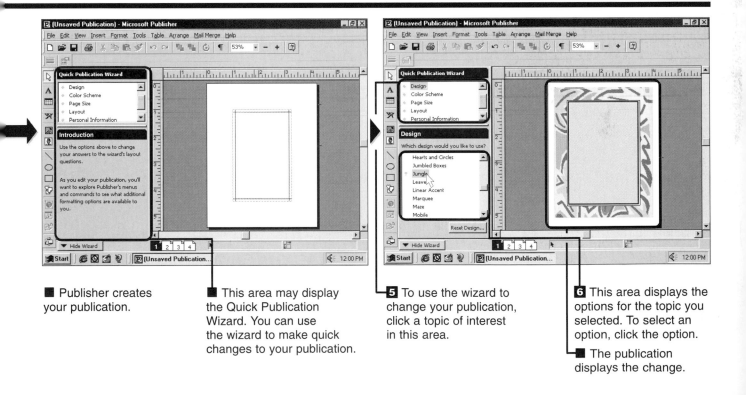

■ Publisher creates your publication.

■ This area may display the Quick Publication Wizard. You can use the wizard to make quick changes to your publication.

**5** To use the wizard to change your publication, click a topic of interest in this area.

**6** This area displays the options for the topic you selected. To select an option, click the option.

■ The publication displays the change.

# SAVE A PUBLICATION

You can save your
publication to store
it for future use.
This allows you to
later review and
make changes to
the publication.

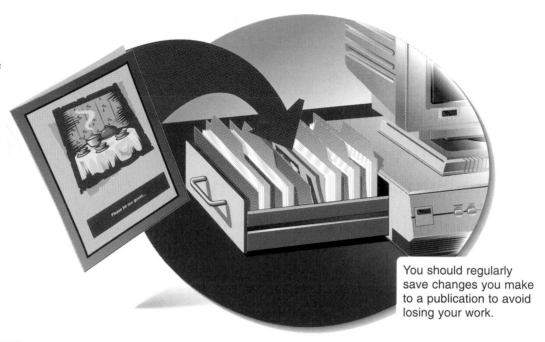

You should regularly
save changes you make
to a publication to avoid
losing your work.

## SAVE A PUBLICATION

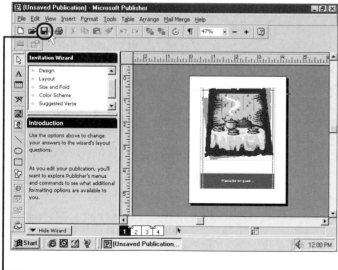

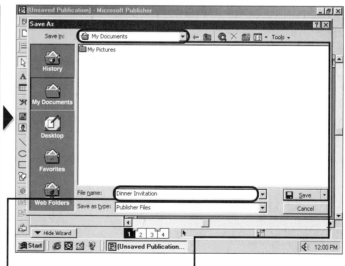

**1** Click 🖫 to save
your publication.

■ The Save As dialog
box appears.

*Note: If you previously saved
your publication, the Save As
dialog box will not appear
since you have already
named the publication.*

**2** Type a name for
the publication.

■ This area shows the
location where Publisher
will store your publication.
You can click this area to
change the location.

**?** **What are the commonly used folders I can access?**

**History**

Provides access to folders and publications you recently used.

**My Documents**

Provides a convenient place to store a publication.

**Desktop**

Lets you store a publication on the Windows desktop.

**Favorites**

Provides a place to store a publication you will frequently access.

**Web Folders**

Can help you store a publication on the Web.

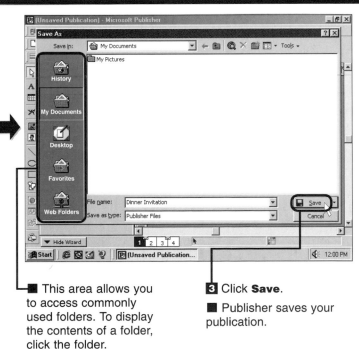

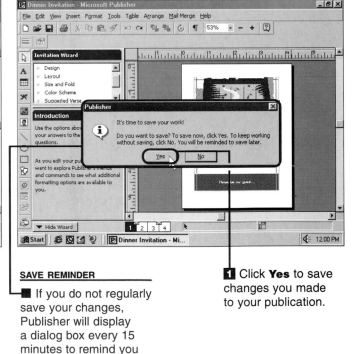

■ This area allows you to access commonly used folders. To display the contents of a folder, click the folder.

**3** Click **Save**.

■ Publisher saves your publication.

**SAVE REMINDER**

■ If you do not regularly save your changes, Publisher will display a dialog box every 15 minutes to remind you to save your publication.

**1** Click **Yes** to save changes you made to your publication.

# OPEN A PUBLICATION

You can open a saved publication and display it on your screen. This lets you review and make changes to the publication.

You can have only one publication open at a time. Publisher will close a publication displayed on your screen when you open another publication.

## OPEN A PUBLICATION

■ The Catalog dialog box appears each time you start Publisher.

**1** Click **Existing Files** to open a publication you previously created.

■ The Open Publication dialog box appears.

■ This area shows the location of the displayed publications. You can click this area to change the location.

■ This area allows you to access commonly used folders. To display the contents of a folder, click the folder.

*Note: For information on the commonly used folders, see the top of page 331.*

**?**

**While working in Publisher, can I quickly open a publication I recently worked with?**

Publisher remembers the names of the last four publications you worked with. You can quickly open one of these publications.

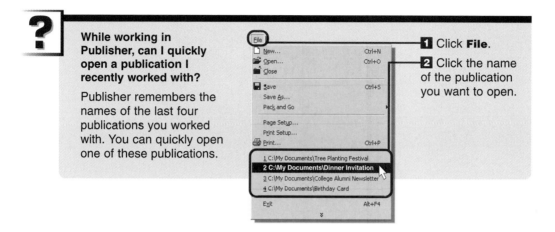

**1** Click **File**.

**2** Click the name of the publication you want to open.

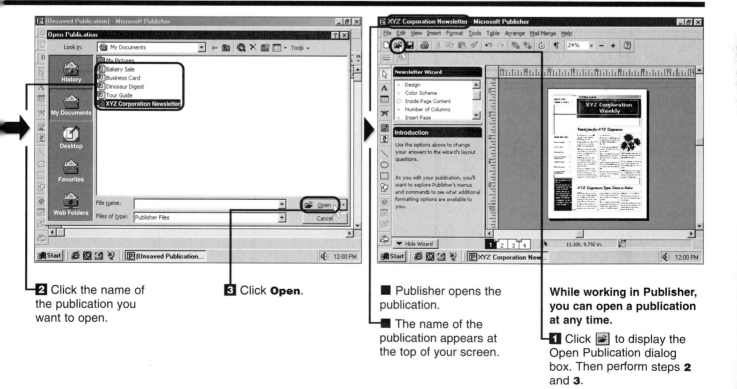

**2** Click the name of the publication you want to open.

**3** Click **Open**.

■ Publisher opens the publication.

■ The name of the publication appears at the top of your screen.

**While working in Publisher, you can open a publication at any time.**

**1** Click 📂 to display the Open Publication dialog box. Then perform steps **2** and **3**.

# ADD A NEW PAGE

You can add a
new page to your
publication to
include additional
information.

## ADD A NEW PAGE

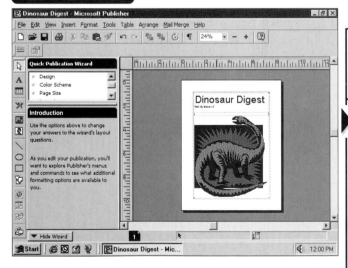

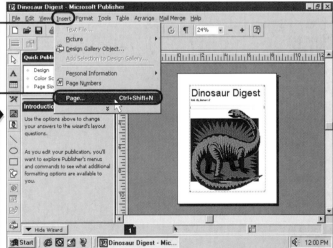

**1** Display the page you
want to appear before
or after a new page.

*Note: To move through the
pages in your publication,
see page 336.*

**2** Click **Insert**.

**3** Click **Page**.

■ The Insert Page dialog
box appears.

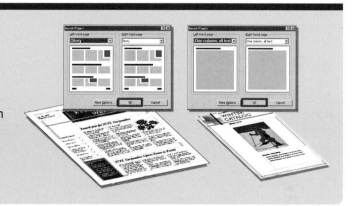

**?**

**Why does the Insert Page dialog box look different on my screen?**

The appearance of the Insert Page dialog box depends on the type of publication you are working with. Publications such as newsletters, Web sites and catalogs display a different dialog box. Click **OK** to add a new page to your publication.

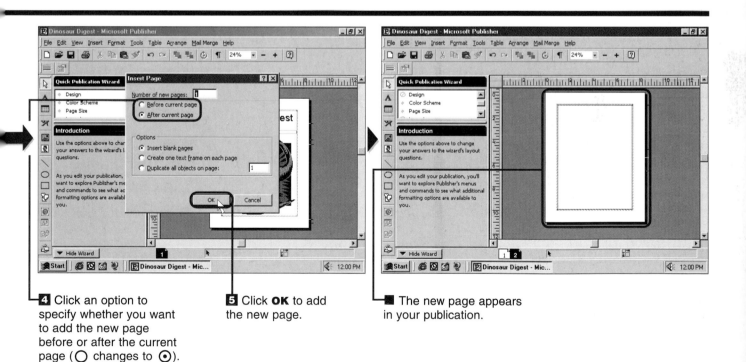

**4** Click an option to specify whether you want to add the new page before or after the current page (○ changes to ⊙).

**5** Click **OK** to add the new page.

■ The new page appears in your publication.

# MOVE THROUGH PAGES

If your publication contains more than one page, you can easily display the contents of another page.

MOVE THROUGH PAGES

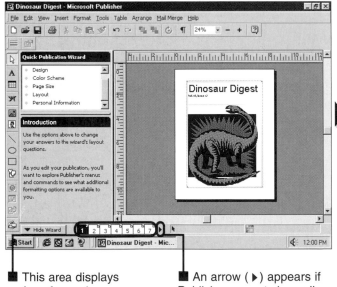

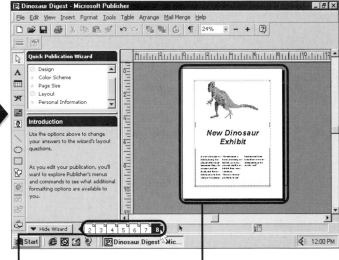

■ This area displays an icon for each page in your publication. The icon for the current page is highlighted.

■ An arrow ( ▶ ) appears if Publisher cannot show all the page icons. You can click the arrow to display the other page icons.

**1** Click the icon for the page you want to view.

■ The page you selected appears.

*Note: Two pages may appear on your screen if your publication has facing pages like those in a book. Publications such as newsletters and catalogs often have facing pages.*

# PRINT A PUBLICATION

**You can produce a paper copy of your publication.**

Before printing, you should make sure your printer contains the type and size of paper your publication requires. For example, you may want to use specialty paper to print a postcard. The type and size of paper you can use depends on your printer.

## PRINT A PUBLICATION

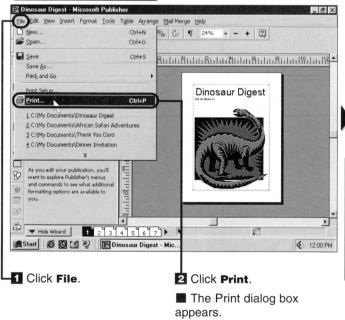

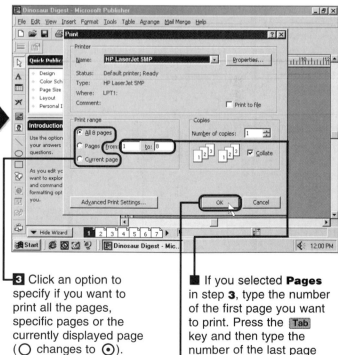

**1** Click **File**.

**2** Click **Print**.

■ The Print dialog box appears.

**3** Click an option to specify if you want to print all the pages, specific pages or the currently displayed page (○ changes to ⊙).

■ If you selected **Pages** in step **3**, type the number of the first page you want to print. Press the `Tab` key and then type the number of the last page you want to print.

**4** Click **OK**.

# ADD A TEXT FRAME

Before you can
add text to your
publication, you
must first add
a text frame to
hold the text.

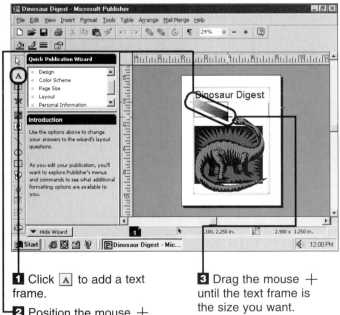

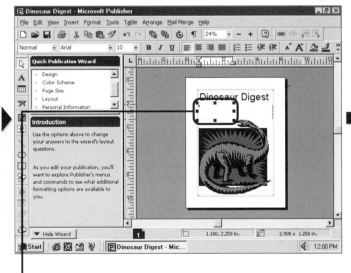

**1** Click ▲ to add a text
frame.

**2** Position the mouse ＋
where you want to begin
drawing the text frame.

**3** Drag the mouse ＋
until the text frame is
the size you want.

■ The text frame appears
in the publication.

**4** Press the F9 key
to increase the size of
the publication so you
can clearly view the
text you type.

338

**?**

**Why does the [A···] symbol appear at the bottom of the text frame I am working with?**

When you type more text than a text frame can hold, Publisher displays the overflow indicator ([A···]). You can increase the size of the text frame to display the extra text. To size a text frame, see page 347.

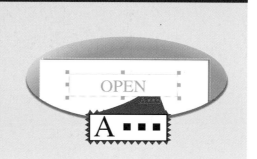

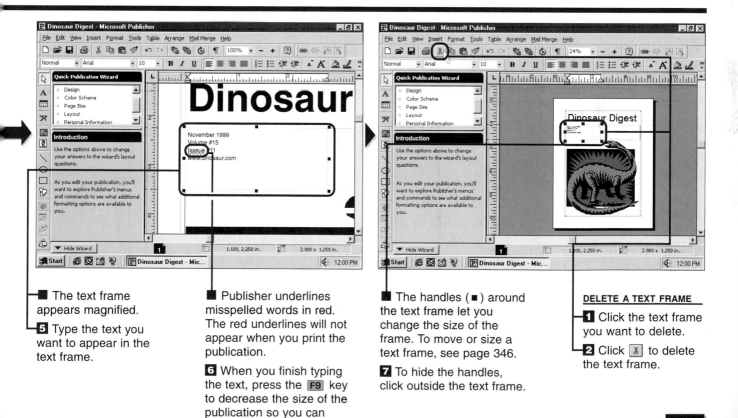

■ The text frame appears magnified.

**5** Type the text you want to appear in the text frame.

■ Publisher underlines misspelled words in red. The red underlines will not appear when you print the publication.

**6** When you finish typing the text, press the **F9** key to decrease the size of the publication so you can clearly view the publication.

■ The handles (■) around the text frame let you change the size of the frame. To move or size a text frame, see page 346.

**7** To hide the handles, click outside the text frame.

**DELETE A TEXT FRAME**

**1** Click the text frame you want to delete.

**2** Click [✂] to delete the text frame.

# ADD CLIP ART

You can add a clip art image to your publication to make your publication more interesting or help express an idea.

**BEAUTIFUL FLOWERS CATALOG**

**SUMMER 1999**

Publisher provides thousands of clip art images that you can choose from.

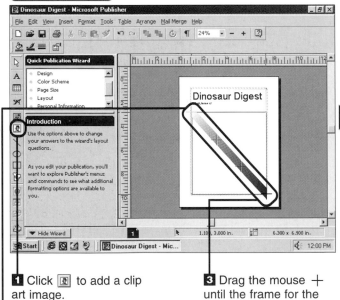

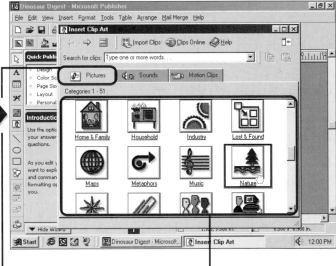

**1** Click  to add a clip art image.

**2** Position the mouse + where you want to begin drawing the frame for the clip art image.

**3** Drag the mouse + until the frame for the clip art image is the size you want.

■ The Insert Clip Art window appears.

**4** Click the **Pictures** tab.

**5** Click the category of clip art images you want to display.

■ The clip art images in the category you selected appear.

**Where can I find more clip art images?**

If you are connected to the Internet, you can visit Microsoft's Clip Gallery Live Web site to find additional clip art images. In the Insert Clip Art window, click **Clips Online**. In the dialog box that appears, click **OK** to connect to the Web site.

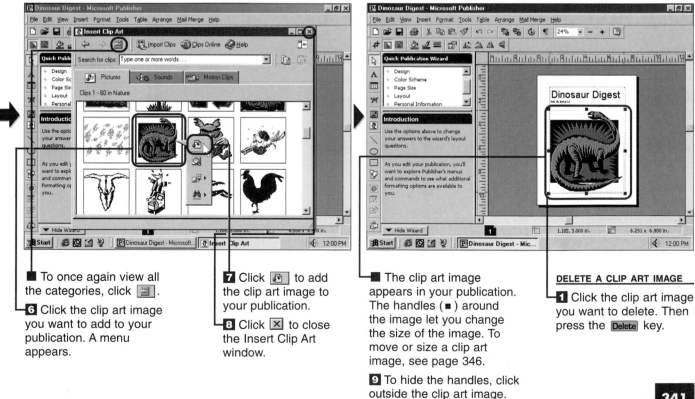

■ To once again view all the categories, click 🔠 .

**6** Click the clip art image you want to add to your publication. A menu appears.

**7** Click 🔊 to add the clip art image to your publication.

**8** Click ✕ to close the Insert Clip Art window.

■ The clip art image appears in your publication. The handles ( ■ ) around the image let you change the size of the image. To move or size a clip art image, see page 346.

**9** To hide the handles, click outside the clip art image.

**DELETE A CLIP ART IMAGE**

**1** Click the clip art image you want to delete. Then press the Delete key.

# ADD A PICTURE

You can add a
picture stored on
your computer to
your publication.

Adding a picture is useful
if you want to display
your company logo or
a favorite photograph
in your publication.

## ADD A PICTURE

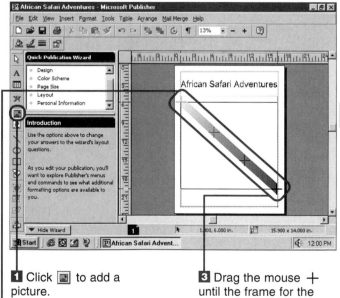

**1** Click 🖻 to add a
picture.

**2** Position the mouse +
where you want to begin
drawing the frame for the
picture.

**3** Drag the mouse +
until the frame for the
picture is the size you
want.

**4** Double-click inside
the frame for the picture.

■ The Insert Picture
dialog box appears.

■ This area shows
the location of the
displayed files. You
can click this area to
change the location.

■ This area allows you
to access commonly
used folders. To display
the contents of a folder,
click the folder.

*Note: For information on the
commonly used folders, see
the top of page 331.*

**?**

**Where can I get pictures to use in my publications?**

You can use a drawing program to create your own pictures or use a scanner to scan pictures into your computer. You can also find collections of pictures at most computer stores and on the Internet.

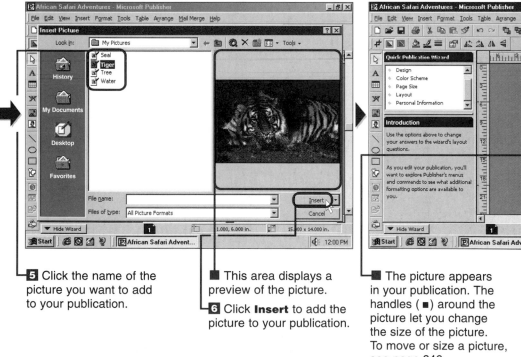

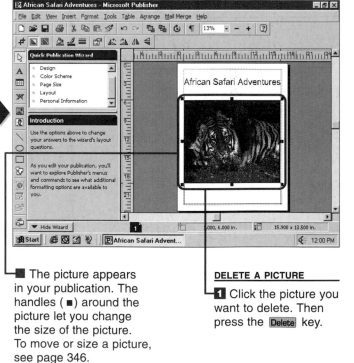

**5** Click the name of the picture you want to add to your publication.

■ This area displays a preview of the picture.

**6** Click **Insert** to add the picture to your publication.

■ The picture appears in your publication. The handles ( ■ ) around the picture let you change the size of the picture. To move or size a picture, see page 346.

**7** To hide the handles, click outside the picture.

**DELETE A PICTURE**

**1** Click the picture you want to delete. Then press the Delete key.

# ADD A TEXT EFFECT

You can add a text effect
to your publication to
enhance the appearance
of a title or draw
attention to important
information.

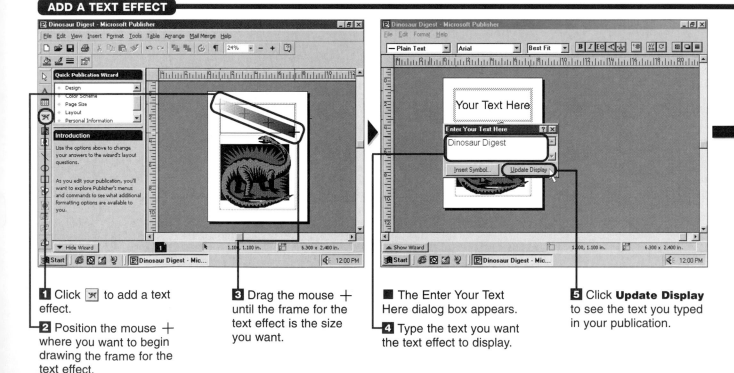

**1** Click 🕱 to add a text
effect.

**2** Position the mouse +
where you want to begin
drawing the frame for the
text effect.

**3** Drag the mouse +
until the frame for the
text effect is the size
you want.

■ The Enter Your Text
Here dialog box appears.

**4** Type the text you want
the text effect to display.

**5** Click **Update Display**
to see the text you typed
in your publication.

**Can I change the text displayed in a text effect?**

Yes. Double-click the text effect to redisplay the Enter Your Text Here dialog box. Type the new text and then click a blank area on your screen.

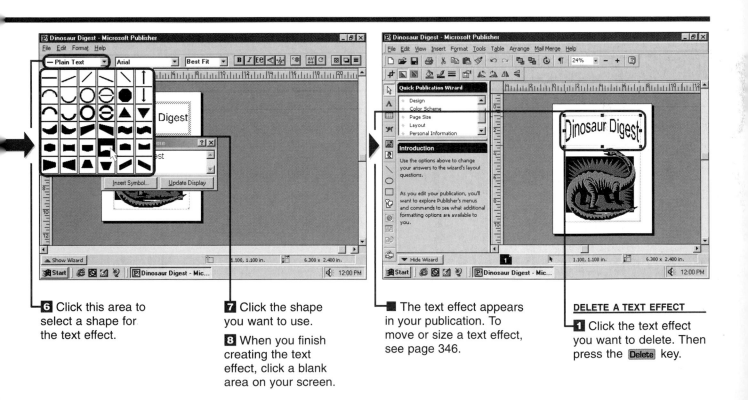

**6** Click this area to select a shape for the text effect.

**7** Click the shape you want to use.

**8** When you finish creating the text effect, click a blank area on your screen.

■ The text effect appears in your publication. To move or size a text effect, see page 346.

**DELETE A TEXT EFFECT**

**1** Click the text effect you want to delete. Then press the Delete key.

# MOVE OR SIZE AN OBJECT

**You can change the location or size of an object in your publication.**

For example, you may want to increase the size of a text frame to display more text or move a picture to a new location.

## MOVE AN OBJECT

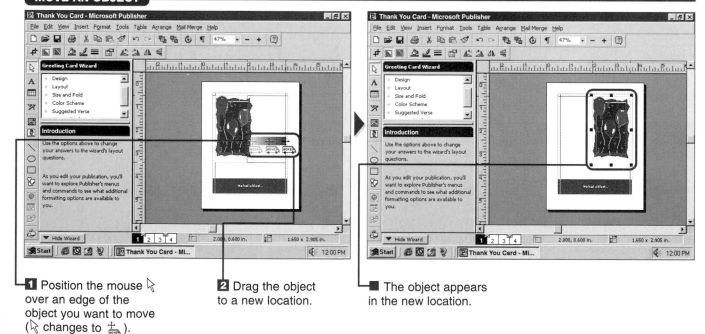

**1** Position the mouse ⌖ over an edge of the object you want to move (⌖ changes to ⊞).

**2** Drag the object to a new location.

■ The object appears in the new location.

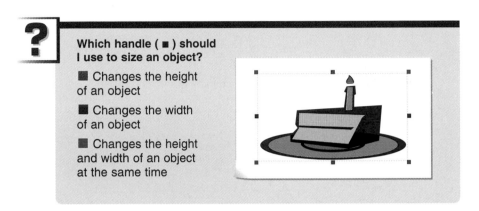

**?** **Which handle ( ■ ) should I use to size an object?**

■ Changes the height of an object

■ Changes the width of an object

■ Changes the height and width of an object at the same time

## SIZE AN OBJECT

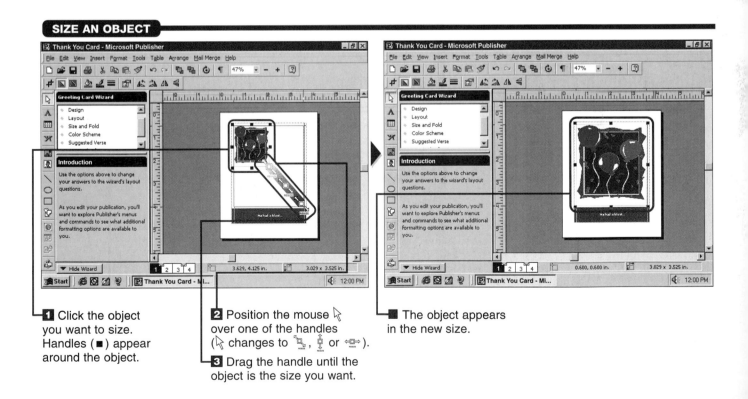

**1** Click the object you want to size. Handles (■) appear around the object.

**2** Position the mouse over one of the handles ( changes to , or ).

**3** Drag the handle until the object is the size you want.

■ The object appears in the new size.

# Using Outlook

| Time | Activities |
|------|-----------|
| 9:00 | Sales meeting |
| | Lunch with Neil |

12

Outlook can help you manage your e-mail messages, appointments, contacts, tasks and notes.

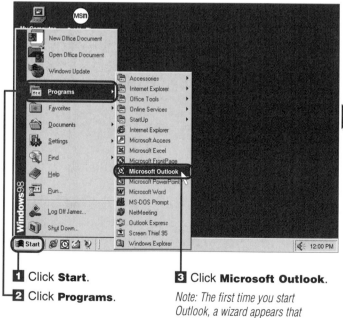

**1** Click **Start**.

**2** Click **Programs**.

**3** Click **Microsoft Outlook**.

*Note: The first time you start Outlook, a wizard appears that allows you to set up Outlook on your computer. Follow the instructions on your screen to set up Outlook.*

■ The Microsoft Outlook window appears.

■ The Office Assistant welcome also appears the first time you start Outlook.

*Note: For information on the Office Assistant, see page 14.*

**4** To maximize the window to fill your screen, click ▢.

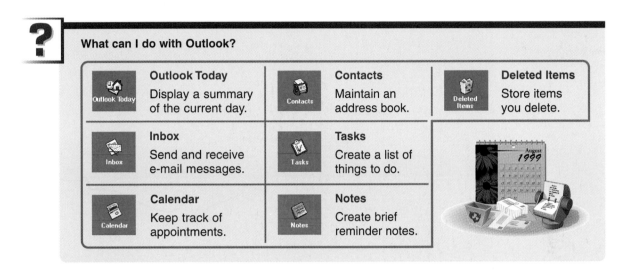

## ? What can I do with Outlook?

**Outlook Today**
Display a summary of the current day.

**Contacts**
Maintain an address book.

**Deleted Items**
Store items you delete.

**Inbox**
Send and receive e-mail messages.

**Tasks**
Create a list of things to do.

**Calendar**
Keep track of appointments.

**Notes**
Create brief reminder notes.

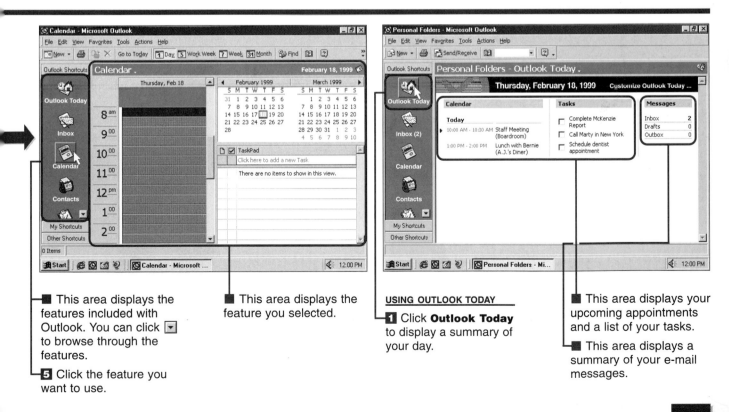

■ This area displays the features included with Outlook. You can click ▼ to browse through the features.

**5** Click the feature you want to use.

■ This area displays the feature you selected.

USING OUTLOOK TODAY

**1** Click **Outlook Today** to display a summary of your day.

■ This area displays your upcoming appointments and a list of your tasks.

■ This area displays a summary of your e-mail messages.

# READ A MESSAGE

The Inbox stores all the e-mail messages you receive. You can display the contents of a message to read the message.

## READ A MESSAGE

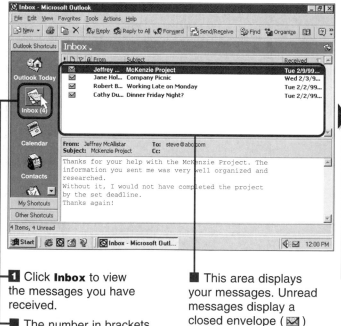

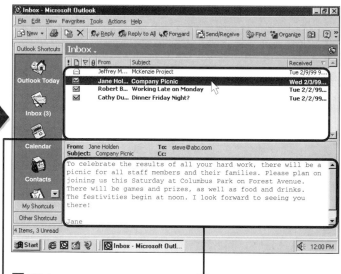

**1** Click **Inbox** to view the messages you have received.

■ The number in brackets beside the Inbox indicates the number of messages you have not read.

■ This area displays your messages. Unread messages display a closed envelope (📩) and appear in **bold**.

**2** Click a message you want to read.

■ This area displays the contents of the message.

■ To view the contents of another message, click the message.

352

# DISPLAY THE MAIL FOLDERS

**Outlook uses three mail folders to store e-mail messages you have created.**

Drafts — Stores messages you have not completed.

Outbox — Temporarily stores messages that have not yet been sent.

Sent Items — Stores copies of messages you have sent.

## DISPLAY THE MAIL FOLDERS

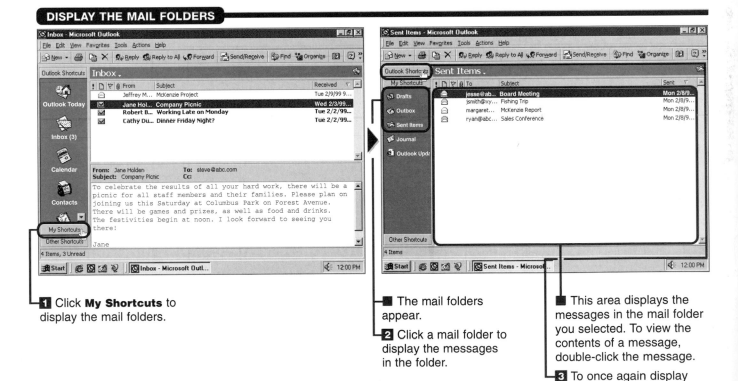

**1** Click **My Shortcuts** to display the mail folders.

■ The mail folders appear.

**2** Click a mail folder to display the messages in the folder.

■ This area displays the messages in the mail folder you selected. To view the contents of a message, double-click the message.

**3** To once again display the Outlook features and hide the mail folders, click **Outlook Shortcuts**.

# CREATE A MESSAGE

You can create and
send an e-mail message
to exchange ideas or
request information.

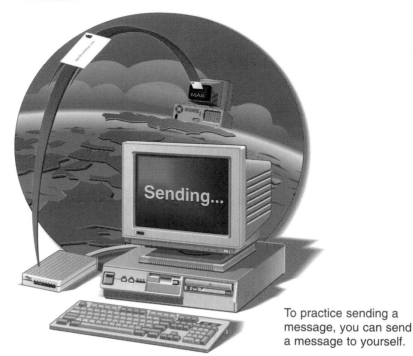

To practice sending a
message, you can send
a message to yourself.

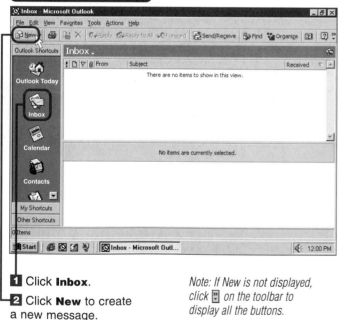

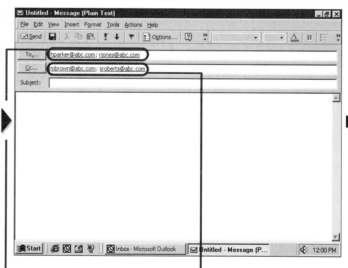

**1** Click **Inbox**.

**2** Click **New** to create
a new message.

*Note: If New is not displayed,
click ⯮ on the toolbar to
display all the buttons.*

■ A window appears
for you to compose
the message.

**3** Type the e-mail address
of each person you want
to receive the message.
Separate each address
with a semicolon (;).

**4** To send a copy of the
message, click this area
and then type the e-mail
address of each person
you want to receive a copy.
Separate each address
with a semicolon (;).

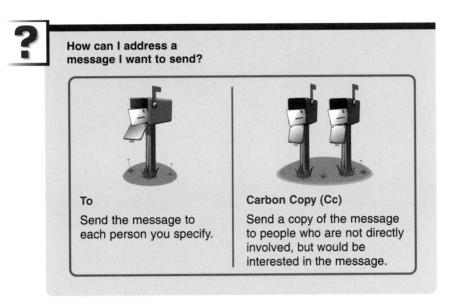

**How can I address a message I want to send?**

**To**

Send the message to each person you specify.

**Carbon Copy (Cc)**

Send a copy of the message to people who are not directly involved, but would be interested in the message.

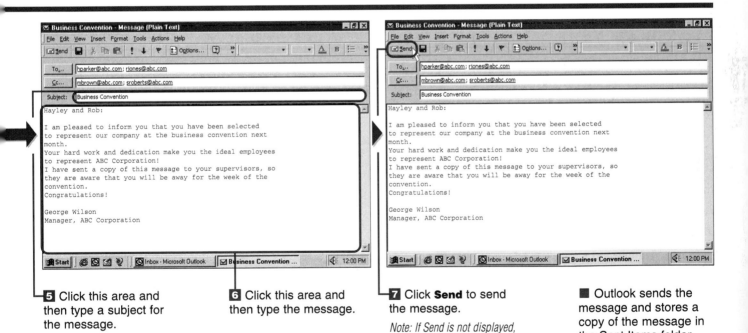

**5** Click this area and then type a subject for the message.

**6** Click this area and then type the message.

**7** Click **Send** to send the message.

*Note: If Send is not displayed, click ⏹ on the Standard toolbar to display all the buttons.*

■ Outlook sends the message and stores a copy of the message in the Sent Items folder.

*Note: To display the messages in the Sent Items folder, see page 353.*

# ATTACH A FILE TO A MESSAGE

You can attach a file
to a message you are
sending. Attaching a
file is useful when
you want to include
additional information
with a message.

To:
Cc:
Subject:

*Fishing Derby Winner*

Congratulations on your
achievement! I'm looking forward
to seeing you at the awards
ceremony! I've also included photos
from the event in an attached file.

**1** To create a message,
perform steps **1** to **6**
starting on page 354.

**2** Click 📎 to attach
a file to the message.

*Note: If 📎 is not
displayed, click 》 on
the Standard toolbar to
display all the buttons.*

■ The Insert File
dialog box appears.

■ This area shows the
location of the displayed
files. You can click this
area to change the
location.

**3** Click the name of the
file you want to attach
to the message.

**4** Click **Insert** to attach
the file to the message.

**?**

**What types of files can I attach to a message?**

You can attach many different types of files to a message, including documents, pictures, videos, sound recordings and programs. The computer receiving the message must have the necessary hardware and software installed to display or play the file you attach.

Attachments

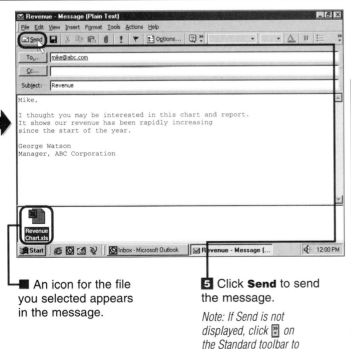

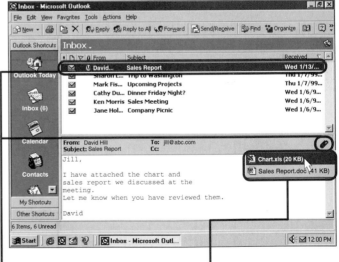

■ An icon for the file you selected appears in the message.

**5** Click **Send** to send the message.

*Note: If Send is not displayed, click ⯮ on the Standard toolbar to display all the buttons.*

**VIEW AN ATTACHED FILE**

**1** Click a message with an attached file. A message with an attached file displays a paper clip icon ( 📎 ).

**2** Click this area to display a list of the files attached to the message.

**3** Click the name of the file you want to view.

■ A dialog box may appear, asking if you want to open or save the file.

# REPLY TO A MESSAGE

You can reply to a message to answer a question, express an opinion or supply additional information.

## REPLY TO A MESSAGE

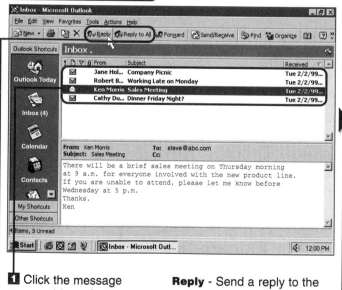

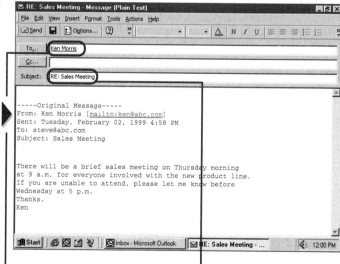

**1** Click the message you want to reply to.

**2** Click one of the following buttons.

**Reply** - Send a reply to the author only.

**Reply to All** - Send a reply to the author and everyone who received the original message.

*Note: If the button you want is not displayed, click ⯆ on the toolbar to display all the buttons.*

■ A window appears for you to compose your reply.

■ Outlook fills in the e-mail address(es) for you.

■ Outlook also fills in the subject, starting the subject with **RE:**.

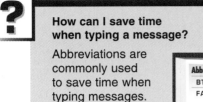

**How can I save time when typing a message?**

Abbreviations are commonly used to save time when typing messages.

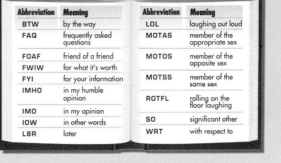

| Abbreviation | Meaning |
|---|---|
| BTW | by the way |
| FAQ | frequently asked questions |
| FOAF | friend of a friend |
| FWIW | for what it's worth |
| FYI | for your information |
| IMHO | in my humble opinion |
| IMO | in my opinion |
| IOW | in other words |
| L8R | later |

| Abbreviation | Meaning |
|---|---|
| LOL | laughing out loud |
| MOTAS | member of the appropriate sex |
| MOTOS | member of the opposite sex |
| MOTSS | member of the same sex |
| ROTFL | rolling on the floor laughing |
| SO | significant other |
| WRT | with respect to |

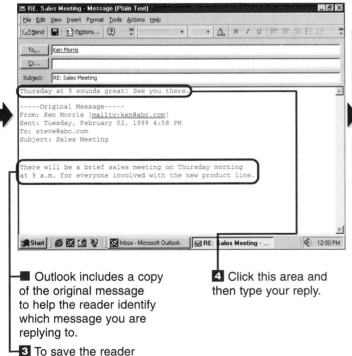

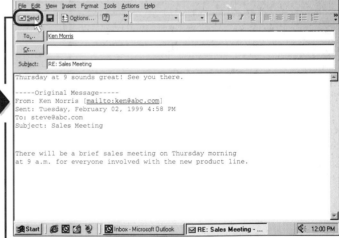

■ Outlook includes a copy of the original message to help the reader identify which message you are replying to.

**3** To save the reader time, delete all parts of the original message that do not directly relate to your reply.

**4** Click this area and then type your reply.

**5** Click **Send** to send the reply.

*Note: If Send is not displayed, click 📄 on the Standard toolbar to display all the buttons.*

■ Outlook sends the reply and stores a copy of the reply in the Sent Items folder.

*Note: To display the messages in the Sent Items folder, see page 353.*

# FORWARD A MESSAGE

After reading a message you received, you can add comments and then send the message to a friend, family member or colleague.

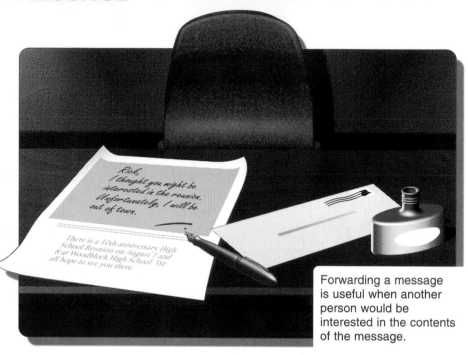

Forwarding a message is useful when another person would be interested in the contents of the message.

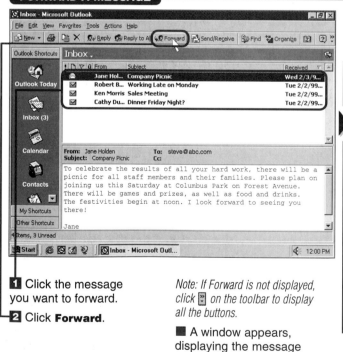

**1** Click the message you want to forward.

**2** Click **Forward**.

*Note: If Forward is not displayed, click ⏷ on the toolbar to display all the buttons.*

■ A window appears, displaying the message you are forwarding.

**3** Type the e-mail address of the person you want to receive the message.

■ Outlook fills in the subject for you, starting the subject with **FW:**.

**4** Click this area and then type any comments about the message.

**5** Click **Send** to forward the message.

*Note: If Send is not displayed, click ⏷ on the Standard toolbar to display all the buttons.*

# DELETE A MESSAGE

You can delete a message you no longer need. Deleting messages prevents your folders from becoming cluttered with messages.

## DELETE A MESSAGE

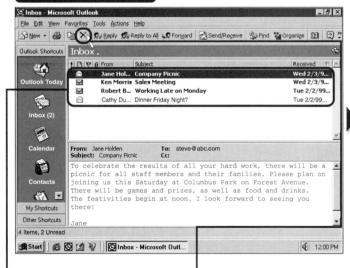

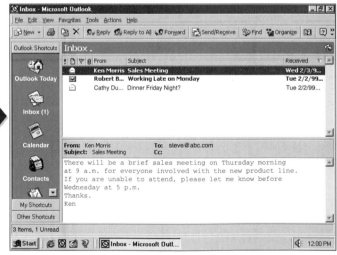

**1** Click the message you want to delete.

**2** Click ⊠ to delete the message.

*Note: If ⊠ is not displayed, click ⊞ on the toolbar to display all the buttons.*

■ The message disappears.

■ Outlook places the message in the Deleted Items folder. For information on the Deleted Items folder, see page 374.

# USING THE CALENDAR

You can use the Calendar to keep track of your appointments, such as meetings, lunch dates or dentist appointments.

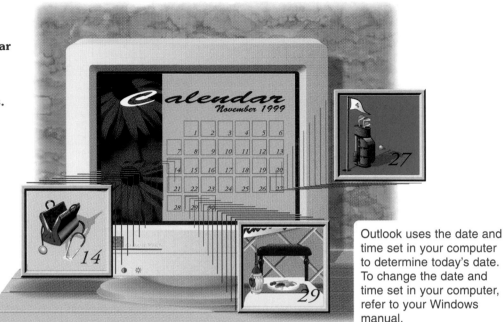

Outlook uses the date and time set in your computer to determine today's date. To change the date and time set in your computer, refer to your Windows manual.

## DISPLAY THE CALENDAR

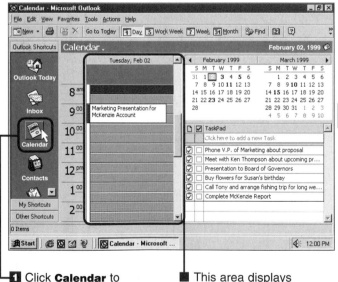

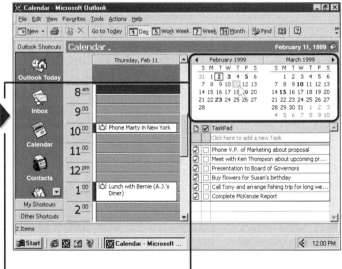

**1** Click **Calendar** to display the Calendar.

■ This area displays the appointments for the current day.

*Note: To add an appointment, see page 364.*

■ This area displays the days in the current month and the next month. Days with appointments are shown in **bold**.

**2** To display the appointments for another day, click the day. The day you select is highlighted.

■ The current day displays a red outline.

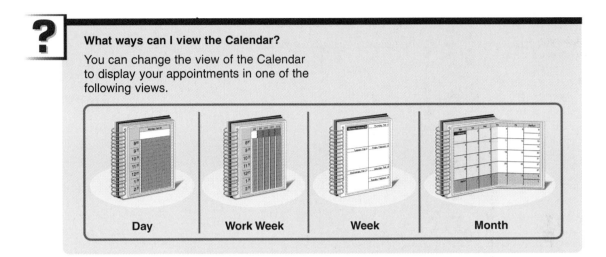

**What ways can I view the Calendar?**

You can change the view of the Calendar to display your appointments in one of the following views.

Day     Work Week     Week     Month

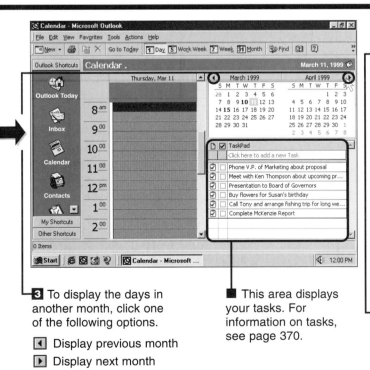

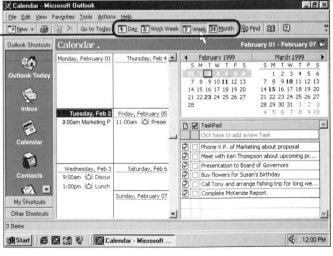

**3** To display the days in another month, click one of the following options.

◄ Display previous month

► Display next month

■ This area displays your tasks. For information on tasks, see page 370.

**CHANGE VIEW OF CALENDAR**

**1** Click the way you want to view the Calendar.

| 1 Day | Day |
| 5 Work Week | Work Week |
| 7 Week | Week |
| 31 Month | Month |

*Note: If the button you want is not displayed, click* ⏵ *on the toolbar to display all the buttons.*

# USING THE CALENDAR

You can add an appointment to the Calendar to remind you of an activity such as a seminar or doctor's appointment.

## SCHEDULE AN APPOINTMENT

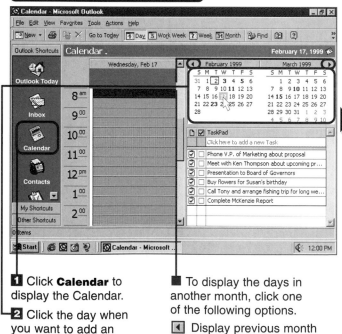

**1** Click **Calendar** to display the Calendar.

**2** Click the day when you want to add an appointment.

■ To display the days in another month, click one of the following options.

◀ Display previous month

▶ Display next month

**3** Position the mouse ▷ over the starting time for the appointment.

**4** Drag the mouse ▷ to select the time you want to set aside for the appointment.

**?** **Will Outlook remind me of an appointment I have scheduled?**

Outlook will play a brief sound and display the Reminder dialog box 15 minutes before a scheduled appointment.

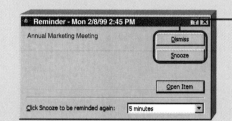

■ To close the Reminder dialog box, click one of the following options.

**Dismiss** - Close the reminder

**Snooze** - Remind again in five minutes

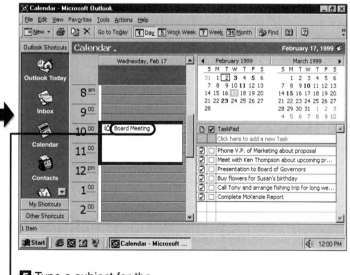

**5** Type a subject for the appointment and then press the [Enter] key.

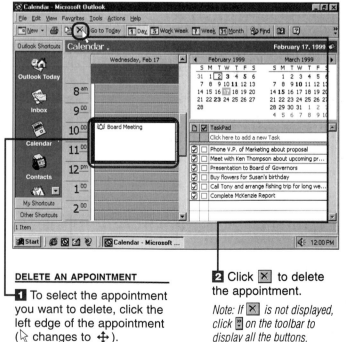

**DELETE AN APPOINTMENT**

**1** To select the appointment you want to delete, click the left edge of the appointment (↖ changes to ✥).

**2** Click ✕ to delete the appointment.

*Note: If ✕ is not displayed, click ⯮ on the toolbar to display all the buttons.*

# USING CONTACTS

Outlook allows you to keep detailed information about your friends, family members, colleagues and clients.

## CREATE A NEW CONTACT

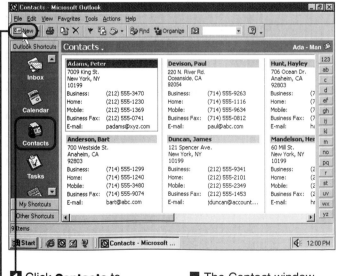

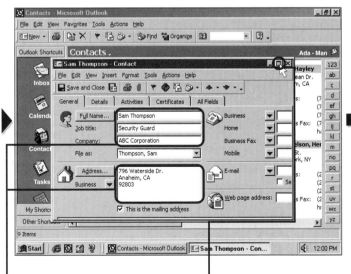

**1** Click **Contacts** to display your contacts.

**2** Click **New** to create a new contact.

■ The Contact window appears, displaying areas where you can enter information about a contact.

*Note: You do not need to enter information in every area.*

**3** Click an area and type the contact's full name, job title and company name.

**4** Click this area and type the contact's address.

**5** To enlarge the window so you can clearly see all the areas in the window, click ▣.

? Why did the Check Address dialog box appear after I entered an address?

If the address you entered is incomplete, Outlook displays the Check Address dialog box to help you complete the address.

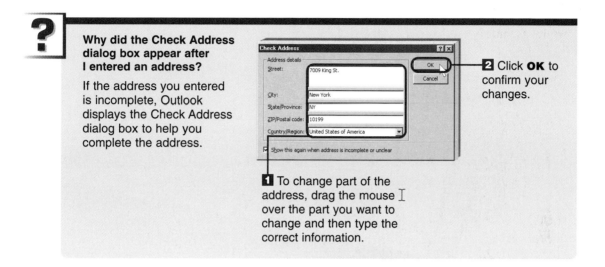

2 Click **OK** to confirm your changes.

1 To change part of the address, drag the mouse I over the part you want to change and then type the correct information.

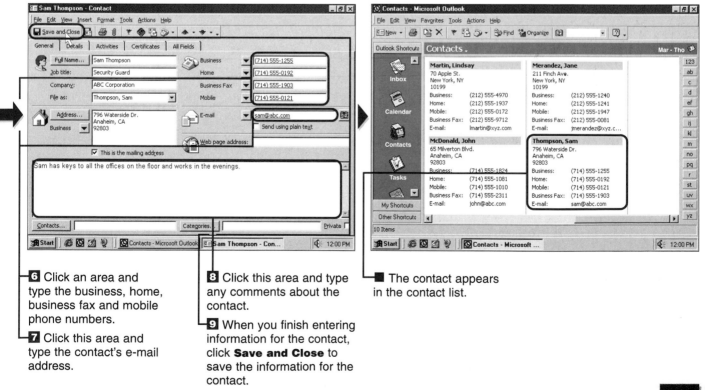

6 Click an area and type the business, home, business fax and mobile phone numbers.

7 Click this area and type the contact's e-mail address.

8 Click this area and type any comments about the contact.

9 When you finish entering information for the contact, click **Save and Close** to save the information for the contact.

■ The contact appears in the contact list.

# USING CONTACTS

You can browse through your contacts to find the contact you want to work with. After you find the contact, you can remove the contact or update the information for the contact.

## WORK WITH CONTACTS

### BROWSE THROUGH CONTACTS

■ These tabs allow you to browse through your contacts alphabetically.

**1** Click the tab for the contacts you want to view.

■ Contacts beginning with the letter(s) you selected appear.

### DELETE A CONTACT

**1** Click the contact you want to delete.

**2** Click ⊠ to delete the contact.

■ The contact disappears from the list.

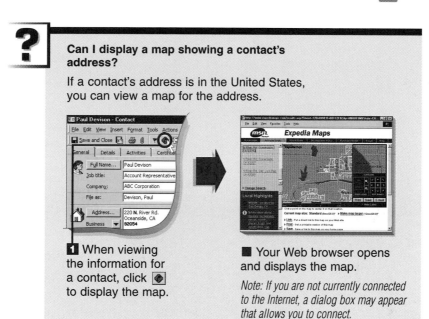

**?** Can I display a map showing a contact's address?

If a contact's address is in the United States, you can view a map for the address.

**1** When viewing the information for a contact, click ◈ to display the map.

■ Your Web browser opens and displays the map.

*Note: If you are not currently connected to the Internet, a dialog box may appear that allows you to connect.*

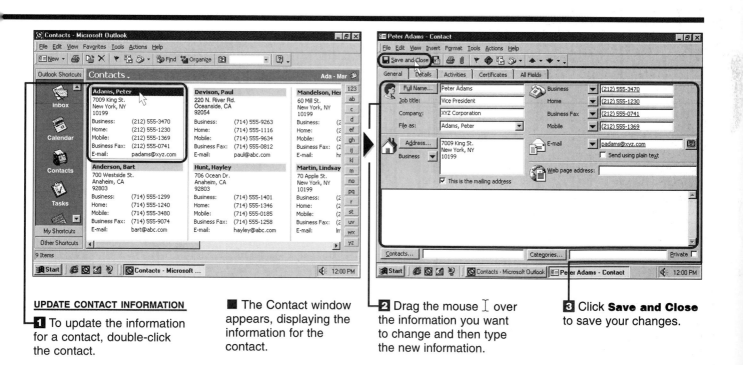

**UPDATE CONTACT INFORMATION**

**1** To update the information for a contact, double-click the contact.

■ The Contact window appears, displaying the information for the contact.

**2** Drag the mouse I over the information you want to change and then type the new information.

**3** Click **Save and Close** to save your changes.

# USING TASKS

You can create an electronic to-do list of personal and work-related tasks that you want to accomplish.

## USING TASKS

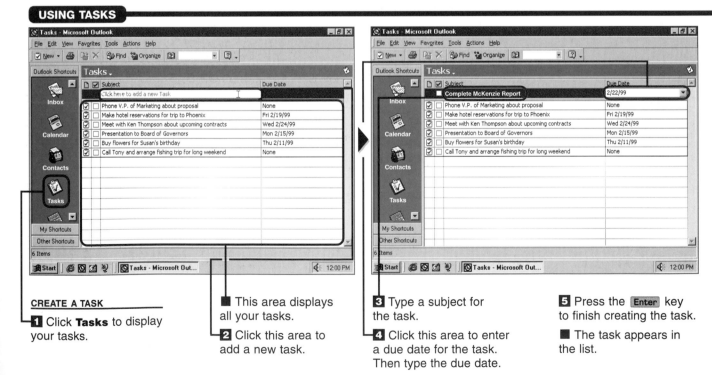

**CREATE A TASK**

**1** Click **Tasks** to display your tasks.

■ This area displays all your tasks.

**2** Click this area to add a new task.

**3** Type a subject for the task.

**4** Click this area to enter a due date for the task. Then type the due date.

**5** Press the Enter key to finish creating the task.

■ The task appears in the list.

**Is there a quick way to enter a due date for a task?**

Yes. Instead of typing a date, you can type a brief description of the date, such as "Friday", "tomorrow", "next Thursday", "one month from now" or "Valentine's Day".

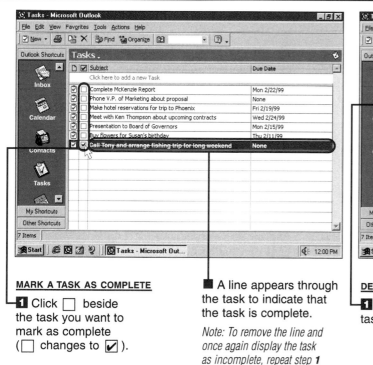

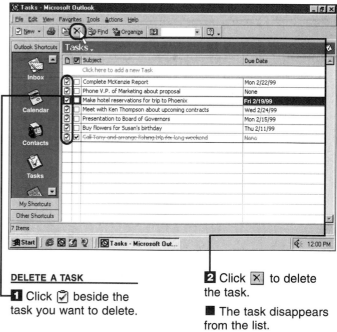

## MARK A TASK AS COMPLETE

**1** Click ☐ beside the task you want to mark as complete (☐ changes to ☑ ).

■ A line appears through the task to indicate that the task is complete.

*Note: To remove the line and once again display the task as incomplete, repeat step 1 (☑ changes to ☐ ).*

## DELETE A TASK

**1** Click ☑ beside the task you want to delete.

**2** Click ☒ to delete the task.

■ The task disappears from the list.

# USING NOTES

You can create
electronic notes
that are similar to
paper sticky notes.

Notes are useful for storing
small pieces of information
such as reminders,
questions, ideas and
anything else you would
record on notepaper.

USING NOTES

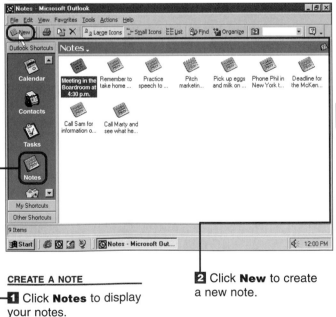

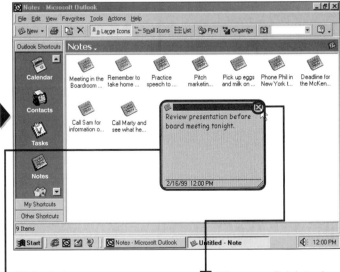

**CREATE A NOTE**

**1** Click **Notes** to display
your notes.

**2** Click **New** to create
a new note.

**◼** A window appears
where you can type the
note. The bottom of the
window displays the
current date and time.

**3** Type the text for
the note.

**4** When you finish typing
the text, click **✕** to close
the note.

**Can I change the size of a note?**

When viewing a note, you can change the size of the note. This is useful when the note is too small to display all the text.

■ Position the mouse � over the bottom right corner of the note ( � changes to ↖ ). Then drag the corner of the note until the note is the size you want.

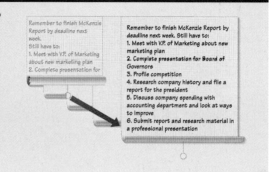

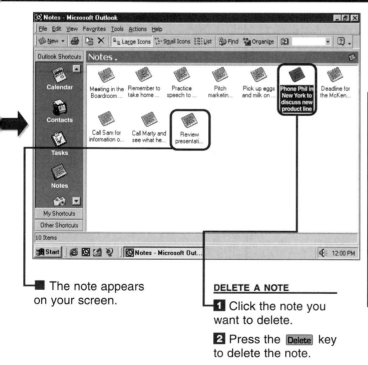

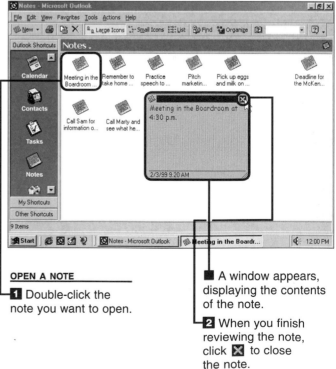

■ The note appears on your screen.

**DELETE A NOTE**

**1** Click the note you want to delete.

**2** Press the `Delete` key to delete the note.

**OPEN A NOTE**

**1** Double-click the note you want to open.

■ A window appears, displaying the contents of the note.

**2** When you finish reviewing the note, click ✕ to close the note.

# USING DELETED ITEMS

The Deleted Items folder stores all the items you have deleted in Outlook. You can recover an item you accidentally deleted.

You can also empty the Deleted Items folder to permanently remove all the items from the folder. You should regularly empty the folder to save space on your computer.

**USING DELETED ITEMS**

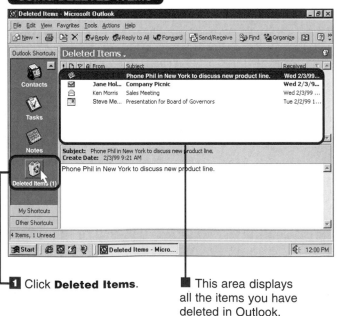

**1** Click **Deleted Items**.

■ This area displays all the items you have deleted in Outlook.

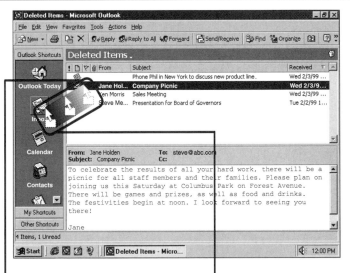

**RECOVER A DELETED ITEM**

**1** Position the mouse ⤡ over the item you want to recover.

**2** Drag the item to the appropriate Outlook feature.

■ The item disappears from the list. Outlook places the item in the feature you selected.

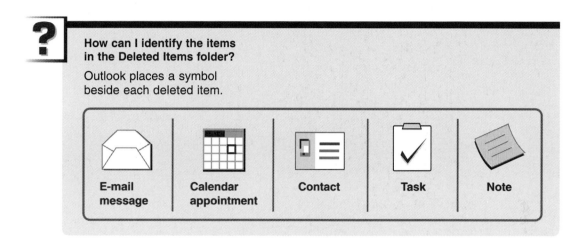

**?**

**How can I identify the items in the Deleted Items folder?**

Outlook places a symbol beside each deleted item.

E-mail message | Calendar appointment | Contact | Task | Note

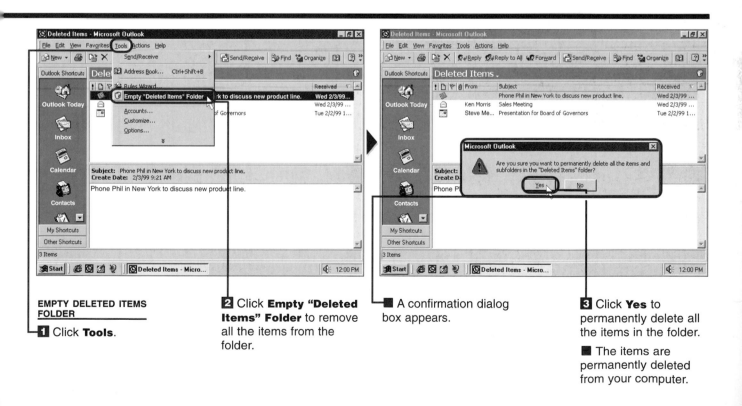

**EMPTY DELETED ITEMS FOLDER**

**1** Click **Tools**.

**2** Click **Empty "Deleted Items" Folder** to remove all the items from the folder.

■ A confirmation dialog box appears.

**3** Click **Yes** to permanently delete all the items in the folder.

■ The items are permanently deleted from your computer.

# Microsoft Office
# and the Internet

# FISHING GUIDE

**W**hen was the last time you heard someone boast about the trophy largemouth bass they reeled in on their last fishing outing? Have you always wanted to go fishing but didn't know where to start? Whether you assume this popular sport is as easy as finding a pond and plopping yourself down with a line, or whether you are intimidated by the large array of rods, reels, baits, lures and fish,

comfortable sticking to shore?

No matter what your preferences are, try to choose a quiet location in the cool still of the early morning or evening. Make sure you are aware of the weather forecast before you set out so you can dress appropriately. Remember that temperatures are often cooler by the water, with different wind factors. Don't be

# CREATE A HYPERLINK

You can create a
hyperlink to connect
a word or phrase in
your document to
another document
on your computer,
network, corporate
intranet or the
Internet.

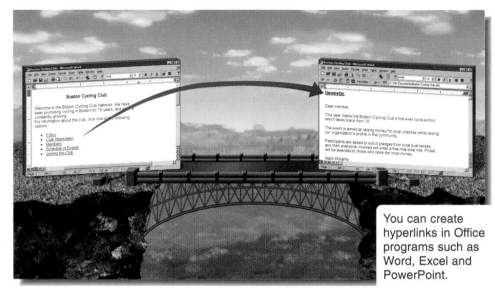

An intranet is a
small version of
the Internet within
a company or
organization.

You can create
hyperlinks in Office
programs such as
Word, Excel and
PowerPoint.

## CREATE A HYPERLINK

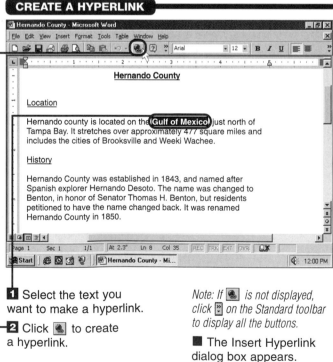

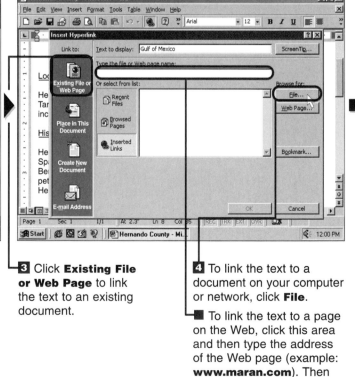

**1** Select the text you
want to make a hyperlink.

**2** Click 🔗 to create
a hyperlink.

*Note: If 🔗 is not displayed,
click ⏵ on the Standard toolbar
to display all the buttons.*

■ The Insert Hyperlink
dialog box appears.

**3** Click **Existing File
or Web Page** to link
the text to an existing
document.

**4** To link the text to a
document on your computer
or network, click **File**.

■ To link the text to a page
on the Web, click this area
and then type the address
of the Web page (example:
**www.maran.com**). Then
skip to step **7**.

**Can an Office program automatically create a hyperlink for me?**

When you type the address of a document located on your network or the Internet, the Office program will automatically change the address to a hyperlink for you.

www.sunkist.com

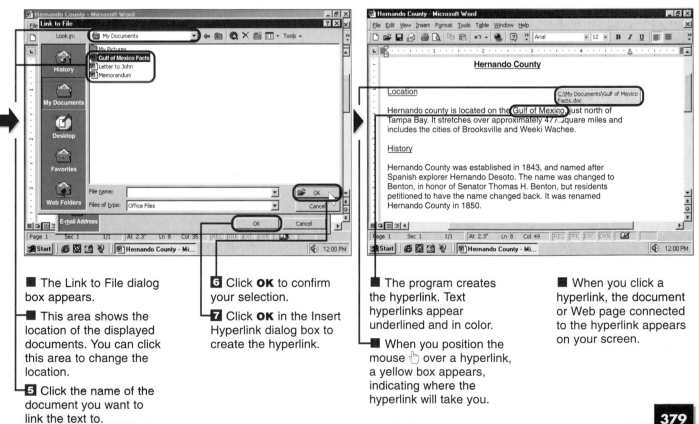

■ The Link to File dialog box appears.

■ This area shows the location of the displayed documents. You can click this area to change the location.

**5** Click the name of the document you want to link the text to.

**6** Click **OK** to confirm your selection.

**7** Click **OK** in the Insert Hyperlink dialog box to create the hyperlink.

■ The program creates the hyperlink. Text hyperlinks appear underlined and in color.

■ When you position the mouse over a hyperlink, a yellow box appears, indicating where the hyperlink will take you.

■ When you click a hyperlink, the document or Web page connected to the hyperlink appears on your screen.

# PREVIEW A DOCUMENT AS A WEB PAGE

You can preview how an Office document will look as a Web page. This allows you to see how the document will appear on the Internet or your company's intranet.

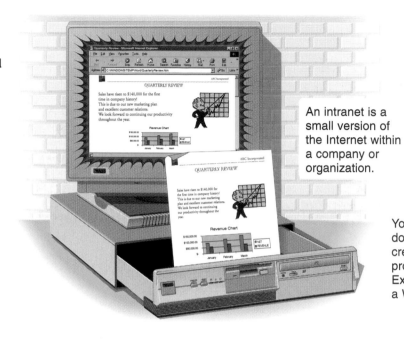

An intranet is a small version of the Internet within a company or organization.

You can preview a document that you created in an Office program such as Word, Excel or PowerPoint as a Web page.

---

## PREVIEW A DOCUMENT AS A WEB PAGE

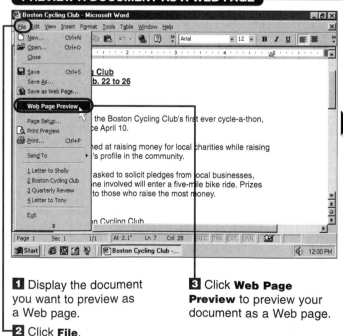

**1** Display the document you want to preview as a Web page.

**2** Click **File**.

**3** Click **Web Page Preview** to preview your document as a Web page.

■ Your Web browser window opens, displaying your document as a Web page. In this example, a Word document is previewed as a Web page.

■ To maximize the Web browser window to fill your screen, click 🗖.

**4** When you finish reviewing the document as a Web page, click ⊠ to close the Web browser window.

**?** **Will my Web page look the same to everyone who views the Web page?**

No. Different Web browsers may display your Web page differently. There are many Web browsers used on the Web. The two most popular Web browsers are Microsoft Internet Explorer and Netscape Navigator.

**Microsoft Internet Explorer**

**Netscape Navigator**

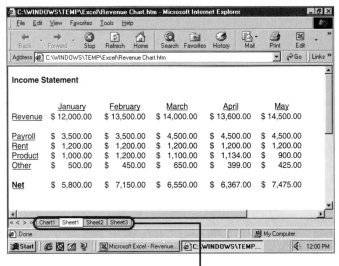

### PREVIEW EXCEL WORKBOOK

■ When you preview an Excel workbook as a Web page, the gridlines that separate each cell do not appear.

■ If your workbook contains data in more than one worksheet, this area displays tabs for each worksheet. You can click a tab to display a different worksheet.

### PREVIEW POWERPOINT PRESENTATION

■ When you preview a PowerPoint presentation as a Web page, this area displays the title of each slide in your presentation. You can click a title to display a different slide.

■ This area displays the current slide.

# SAVE A DOCUMENT AS A WEB PAGE

You can save an Office document as a Web page. This lets you place the document on the Internet or your company's intranet.

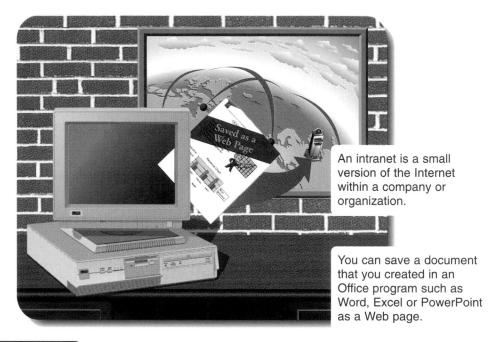

An intranet is a small version of the Internet within a company or organization.

You can save a document that you created in an Office program such as Word, Excel or PowerPoint as a Web page.

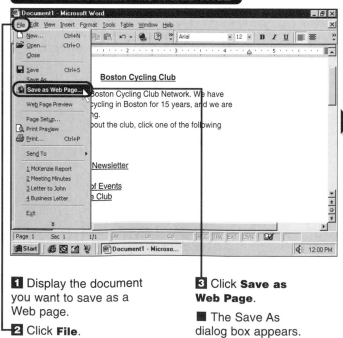

**1** Display the document you want to save as a Web page.

**2** Click **File**.

**3** Click **Save as Web Page**.

■ The Save As dialog box appears.

**4** Type a file name for the Web page. A file name is the name you use to store the page on your computer.

■ This area shows the location where the program will store the Web page. You can click this area to change the location.

■ This area allows you to access commonly used folders. To display the contents of a folder, click the folder.

**?**

**How do I make my Web page available for other people to view?**

After you save a document as a Web page, you can transfer the page to a computer that stores Web pages, called a Web server. Once the Web page is published on a Web server, the page will be available for other people to view. For more information on publishing a Web page, contact your network administrator or Internet service provider.

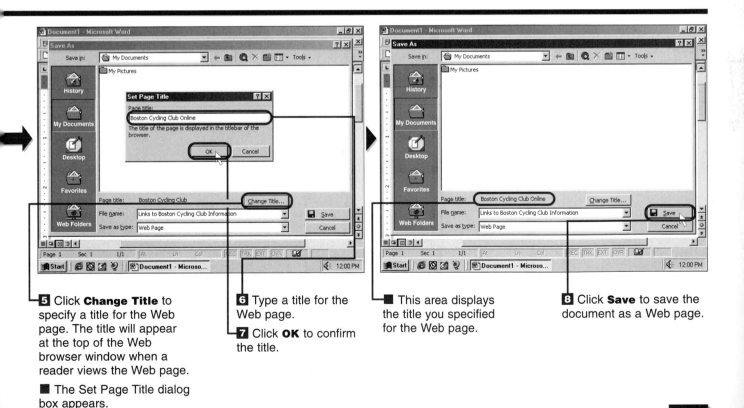

**5** Click **Change Title** to specify a title for the Web page. The title will appear at the top of the Web browser window when a reader views the Web page.

■ The Set Page Title dialog box appears.

**6** Type a title for the Web page.

**7** Click **OK** to confirm the title.

■ This area displays the title you specified for the Web page.

**8** Click **Save** to save the document as a Web page.

# INDEX

# INDEX

electronic mail. *See* e-mail; messages
e-mail. *See also* messages
    documents, in Word, 38-39
    presentations, in PowerPoint, 190-191
    worksheets, in Excel, 114-115
empty
    Deleted Items folder, in Outlook, 375
    fields, criteria, in Access, 311
enter
    data, in Excel, 96-97
    formulas, in Excel, 128-129
    functions, in Excel, 132-135
    text, in Word, 21
        in tables, 79
error messages, in formulas, 127
exact matches (=), criteria, in Access, 311
Excel. *See also specific subject or feature*
    overview, 2, 92
    screen, parts of, 94
    start, 93
exit. *See also* close
    Office programs, 7
exponents. *See* formulas; functions

## F

Favorites folder
    in Access, 255
    in Excel, 109
    in PowerPoint, 187
    in Publisher, 331
    in Word, 29
field
    names, in Access, 261, 279
    properties, in Access, 279
fields, in Access. *See also* columns
    add in tables, 266
    data type, change, 282-283
    delete
        in queries, 309
        in tables, 267
    hide, in queries, 308
    overview, 244, 261
    planning, 246
    rearrange in tables, 265
    rename in tables, 264
    scroll through, in tables, 269
    select in tables, 270

files
    Access. *See* databases
    attach to messages, in Outlook, 356-357
    Excel. *See* workbooks; worksheets
    PowerPoint. *See* presentations
    Publisher. *See* publications
    Word. *See* documents
filter data, in Access, 300, 301
find
    data, in Access, 298-299
    text, in Word, 46-47
find list of items, criteria, in Access, 311
folders
    Deleted Items, empty, in Outlook, 375
    Desktop
        in Access, 255
        in Excel, 109
        in PowerPoint, 187
        in Publisher, 331
        in Word, 29
    Drafts, in Outlook, 353
    Favorites
        in Access, 255
        in Excel, 109
        in PowerPoint, 187
        in Publisher, 331
        in Word, 29
    History
        in Access, 255
        in Excel, 109
        in PowerPoint, 187
        in Publisher, 331
        in Word, 29
    My Documents
        in Access, 255
        in Excel, 109
        in PowerPoint, 187
        in Publisher, 331
        in Word, 29
    Outbox, in Outlook, 353
    Sent Items, in Outlook, 353
    Web Folders
        in Excel, 109
        in PowerPoint, 187
        in Publisher, 331
        in Word, 29
fonts
    data, change, in Excel, 144
    text, change
        in PowerPoint, 220
        in Word, 52

# INDEX

# INDEX

# INDEX

# OVER 6 MILLION

## OTHER 3-D Visual SERIES

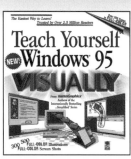

# ORDER FORM

**IDG BOOKS** ®

**TRADE & INDIVIDUAL ORDERS**

Phone: **(800) 762-2974**
or **(317) 596-5200**
*(8 a.m. – 6 p.m., CST, weekdays)*
FAX : **(800) 550-2747**
or **(317) 596-5692**

**EDUCATIONAL ORDERS & DISCOUNTS**

Phone: **(800) 434-2086**
*(8:30 a.m.–5:00 p.m., CST, weekdays)*
FAX : **(317) 596-5499**

**CORPORATE ORDERS FOR 3-D VISUAL™ SERIES**

Phone: **(800) 469-6616**
*(8 a.m.–5 p.m., EST, weekdays)*
FAX : **(905) 890-9434**

| Qty | ISBN | Title | Price | Total |
|-----|------|-------|-------|-------|
|     |      |       |       |       |
|     |      |       |       |       |
|     |      |       |       |       |
|     |      |       |       |       |
|     |      |       |       |       |
|     |      |       |       |       |
|     |      |       |       |       |
|     |      |       |       |       |
|     |      |       |       |       |
|     |      |       |       |       |
|     |      |       |       |       |
|     |      |       |       |       |
|     |      |       |       |       |
|     |      |       |       |       |
|     |      |       |       |       |

### Shipping & Handling Charges

|  | Description | First book | Each add'l. book | Total |
|--|-------------|-----------|------------------|-------|
| **Domestic** | Normal | $4.50 | $1.50 | $ |
|  | Two Day Air | $8.50 | $2.50 | $ |
|  | Overnight | $18.00 | $3.00 | $ |
| **International** | Surface | $8.00 | $8.00 | $ |
|  | Airmail | $16.00 | $16.00 | $ |
|  | DHL Air | $17.00 | $17.00 | $ |

**Subtotal** _____

*CA residents add*
*applicable sales tax* _____

*IN, MA and MD*
*residents add*
*5% sales tax* _____

*IL residents add*
*6.25% sales tax* _____

*RI residents add*
*7% sales tax* _____

*TX residents add*
*8.25% sales tax* _____

*Shipping* _____

**Total** _____

## Ship to:

Name _____

Address _____

Company _____

City/State/Zip _____

Daytime Phone _____

**Payment:** ☐ Check to IDG Books (US Funds Only)
☐ Visa   ☐ Mastercard   ☐ American Express

Card # _____ Exp. _____ Signature _____

**maranGraphics™**